Motives
and
Goals
in Groups

SOCIAL PSYCHOLOGY

A series of monographs, treatises, and texts

EDITORS

LEON FESTINGER AND STANLEY SCHACHTER

Motives and Goals in Groups

Alvin Zander

Research Center for Group Dynamics
Institute for Social Research
University of Michigan
Ann Arbor, Michigan

1971

ACADEMIC PRESS New York and London

ACADEMIC PRESS, INC.
111 Fifth Avenue, New York, New York 10003

United Kingdom Edition published by
ACADEMIC PRESS, INC. (LONDON) LTD.
Berkeley Square House, London W1X 6BA

LIBRARY OF CONGRESS CATALOG CARD NUMBER: 70-137634

PRINTED IN THE UNITED STATES OF AMERICA

To Patty

Contents

10. Summation and Interpretation

Preface

A working group is more likely to be effective if it has a clear criterion of success since members can better comprehend where the group is going and whether it is getting there when such a criterion is available. This type of goal also helps members define the duties of participants, coordinate their actions, and develop sensible procedures for work. Doubtless a group's objective determines many of its qualities, yet there has been little study of these effects and even less study of the reasons that a particular criterion is chosen.

This book presents a summary of results from a program of studies into group aspirations and members' motives. Primary attention in these investigations has been given to members' plans or actions in behalf of the whole group regardless of the personal gains to be received from participation in the group's work. Little attention has been given to the interaction among members while they make decisions for the group or take part in its endeavors. The group and its needs have been the central concern.

Although later projects were field studies of adult community organizations, the earliest investigations in this program were formulated in a way that was most relevant to an educational setting. At the outset then, volunteer high school students, and in some cases teachers, were the subjects. As results accumulated and new plans developed, it was wisest to continue with such subjects, in laboratory experiments at least, in order to benefit from the supplementation that one study provides another. The boys' vigor, their enthusiasm, and their interest in the experimental tasks made them ideal participants. One may wonder if their immaturity introduced reactions that would not occur among older persons. There is no clear-cut answer to that question, but the studies of adult groups did not provide findings that were different from those of pupils, on items that could be compared. Boys are like people, only more so.

In studies of aspiration setting (by groups, in this instance), it naturally happens that the units attain their goals some of the time and fail some of the time. For certain problems it was necessary to control the number of successes or failures a group experienced. On occasion, we needed to create standard conditions or contrasting ones by describing our intentions in ways that were not strictly true. Whenever such behavior was required, a careful regimen was followed. Officials in the school were fully informed about our proposed procedure and their approval was obtained. The experimental session was planned so that it would be finished ten to fifteen minutes before the end of a class period—except for one experiment, we kept boys for no more than one hour. During the last part of the hour subjects were told in detail about the purposes of the experiment, the procedures followed, and the exact reasons for these. Questions were sought and fully answered. In effect, this discussion became a brief seminar on scientific method in the study of groups. It provided an opportunity for a boy to learn how he and his schoolmates had reacted to particular conditions and to develop an awareness that behavior can be predicted, for him and his friends. We feel confident that the boys left an experiment feeling that they had been part of an interesting and involving demonstration. They certainly did not leave with a cynical reaction or with a sense of disappointment in themselves or others; they repeatedly proved their sympathy by not telling friends or teachers any more about a study than we asked them to say.

Acknowledgments

Some of these projects were done on a shoe string, others were quite expensive. Several field studies in company settings were financed by the firms involved. A survey of board members in United Fund organizations was supported by a grant from the United States Public Health Service to Dr. Irwin Rosenstock in the School of Public Health at The University of Michigan. Happily, our interests coincided with his. Early investigations had help from the United States Office of Education, but most of the research was financed by the United States Air Force Office of Scientific Research. I am deeply grateful for this financial assistance and particularly appreciate the encouragement supplied by Dr. Charles Hutchinson and Dr. Herman Sanders in the latter organization.

A number of associates, graduate students at the time, brought an infusion of new ideas that was invaluable. They include: Rosita Albert, Theodore Curtis, David Dustin, Ronald Efron, Edward Krupat, James Ledvinka, Theodore Newcomb, Jr., Howard Rosenfeld, Cyrus Ulberg, and David Wulff. Two colleagues who had larger responsibilities in this work, John Forward and Herman Medow, contributed more to me and these studies than my thanks to them can convey.

I owe much to the writings of John W. Atkinson. He has also been a wise counselor and an interested critic, yet he doubtless feels that I have created a strange conceptual hybrid by displacing some of his ideas to a social setting. Both the initiation of these studies and their later development were stimulated by the creative help of Dorwin Cartwright—as is always so for staff members in the Research Center for Group Dynamics.

The Swedish Institute for Administrative Research in Stockholm furnished a calm and undemanding environment for the preparation of this volume, and provided an opportunity for me to learn about their work in long-range planning.

To all these people I give my warmest thanks. They should not be held responsible for the use I have made of their ideas.

By now, we have worked with hundreds of young men. Our appreciation for the part they played was expressed at the time we met with them. We thank them again for their help and we thank again the officials in many high schools near Ann Arbor who welcomed us and provided the facilities necessary for a temporary laboratory.

An earlier version of this volume was read by William Haney, Dorwin Cartwright, John Forward, Cyrus Ulberg, and Robert Zajonc. I greatly appreciate their thoughtful advice. Mrs. Carrie Lewis knows that I am thankful for her skill and patience in typing this manuscript and for varied assistance she provided during this series of studies.

Motives
and
Goals
in Groups

CHAPTER 1 | The Study of Group Goals

One often hears members of a group say (with vigor) that their unit has done a good job. Their tone and their comments about the group's performance reveal that the accomplishment pleases them. The source of their satisfaction, they make clear, is in the unit's attainment of a preset goal. On a later occasion, one may hear the same members assert that their group has done poorly, that they are dissatisfied; yet, their group's output is exactly the same as it was when the members were pleased. Apparently in the interim members have changed their group's goal, the criterion they use in evaluating the group's work. A sense of success and pride among these participants, it is plain, depends not only on the group's score, it depends as well on what they expect or intend that score to be.

Members' awareness of accomplishment and their feeling of satisfaction are generally recognized as good things in themselves. In addition, a gratifying success gives rise to other useful properties in a group: members develop a stronger desire for group success, they work harder, they cordinate their efforts more effectively, they have less strain in interpersonal relations, they are more attracted to membership, and the group in fact becomes more productive. A success can foster conditions conducive to further success. A dissatisfying failure, in contrast, may invoke properties quite different from those just mentioned; thus a failure may lead to further failure, a spiraling of events that can be difficult to reverse. It is necessary in short that a group have an appropriate goal if it is to develop the qualities most favorable for its effective operation and survival.

The ability to interpret behavior in working groups would be considerably improved if there was a better understanding of the conditions that determine why a group chooses one goal rather than another, a reasonable goal rather than an unreasonable one. The contents of this volume concern the goal members establish for their group and are mainly focused on a particular kind of goal called a group level of aspiration. It is intended to examine the origin of this aspiration, to spell out its value in the continuing work of the group, and to observe how it affects and is affected by members' motives to achieve success. Such motives, it is assumed, are not merely dispositions to obtain personal gains; they are also inclinations to help the group attain satisfactory outcomes. The primary questions can be stated simply: What causes members to select a particular goal for their joint endeavor? Why do members become involved in the achievement of their group?

There is not a complete absence of information on these matters. But most relevant research has been based on the assumption that a member thinks only about his own interests while participating in a group: he competes, bargains, negotiates, or cooperates with colleagues in order to achieve personal ends. Group objectives, in this view, are only an indirect product of the agreements among self-centered individuals. And, when the members of goal-setting bodies indulge in self-seeking, group objectives do become a compromise among preferences based on personal motives. When one observes group decision making, however, one notes that members often suppress any inclination to put their own needs first, pay little attention to each other's personal desires, and believe it to be an ethical matter to behave in this way. They concentrate instead upon what the total group should do. Choices are made on the basis of what is "good for the group," a matter which can itself generate disharmony and differences. It is understandable then that members' motives to achieve success may not only be dispositions to obtain personal rewards, but may also be inclinations to attain satisfactory outcomes for the group.

Suppose that all the members have a say in the selection of a future goal on a task they have jointly performed a number of times. Several sets of circumstances other than self-focused negotiations might affect their choice.

1.   The participants have to decide what score they can reasonably expect their group to attain. They will want this goal to be possible, yet it should not be too easy. The unit's past performance suggests what its next score might very well be, but there is always the potentiality that the skill of members will improve; or a change in group structure, in assignments, in leadership, in procedure of work, in training, or in the enthusiasm of members, might also make a difference. Are previous scores always the most reliable indicators of the group's true competence? If the group is changed in some way, should expectations be changed?

2.   Some levels of group achievement are more satisfying than others. In a Western society larger rewards are given for, and more satisfaction develops from, accomplishing harder tasks. Pride in group or "team spirit" are not wholly mythical consequences of a success on a challenging task. A successful group, for example, might welcome a greater challenge in the future.

3. Members frequently receive information from external sources that have an impact, intended or otherwise, upon future plans for the unit. Because the product of a group is seldom for the use of members alone, participants often suit their objectives to the wishes and reactions of agents outside the group.

4. The members of a group may differ in the strength of their desire to have their group achieve success. A unit's past history of success or failure will doubtless influence such a group-oriented motive but other circumstances also have an effect. Those in a better organized or more attractive collectivity might have a stronger desire to do well. Members who feel that the work of their group is important in itself or of use to a larger organization may be more eager to ensure that the group sets proper yet satisfying goals.

5. Even the personal dispositions a member brings to his group, or develops there, can determine his plans for the group. If he is the type who appreciates challenging tasks, whether alone or with others, involvement in the group's endeavors and his reactions to its performance may be quite different from what they would be if he dislikes competing against standards of excellence.

The nature of the goal can, in turn, determine what events occur within the group: its level of performance, the pride of members in their organization, their personal self-regard, the aims they develop for their own jobs, the attitudes and beliefs they invent about the organization or its work, and the survival of the unit itself.

In sum, the goal men choose for their group can be influenced by conditions in the group as well as their individual motives, and their choice has a potentially strong effect upon the life of the group. Group leaders and members commonly develop concepts for use in thinking about these issues and create their own explanations about why things happen as they do. There is, however, little scientific understanding of such matters.

APPROACH TO THE STUDY OF GOAL SETTING

Given the questions we wish to answer, the results of previous investigations are largely truncated. On the one hand, students of social institutions have written about group goals but have avoided making assumptions about motives of members. They have been interested in the abstract meaning of the term goal, how one discovers what the goal of a group is (if any), who sets the goal, and the character of multiple goals within a larger organization. Students of individual motives, on the other hand, have had little interest in groups, except as they provide a locus for arousing particular needs. They have studied the nature of a member's personal motivation, but not the effect of a group's goal on this motivation. The study of the origins (and effects) of group goals has largely fallen between disciplinary chairs.

At first glance, one might think that investigations of group decision making or problem solving are pertinent to present purposes. However, most such studies do not require participants to commit themselves to their decisions, or to live with them; instead, the studies concentrate upon the effects of reasoning, cognitive clarity, or interpersonal influence among members.

Investigations of "risk taking" by groups (6, 71, 72) reveal that group decisions are often quite different from personal and private judgments made by members prior to a group discussion. These experiments appear to be related to the present interests since they concern choices in which there is a greater or lesser probability of favorable or unfavorable consequences for somebody. Apparently groups make more "risky" choices than individuals do, but not always. As the reasons for these interesting findings are not yet understood, it is not possible to say what the precise relationship between them and the results in this volume will turn out to be.

Studies in the dynamics of groups, particularly those on the nature of cooperation, cohesiveness, and group performance, have been useful in ways that will be evident later as pertinent findings are presented when they relate to a given topic.

All in all, the results of prior research provide few leads suggesting where one might best begin to study the origins of group goals and the interest of members in these goals. In the absence of descriptive data and relevant theory, it appeared that a study of how a group goes about establishing its future expectations would initially be most useful. It was decided to begin with observations of simple experimental groups in the laboratory and to move on thereafter to the study of group properties, taking them one by one, that appear to have an impact on the selection of a group's goal. This plan was accompanied by several working assumptions.

First, the ends that members select for their group were conceived as part of the unit's ongoing procedure in doing work, subject to change as a result of feedback on the group's performance.

This assumption is in accord with a proposal made by Lewin (46) in an essay on social diagnosis and action. As he saw it, a plan for group work exists when the group's purposes have been defined, a relevant goal and the means for its attainment have been determined, and a strategy for action laid out. Assuming that this plan should be flexible and subject to change as actions by the group make this necessary, he displaces the basic principles of feedback to the social realm. Emphasizing the major proposition in such self-steering—that a means exists for determining the desired performance and the proximity of this performance to the desired state—he then asserts that "a discrepancy between the desired and the actual direction leads automatically to a correction of actions or to a change in planning."

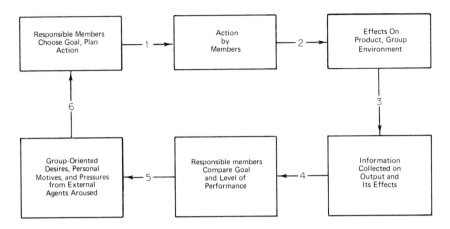

Fig. 1-1 The process of feedback in a group.

Typical stages in his model of feedback are shown in Fig. 1-1: (1) Decision makers establish a goal and the methods to be used in attaining it. (2) Action is taken which has effects upon the group and on relevant conditions outside the group. (3) Information about the movement of the group toward its goal (the output of the group) is obtained and reported back to the decision makers. (4) The decision makers observe any deviation between the original goal and the group's performance. (5) Desires members have for the group, their personal motives, and pressures arising from external agents influence the members' reactions to this evaluation (this stage is not explicitly stated but is implied in the model). (6) If the deviation between score and expectation is greater than is tolerable, the decision makers take steps to reduce this discrepancy either by changing the nature of actions in the future or by changing the group's goal. The important point is that the meaning of the group's performance is not simply

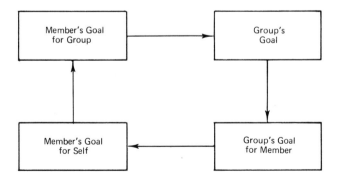

Fig. 1-2 Relations among individual and group goals.

something in the score itself or in the group itself but in the relationship between performance and what is desired. When a feedback loop exists, that is, when members obtain evidence about the group's performance on a series of attempts, we can expect a type of motivated behavior to be invoked.

Second, a group's decisions and actions are the behaviors of individuals, even when the decisions are joint agreements among many persons and lead to later teamwork among them. In order that one not mix levels of discourse between group and individual goals, then, it is necessary that one recognize the four types of relations at work, as shown in Fig. 1-2.

The goals and their relationships in Fig. 1-2 remind us that there can be a circular-causal relationship among such and that some (in the left column) are concepts about an individual and others (in the right column) are properties of a group. It is plausible to believe that different matters determine the nature of the goals within each of the four boxes. Planning of research must recognize the distinctive nature of these different variables.

Third, and most important, it was decided that a group level of aspiration was a suitable type of goal for initial study, assuming that a group aspiration may be conceived to be an analog of a personal aspiration. A group level of aspiration is the score members expect their group will attain in the future.

There were several reasons for this decision: the origin and changes in a level of aspiration give operational meaning to the stages in the feedback model discussed above; a fairly standardized procedure exists for studying the level of aspiration and related concepts; there is evidence on hand that a group can influence a member's personal aspiration by establishing a group level of aspiration; and findings from prior research on individual aspirations provide a way of judging intuitively if groups, when they set goals, differ in some way from solo individuals, when they set goals.

It is quite meaningful to ask a group as a single entity to perform a task over and over, to obtain a group score, and to require that the members agree upon a level of aspiration for their group prior to each trial. In addition, each member can be asked, privately, what he prefers the group's aspiration to be, so that the effects of personal desires or of properties of the group can be examined without the confounding created by a group discussion. Certain ground rules are necessary for treating a group in this fashion, these are described in the next chapter. There is a potential problem, however, in the use of aspiration theory for the present purposes. Does the level of aspiration function both as a criterion for evaluating the performance of the group *and* as an objective for guiding performance, or does it have one of these functions under certain conditions and the other function under different conditions? These question will remain unanswered at the outset, and during most of this report. The answers are provided in Chapters 4 and 10.

These decisions were made before research began. Later, it became clear that several others followed naturally. In a typical experimental routine, we asked members to select a group level of aspiration and provided them with information about the score of the group but *not* the member's own performance for each trial. In such a situation a member's cognitions are limited to those concerning the output of the group and he thus develops, can only develop, an interest in the satisfactoriness of the entity—a need to have his group achieve success, either for his own good, the good of the group, or both. Thus, a need to achieve is aroused, but this need under the circumstances is focussed on the achievement of the group. The writings of Atkinson and Feather (4) provided a uniquely helpful model to follow here since much of their theorizing about the need for achievement had grown out of aspiration theory. Moreover, work of McClelland on achieving societies (53, 54) encouraged the belief that high achievers must sometimes work in behalf of an organization and must be concerned about the outcome of that social unit, not only their personal successes, although McClelland did not say this. The concept of group achievement motivation, which has a central place in Chapters 4, 5, and 6, subsequently suggested matters to be explored and measured in field settings: comparative interest in achievement of self versus group, reactions to group success and failure, the origins of impossible group goals, or the effects of a member's responsibility for the fate of a group. Descriptive surveys of groups outside the laboratory occurred late rather than early in this program of research.

SEQUENCE OF TOPICS

In Chapter 2 the nature of group aspirations under the simplest of conditions is examined. These results will help clarify whether groups chooose and change aspirations on grounds similar to those that usually affect individual choices. The issue in the third chapter is the influence of the social environment on a group's aspirations. What makes it possible for external agents to affect these?

It was proposed earlier that some members, compared to others, may be more deeply engaged in the attainment of their unit. What are the sources of this greater or lesser involvement in the group? What difference does it make in the group's aspirations if members are interested or disinterested in their group's outcomes? Attention is turned to such questions in Chapter 4. Immediately thereafter, in Chapter 5, the influence of the individual need for achievement is considered. Here it is asked if this motive affects a member's interest in his group and if the group's performance is a means to self-satisfaction.

The motives of members can be revealed in various behaviors, beliefs, or attitudes, often popularly conceived to be signs of a group's morale, or of the loyalty of members. The sources and nature of what are called motivated beliefs provide, in Chapter 6, an awareness of the ways that purposive behavior is expressed in a variety of views about the group. In Chapter 7 members' evaluations of their group and themselves under different conditions are observed. With these data it can be determined whether members use the group's aspiration level as a criterion of success and what kinds of situations cause them to avoid blame for or accept credit for its output.

In Chapter 8 some of the many problems in understanding the nature of a group's performance are considered. How do goals and group-oriented motives affect productivity?

A group may set an aspiration level for an individual and a member may have his own aspiration for the duty he is to perform. The last chapter on research explores why a member sets his own aspiration close to the one his colleagues prefer him to have.

In Chapter 10 a summary is presented that reveals the coherence among the results, explains what leads to what, and prepares the way for further investigation. A number of basic assumptions are offered as well as the outcomes of research relevant to each.

CHAPTER 2 | The Group Level of Aspiration

How can we use aspiration-level theory in studying group goals? A group is not a person. Yet, a working group is an acting entity that has singular importance for a member. He and others can conceive of it as a unit, they can make decisions about the whole, their agreements can be unanimous if necessary, a score can be attributed to the group not only to the sum of individual efforts, and members can evaluate the performance of the group. It is feasible then to think of a group as a unit and to observe its aspirations as well as its scores.

In research on the individual level of aspiration a subject is usually given a task in which different levels of performance are possible. His task might be a set of arithmetic problems with a limited time period to finish as many as he can, a series of jigsaw puzzles graded for difficulty from which he chooses the one he wishes to attempt, a ring-toss game, or some other test of skill. He is asked to repeat the activity a number of times and, before each trial, to state the score he is going to try for on his next attempt. This simple procedure has been used to observe what tasks a person believes to be hard or easy, what level he chooses, what changes in choice he makes over time, how he reacts to success or failure, and, more recently, how his personal motives are revealed in his goals. The classic paper by Lewin *et al.* (45) summarizes early studies in the level of aspiration and advances an explanation for their results.

When asked to engage in an aspiration-setting experience, will a group choose its aims on the same grounds as an individual? To some, the answer is obvious; there would be no difference, sets of individuals decide matters as solo persons do. To others, a contrasting answer is the obvious one; there would be a distinct difference because a group has properties that generate decisions unlike those of solo persons. Any question with two obvious answers requires elementary facts. The following small experiment was constructed to obtain some of them (Zander & Medow, *80*).

9

EXPERIMENTAL PROCEDURE

The subjects, high schools boys in a small city, were approached in their study hall and invited to participate in a survey of "teamwork in muscle control." This sounded interesting to 59 young men who were then taken (in groups of three or five) to a small room in the school building.* Most of them knew one another; some were friends.

When they entered the laboratory, they encountered a board 12 ft. long bridging several tables. Along the length of the board was a channel wide enough to contain a wooden croquet ball. A 6-ft. aluminum pole was nearby. After introducing the teammates to one another, the experimenter began:

> I am from the University Testing Service. I and my organization have been asked by the government to make a survey of a special ability called *teamwork in muscle control.* Men in our government want to know how much of this ability high school students have so that they can plan for the future. You are used to the idea that careful control of your movements is necessary in lots of things you do, as in sports, music, drawing, fixing cars, dancing, or whatever. You know too, that teamwork among people is necessary in all kinds of activities. In recent years more and more types of jobs have developed that demand teamwork *as well as* muscle control: flying an airplane, guiding a space capsule, running a computer, making an automobile, filming a television show, or playing on a professional ball team all require this ability. We are going to measure how much of this capacity you have. See how well you can do on the test we are going to give you today. It was especially designed to measure this ability.

After a bit more talk about the importance of this skill, the participants were lined up, one behind the other, at the end of the board. They took the pole in one hand, arms at their sides, and were shown that they could move its rubber tip against the wooden ball, by swinging their arms forward in unison. A quick swing sent the ball rolling noisily down the channel. They were to make it stop as closely as they could to a Number 10 posted on the side of the board. Numbers from 9 to 1 were placed at regular intervals above and below the 10; the value reached by the ball was the score for that shot regardless of whether it was before or beyond the 10. Holes drilled in the floor of the channel beside each number stopped movement of the ball next to one of the score points. Five shots equaled one trial; thus, the maximum score for a trial was 50. This experimental activity is a giant-size version of one originally developed by Rotter (62) for studying the aspiration behavior of individuals.

To make sure that it was noticed, the experimenter announced the group's score after each shot and stated the accumulated point total. At the finish of five shots he wrote this total on the blackboard. After a group had had three practice trials, the experimenter proceeded:

*Actually, these are control groups from an investigation with two experimental conditions. The rest of the study is discussed in the next chapter.

> We have become interested in how well young men can judge the amount of teamwork in muscle control within their group and would like to get information on that as well. Before each set of five shots, therefore, we are going to ask each of you to give us your best private estimate about the score your group will try for next time. After you have done this, you will have a group discussion and decide how you all feel about this matter. You are to reach a decision that you all agree on—a unanimous decision. This decision has nothing to do with your score but it will give us some idea of how well you can estimate the amount of team control you have over your movements.

In accord with these instructions, prior to each trial, he gave each subject a private ballot requesting the following information: "In my opinion, on the next trial our team will be able to get a score of___." The response is taken to be the *member's aspiration for his group*. After the marked ballots had been given to the experimenter, they discussed the same question until a unanimous decision was reached. This is considered as the *group's level of aspiration*. During these meetings the experimenter made the appearance of being busy elsewhere.

The pattern of discussion in these conversations was remarkable for its consistency. A conference began with each subject stating in turn what he expected the group's score would be on the next trial. Members then gave reasons for their beliefs or offered advice to one another on ways of improving their performance until someone made an informal "motion" by suggesting a level the group might consider. This was invariably a compromise among the various levels originally offered. Modifications of this motion were then discussed until an agreement was reached. The meetings were brief, informal (a vote was never taken), calm, and characterized by harmony.

During work on the task the groups were noisier than they were in the meetings. The participants talked freely and loudly, criticized individuals or congratulated the team. The first man in line often became the "coxswain" and counted out a rhythm for swinging the pole; others joined in. As the trials progressed (14 in all), each team became orally more involved in improving its score.

In a solo condition, eight additional subjects worked on the same task, alone. The pole was light enough so that one could play the game alone with no problem. A solo participant was given the same explanation about the importance of muscle control and the experimenters' desire to see how well he could judge his ability. In all respects he had the same experience as the teams except of course he heard nothing about teamwork in the experimenter's opening recital and did not participate in the group discussion.

Comment on Procedure. Because this experimental procedure, or something akin to it, is used in a number of experiments, it is useful to note its characteristics. They indicate what was believed were the minimal conditions for initiating study of group aspirations and were intended to create as simple a group as possible.

a. A group exists for doing work.

b. All members interdependently engage in the group's activity.

c. Each member does exactly the same thing at precisely the same time. There is no flow of work, no distinction in status levels, no designated leader.

d. No member, compared to others, has more responsibility for the score of the group.

e. The work is repeatedly performed for a number of trials.

f. The score of the unit is evident to a member but he does not know his personal score.

g. One in a number of scores may be earned by the group on any trial.

h. The scores each occupy some point on an objective scale of difficulty from easier to harder.

i. The level of aspiration is for the group's future level of performance as a unit.

Some of these conditions will serve as variables in later studies.

Results

The main results were these.

1. Groups and individuals were not notably different. In none of the findings to be described concerning performance level, aspiration level, direction of shifts in aspiration level, amount of shift in aspiration level, or the d value (discrepancy between prior performance and future aspiration), were the results for individuals and groups reliably dissimilar. There is little point then in presenting the comparative data for individuals and groups since those for groups describe fairly well what the solo performers did. Under the conditions employed, the assumptions and concepts in aspiration theory can reasonably be used in interpreting the actions members make in behalf of their group.

2. Groups with three members were no different from those with five members—the results from the two sizes will be pooled hereafter.

3. The mean of the aspirations members privately set for their group were not significantly different from the aspirations the same persons chose as the result of a group discussion. Groups did not favor harder or easier group goals than did individuals.

4. The mean performance score for all groups was 36 (S.D. = 3.68) and the mean group level of aspiration was 38 (S.D. = 2.29). The level of aspiration was slightly more difficult than the level of performance.

5. When a group score on one trial was better than the score on an immediately prior one, the aspiration level for the next trial was raised; when the performance was worse, the aspiration level was lowered. The correlation

between amount of change in performance and the amount of change in aspiration level was +.60 ($p < .01$).

6. Aspiration levels were more consistently raised when the performance improved than they were lowered when the performance worsened. (The effects of failure or success in efforts to attain the level of aspiration are presented below.)

An explanation commonly offered in writings on the level of aspiration is suitable for interpreting these results. Consider the following, stated in terms of group behavior.

The choice of a group aspiration is assumed to be a function of the perceived probability of a group's attaining a given score and the satisfaction members believe they will derive from its doing so. In the present case subjects know that their group may obtain a tally from 0 to 50 on any trial (five shots). As their group progresses on the test, they begin to see approximately what scores it is most likely to earn and what scores are less likely. A member's *subjective probability of success by his group* (Pgs) is his judgment as to the probability, from 0 to 1.00, that it will attain a given score; this probability will be smaller for a difficult score and larger for an easier one. A member's *subjective probability of failure by his group* (Pgf) is his judgment as to the probability that it will fail to attain a given score; this probability will be larger for a difficult score and smaller for an easier one. The subjective Pgf is the inverse of Pgs, that is, Pgf decreases as Pgs increases and the sum of the two probabilities equals unity.

Expectation of a specific future score generates anticipation of a future degree of satisfaction. The *incentive value of group success* (Igs) is the amount of satisfaction with his group that a member anticipates he will develop if the group attains a given score. The *incentive value of failure* (Igf) is the amount of dissatisfaction with his group that a member anticipates he will develop if the group fails to attain a given score.

The amount of satisfaction an individual anticipates if his group should attain a particular score (Igs) is inversely related to his perceived probability of group success in attaining that score (Pgs), that is, he expects his satisfaction will be greater if the group earns a harder score than if it earns an easier one. The amount of dissatisfaction he anticipates if his group should fail to attain a given score (Igf) is inversely related to the perceived probability of failure to attain that score (Pgf), that is, he expects his dissatisfaction will be less after a failure to reach a harder score than after a failure to reach an easier one.

The level of aspiration an individual selects for his group is one that best resolves the conflict between the attractiveness of success, repulsiveness of failure, and the perceived probabilities of success and failure. It is set at a location that will provide as much satisfaction as is reasonably probable.

Effects of Group Success or Failure. A chosen level of aspiration provides a criterion for judging whether a given score is better or worse than had been expected, this judgment then leads to a reappraisal of what the group can do in the future.

Suppose a team achieves its level of aspiration. The expectancy of future success on that level we assume is thereby strengthened, that is, the Pgs for that level becomes larger. Members, in addition, become increasingly certain that their group can accomplish an easier level and their confidence also improves that the group can attain an even harder one. Imagine, instead, that a team fails to achieve its level of aspiration. Here the expectancy of future failure on that level is increased, that is, the Pgf becomes larger, and the perceived likelihood of failing on other levels is also changed. Recalling the above relationship between incentive and probability, it is evident that success heightens the attractiveness of success and failure heightens the repulsiveness of failure. Success, in short, invokes a tendency to set a higher level of aspiration, failure a tendency to set a lower level. The rule is: *succeed, raise; fail, lower.*

The direction of shifts in aspiration for teams engaged in the ball-propelling task are displayed in Table 2-1. These results are in accord with the rule.* Similar support for this rule was obtained in several other experiments (*83, 85, 86, 89*).

After a group successfully attains a goal, then, its members perceive that the task is too easy for a fully satisfactory outcome and shift their aspiration level in a more difficult direction. After a group fails, members perceive that the goal is too hard for them and move their subsequent aspirations to an easier level.

There was one exception, however. Members were less willing to lower their group's goal following a failure than to raise it after a success. This reluctance to lower the goal after a failure could mean that they wished to reduce the dissatisfaction that would follow another failure and were aware they could reduce this dissatisfaction somewhat by failing at a harder task, it may mean that they regarded a failing performance as not typical of the group's true ability, or

TABLE 2-1   DIRECTION OF CHANGES IN GROUP LEVELS OF ASPIRATION

Performance on trial k	N of trials	Aspiration for trial k + 1 (%)		
		Raised	Lowered	Kept same
Sucess	103	79	1	20
Failure	118	8	69	23

*The only significant difference between groups and solo individuals occurred at this point. Groups were less likely to lower their goals after a failure than were individuals. Does this mean that groups were less willing than individuals to accept that their team had failed?

it may mean that they felt restraints from some source against lowering the aspiration level. This matter will be taken up again.

In sum, a member's aspiration for his group may be accounted for by the same factors that are thought to influence the choice of an individual's aspiration. The group aspiration is assumed to be a function which *either* maximizes the expected satisfaction of group success (Pgs X Igs) *or* minimizes the expected dissatisfaction from group failure (Pgf X Igf).

GROUP SUCCESS OR FAILURE IN A MORE DEMANDING SITUATION

Choosing a group level of aspiration in the laboratory, even when the activity is billed as a test of masculine skills, is probably less important to participants than the goals members establish in real life. Outside the laboratory, members doubtless give more thought to the selection of a goal than they do in an experimental setting. Moreover, outside the laboratory, they are not subject to the influence of an experimenter. It will be informative then to consider comparable data from a goal-setting, formal, organization where success and failure are truly important and wholly autonomous matters.

The annual cycle of events in a local United Fund organization is similar in most respects to the sequence in one trial of an aspiration-level experiment. The Fund establishes a goal, runs a financial campaign to fulfill that goal, notes any discrepancy between goal and performance, and next year sets another goal to begin a new cycle. There are over 2500 of these organizations in the United States and Canada, the campaigns are similar from town to town in their structure, methods, and administration. The money they raise provides careers and services for many persons.

A sample of 149 cities between 55,000 and 140,000 in population was selected and a study made of the goals and performance levels in each, year by year (Zander & Newcomb, 87). The changes in the goals during four consecutive trials are shown in Table 2-2. Clearly, Funds raise their goals after a success more often than they lower them after a failure. The reluctance to lower after a failure is considerably stronger than in the laboratory groups (see Table 2-1).

TABLE 2-2   DIRECTION OF CHANGES IN UNITED FUND GOALS (N = 149 FUNDS)[a]

Performance in year y	N of campaigns	Goal for year y + 1 (%)		
		Raised	Lowered	Kept same
Success	207	80	14	6
Failure	240	52	40	8

[a] After Zander and Newcomb (87).

More than experimental groups, however, the properties of a Fund are likely to change from trial to trial (year to year). It is wiser then to include each Fund in these analyses only once. In order to do this the 149 organizations were divided into four types: those with no successes and three failures ($N = 44$), those with one success and two failures ($N = 40$), those with two successes and one failure ($N = 33$), and those with three successes and no failures ($N = 32$). The dominant direction of the shift in goals was determined by an index score in which each Fund received a larger count for a given trial when a shift in goal was upward one year to the next, a smaller count when there was no change in goals, and a still smaller count when the shift was downward. The sum of these tallies thus collapsed into one index the tendencies to raise, lower, or stay. The results are shown in Fig. 2-1.

In the consistently failing Funds the median index was at the point indicating that no change in goal up or down was the most typical response; but in the consistently succeeding Funds the index was near the maximum, indicating that these moved their goals upward after almost every success. The distribution among these values was significant by median test ($x^2 = 10.82$, $p < .02$).

The United Fund data are from statistical records. Do the actions implicit in them accurately reflect the views of men who set the campaign goals? There is evidence that they do. We sent questionnaires to board members in 46 Funds (described in Chapter 6) and asked them about their views and preferences on many matters. Among the questions was this one: "Suppose for the moment that your campaign this fall does not attain the official community goal, and suppose that a proposal is made next year to set a lower goal than the one your community failed to reach this fall. Would you be inclined to support this proposal to lower next year's goal?" Nearly every respondent indicated that he

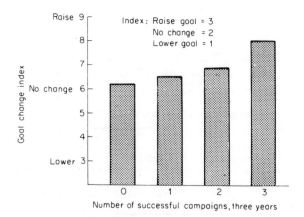

Fig. 2-1   Medians, direction of change in goals index.

would not be willing to do so. At another point in the questionnaire they were asked: "If it happened that the campaign goal was not attained this fall, which of the following do you think would best describe your view for next year?" They were then given three alternatives: (a) set the goal low enough to have a good chance of attaining it, (b) keep the same goal even if we might not be likely to make it next year, or (c) raise the goal some reasonable amount. Only 14% of the respondents chose to lower the goal after the hypothetical failure, while 47% chose to keep it the same and 39% chose to raise it, little support for lowering the goal.

Summary. Thus far, there are three noteworthy findings and typical assumptions from the theory of aspiration setting that account for these reasonably well.

1. A group's level of aspiration tends to be higher than its recent level of performance, explained by the assumption that success on a harder task is perceived to be more satisfying than success on an easier task.

2. Groups shift their aspiration levels in accord with the rule: succeed, raise; fail, lower, explained by the assumption that the perceived probability of achieving a given score increases after a success and decreases after a failure.

3. Groups more often raise their aspiration level after a success than they lower it after a failure, explained by the assumption that the dissatisfaction anticipated from a failure on an easy task is greater than the dissatisfaction anticipated from failure on a difficult task. The easier the goal a team fails to reach, the worse members feel about it. The expected dissatisfaction can be reduced somewhat by selecting a more difficult goal for the next trial rather than an easier one.

A succinct statement concerning reactions to group success and failure can now be made: the perceived value of the consequences from a group success is greater as the subjective probability of the group's success is less (task is harder) and the perceived repulsiveness of the consequences from a group failure is greater as the subjective probability of success is greater (task is easier). This assumption is similar to one advanced by Feather concerning individual aspirations (22).

AMOUNT OF CHANGE IN GOALS

Taken together, the foregoing suggests that there are stronger forces toward choosing a more difficult goal after a success than toward choosing an easier goal after a failure. Thus, one may expect a larger change in goals (covering a greater number of units in the scale of difficulty) after a success than after a failure—upward in the former case, downward in the latter. Support for this hypothesis can be stated briefly.

In an experiment that required groups to engage in tasks differing widely in difficulty, the average amount of shift upward following a success was +1.12 and the average amount of shift downward after a failure was −.16 regardless of the difficulty of the group's task (82). These results are reliably different ($p < .005$). In another study (83), the mean amount of shift upward following a success was +1.47, the mean amount of downward shift following a failure was −1.15, and the mean amount of shift in a control condition in which the members had no idea about how well they were doing was +1.29. The differences among these three means was statistically significant ($p < .001$).

In the study of United Funds, the median amount that a goal was moved from the goal of the previous year increased as the frequency of successful campaigns in a town increased. In communities with three failures and no successes in a row, the median amount of upward shift in the goal was $.04 per capita, but in those with three successes and no failures, the median upward shift was $.13. The trend between these extremes was in regular order. The values in this distribution were significantly different by median test ($\chi^2 = 19.41$, $p < .001$).

DISCREPANCY BETWEEN PRIOR PERFORMANCE
AND GROUP ASPIRATION

It was noticed earlier that the boys working on the ball-rolling test most often set their level of aspiration a bit above their immediately past score. There also are occasions when a group sets its aspiration below its most recent score. A discrepancy between previous performance and future aspiration is called a *d value*, which is positive, if the new aim is higher, negative if it is lower, than the prior performance level.

In a sense the d value indicates the appropriateness of a level of aspiration. The larger its size, the more it is likely that members have set either too easy or too difficult a goal line, as the case may be. Even when this value is not very large, it is of interest because a positive d value means that the members are moving toward a higher goal, while a negative d value implies that participants have faced the need for a lower appraisal of their unit's output. What circumstances, inherent in the dynamics of aspiration setting affect the size of the d value? This issue will be a matter of recurring interest in later chapters.

As would be expected, a unit's d value after a successful trial is different from its value after a failing trial. But, in the light of previous findings, the nature of this difference may at first seem strange. Notice these results.

1. In the United Funds the size of the d value was the amount that the official goal for the year $y + 1$ exceeded the amount collected in the year y.

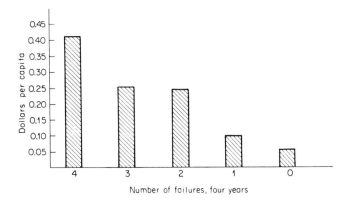

Fig. 2-2 Mean d values in 149 local United Fund organizations.

Following successful campaigns, the mean d value was $.09 per capita, but following failing campaigns, the mean was $.31. The difference between these means is reliable ($p < .001$). The d value was larger after a failure than after a success.

2. The 149 communities were separated into sets, each having a different record of success during the years observed, as shown in Fig. 2-2. The mean d value was greater as the number of past failures increased and the distribution among these values was significantly different by median test ($\chi^2 = 46.33$, $p < .001$).

3. In a second study of United Funds we observed 23 towns that had failed in all of their last four campaigns and 23 towns that had succeeded during the same period. In order to have some kind of control on "ability," each successful town was matched with a failing one on both the size of population and the *Effective Buying Income*, an index used nationally by the Funds to measure the wealth citizens have available for disbursement. The d value of the 1968 campaign goal was calculated. The successful communities had a d value of $.06 per capita while the failing ones had a d value of $.18 ($F = 6.19, p < .01$). A history of failure preceded a larger d value than did a history of success, when determinants of the town's capacity to perform were controlled.

4. The results from several laboratory experiments were essentially the same (*86, 88*).

Why does a group's d value tend to be larger after a failure than after a success? A reasonable explanation can be offered in terms of the assumptions already made. In order to do so, however, it will be helpful to review the step-by-step contrasts after a success and after a failure.

On a successful trial a goal has earlier been set at a given level (Step 1) and the subsequent performance exceeds that level by some amount (Step 2). A fresh goal is then set which is usually higher than the previous aspiration (Step

3). Note that the new goal almost always exceeds the prior goal by a larger amount than it exceeds the most recent level of performance. Thus, the d value is a modest one.

On a failing trial, a goal has been set at a given level (Step 1), the subsequent performance falls short of that level by some amount (Step 2), and the new goal is then set at the same level as the prior goal (Step 3), or lowered a bit. Because the new goal is not lowered much, and because the past level of performance is short of the prior goal, the new goal is located a greater distance above the immediate past level of performance than above the past goal. Clearly, the greater the size of a failure, the more the d value increases in size, if the future aspiration level is not lowered; the d value increases even more if the aspiration level is raised.

The selection of a more difficult goal after a success, as already shown, is a result of the awareness, created by the success, that the social unit can accomplish a more difficult level than it had previously attempted. A fairly large upward shift in a successful group thus results in a modest d value. The tendency to lower the goal after a failure, as also shown, is countered by the perception that unfavorable consequences are greater for failure on an easier task than on a harder one. Thus, in a failing group there are stronger forces toward raising the goal, or keeping it at the same level, than there are toward lowering it. Whether the members make an upward shift in the goal, stay at the same level, or even reduce the level a small amount, the result after a failure is an immodest d value.

Returning to the United Funds, the failing organizations collected significantly less money on a per capita basis than did the successful ones ($p < .02$). The official campaign goals of the failing Funds were also significantly lower than those in the succeeding Funds ($p < .002$). The differences in the d values of succeeding and failing towns was not created then by the tendency of failers to aim higher than succeeders. Instead, it was created by their poorer level of performance and their unwillingness to lower their goals.

The restraints against lowering the goal after a failure have been ascribed thus far to a desire to reduce the dissatisfaction that follows failure. The results from the United Fund create the suspicion that influences may be operating on the decision makers in such an organization that are not wholly captured by the term dissatisfaction. Doubtless a Fund has pressures upon it toward increasing the amount it raises; probably there is no upper limit to the amount that the pressure sources consider desirable, but there is certainly a base line below which they believe the budget should not fall. Whatever the origins of the pressure against lowering the goal, and these will be considered in due course, it is evident that problems arise for a failing Fund because its performance initially is a poor one.

To round out the study, it is interesting to inquire why the goal was set unreasonably high in the failing towns. Perhaps, as a result of local conditions, they needed more money. If so, the restraints against lowering the goal would be easier to understand. An attempt was made to determine if the average size of the d value (per capita) was related to the local need for programs in social welfare. To do this the relationship between the mean size of the d value and the following demographic variables was computed for each of the five types of towns noted in Fig. 2-2. The variables were: Effective Buying Income (assuming that a community with less wealth per citizen requires more social services), percentage loss of Effective Buying Income during four years (same type of assumption), size of town (larger towns often have areas with greater needs for social welfare services), and rate of growth in community population (rapidly growing towns have increasing demands). None of these variables was significantly related to the size of the d value. The results also indicate, one should note, that towns with separate records of success or failure did not differ in these social characteristics.

It cannot be said then whether larger d values in a United Fund are due to greater need for welfare services. One is left, insofar as the present data are concerned, with the evidence that Funds with records of failure have poorer records of performance, and, because they do not lower their goals, they develop larger d values. It is quite possible, as will be seen in Chapter 8, that the poor performance itself occurred because the goal was seen to be "impossible" rather than a "challenge." Board members in such Funds were asked why they remained with the too-hard goals after a failure. The reasons they gave would take the reader too far afield at this point; they will be explored at length later.

A further comment should be made about the larger d values in failing Funds: it increases the chances that a failure will occur again. When a Fund fails, it tends to set or stay with what amounts to an unreasonably difficult goal. This new goal is likely to cause another failure, which is followed by another too-difficult goal and by an additional failure. Thus, a failure tends to induce a failure, in a continuing cycle. The direction of such a cycle is apparently the opposite in a successful Fund since a success leads to a modestly challenging goal, which is followed by a success, and by another attainable goal. These cycles will be considered more fully in Chapter 6.

RELATION BETWEEN PROBABILITY AND INCENTIVE

It will be useful to return for a moment to the assumption that probability and incentive are inversely related (that satisfaction, for example, is proportionally greater on harder tasks) because this proposition has usually concerned the behavior of individuals, has been rejected by some students of organizational decision-making, and is largely based on inferential rather than direct evidence. Does this assumption properly apply to the views members develop about their group?

One cannot get sensible data on this matter by asking subjects trial by trial how satisfied they think they might be if they attain their aspiration level on an upcoming attempt since participants always respond that achievement of their chosen aspiration will be satisfying. A question about their satisfaction after they have tried to attain a given aspiration, moreover, is confounded by the success or failure the group has just experienced. An alternative approach is to make it clear to members that the group is working on either a hard task or an easy one. This method requires the somewhat questionable assumption that the members' subjective probability of group success is what they are told it is by the experimenter. If all else is equal, this is a reasonable working proposition. The hypothesis is that members in a group with a harder goal will have more favorable feelings about their experience than those in a group with an easier goal, as frequency of success or failure on that task are held constant. This hypothesis was tested as a part of an experiment designed for other purposes (Zander & Ledvinka, 82).

The groups, three high schools boys in each, were asked to collaborate in producing a single product—a design made of dominoes. Each participant had a supply of the dominoes and was to fit these into a pattern so that each location in the design had a domino with a particular number. Along one wall were 13 large poster cards, each displaying a design. These regularly increased in complexity and size, from 6 pieces to 18. A prominent numeral on each card indicated the proportion of teams that had been able to finish that design in the allotted time, larger for easier designs and smaller for harder ones. Thus, the set of patterns constituted a 13-point scale of difficulty.

The boys were told that they would choose, after the first trial, whatever level they wished their group to attempt; at the outset, however, they would be assigned a particular level. The time allowed for each trial would be the same regardless of the design they selected.

For the first trial, half of the groups were given design Number 4, toward the easy end of the scale, the other half were given design Number 10, toward the hard end of the scale. The number of successes and failures within these two conditions was controlled by the experimenter and was alike in both.

It was anticipated that the participants in the easy and hard conditions would not move their group's aspirations very much away from the levels originally assigned to them. This anticipation was well met: groups given the easier level on the first trial (Number 4) worked at an average level of 5.12 when they made their own choices, while groups given the more difficult level (Number 10) worked at an average of 10.60.

When five trials had been completed, the subjects filled out a brief questionnaire asking their reactions to the experience. These are indicators of their satisfaction. The mean responses in each group were correlated with the average difficulty of the patterns chosen by their team. These correlations are

TABLE 2-3 DIFFICULTY OF GROUP'S TASK AND ATTITUDES
TOWARD THE TASK (N = 80 GROUPS)

Content of question	r
Value in tests like this?	.235*
Validity of test as measure of coordination in teamwork?	.266*
Importance of succeeding on test?	.236*
How hard do people try on tests like this?	.314*
Importance of skill measured by test?	.231*
How involved were you in test?	.296*

* $p < .01$

displayed in Table 2-3. Although the correlations are not strong, it is evident that members gave more favorable responses when they had worked on more difficult designs than when they had worked on easier ones.

If members are more satisfied when their group works on a more difficult task, they will be more pleased by evidence that the group will subsequently attain a difficult level of performance than by evidence that it will attain an easier level. Thus, they might reasonably feel more approving toward an agent who assures the group that it will attain a difficult level than toward an agent who says that the group will achieve an easier level.

In an experiment to be described more fully in the next chapter (85), a team of three boys worked on the ball-propelling test while a set of three additional boys, waiting their turn to be tested, observed the team at work. Before the performers set their aspiration for each trial the observers held a brief conference and agreed upon the score they unanimously expected the performers to attain on the next trial. This expectation was then allegedly delivered to the performers. In fact, however, the experimenter substituted a previously prepared message. For half of the groups this message was about four points higher than the working group had ordinarily achieved and for the rest about four points lower. Were the performers more favorable toward one type of observer than the other? The relevant data are the attitudes of subjects at the end of the experiment. The mean values on a number of rating scales are shown in Table 2-4. Performers were more favorable toward the observers who had higher expectations than toward those who had lower expectations.

In the situations studied, it is apparent that working on a more difficult task is more satisfying than working on an easier one. Why, then, did members not choose the most difficult task of all for their group? The reason implied earlier is that members consider not only the amount of satisfaction they might derive from a particular score; they also consider the probability that this score will indeed occur, and this estimate in turn is based on prior performance of the group. The cognitive estimate of what the group can probably do, based on its

TABLE 2-4   AVERAGE ATTITUDES OF PERFORMERS TOWARD
OBSERVERS (N = 24 IN EACH COLUMN)[a]

Content of question	Level of observers' expectations		t of diff.
	High	Low	
Accuracy of Os expectations?	4.3	3.7	2.74**
Os ability as judges?	4.7	3.3	5.32***
Care taken by Os?	4.4	3.5	2.94**
Os wanted Ps to do well?	4.0	3.5	3.21**
Os helpful to Ps?	4.0	3.2	2.10*
Confidence Os had in Ps?	5.0	3.8	4.30***

[a] After Zander et al. (85).
*$p < .05$.   **$p < .01$.   ***$p < .001$.

past experience, apparently tempers the members' desire to aim for the hardest goal. If the quality of performance is unknown, ambiguous, or unreliable, this tempering presumably cannot develop. It follows that members should choose harder aspirations when they do not know the scores of their unit than when they do.

This last hypothesis was tested as part of an experiment to be discussed in Chapter 4 (83). In this instance the subjects performed a card-marking activity, each member circling a set of numerals on each of a supply of cards and passing it to his neighbor for him to mark. The group's aspiration was the number of sets it chose to process within a standard period of time. Twenty-four groups engaged in this activity for a series of trials and were given no information about whether their group had succeeded or failed. Forty-eight other groups were told, after each trial, how well their group had performed. The results are shown in Fig. 2-3.

Members with no evidence about their group's performance chose a more difficult task on each new trial, repeatedly placing the group's aspiration level higher than it had been on the previous trial. Those in groups with regular evidence about the quality of performance did likewise, but there was a more moderate increase in the aspiration levels. The contrast between these two curves is significant at the .005 level of confidence. It appears then that members prefer more difficult tasks when the restraints created by knowledge of their group's performance are absent. One wonders how often goal-setting groups elsewhere have unreliable (or no) data about their group's performance, and thereupon hitch their plans to unrealistic but attractive goals. From the findings of these three studies we conclude that future attainment of a more difficult level is likely to be seen as potentially more satisfying.

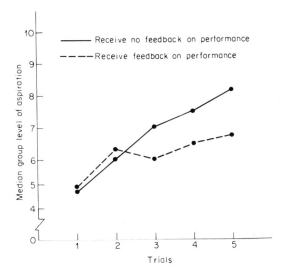

Fig. 2-3 Effect of feedback on group levels of aspiration.

THE SIMILARITY AMONG MEMBERS' ASPIRATIONS
FOR THE GROUP

A group level of aspiration is the result of an agreement among members. In the experiments thus far unanimity was required but this was for purposes of standardization and was not a conceptual necessity. When there is greater similarity in the views of members, a level of aspiration will probably be more easily agreed upon and be better accepted by those who select it. It is pertinent then to identify those conditions that foster greater congruence among the aspirations members privately prefer for their group. Several pieces of evidence are suggestive.

One of the potent sources of influence on a member as he chooses a personal aspiration for his group is an awareness of what others prefer. As part of an experiment described more fully in Chapter 5, Forward (28) examined the degree that past group decisions affected members' private preferences. Before each trial on a group task members indicated (by secret ballot) their personal aspiration for the group. After their marked forms had been collected, the experimenter announced an alleged "majority" vote as the group's aspiration level. For half of the groups he allowed these announced votes to differ very little from trial to trial and made all of them close to the intermediate level in the scale of difficulty. For the other half of the groups he varied the majority widely from trial to trial, making them either very easy or very difficult and moving randomly between these two extremes. Under these conditions, it was evident that some members noticed a discrepancy between their own vote and the subsequent majority and on the trial thereafter moved their vote so that it conformed more closely to the majority.

In a further investigation of the conformity between a member's aspiration for his group and the group's immediately past aspiration level, Zander and Ulberg (92) observed that the degree of conformity was greater after the group had succeeded and it was subsequently urged (by agents outside the group) to take it easy, or after the group had failed and it was urged by such agents to attain a harder score. Conformity occurred less often in contrast if a success was followed by a message asking the group to improve or a failure was followed by a message asking the group to take it easy ($p < .01$). It appeared then that members placed greater reliance on the beliefs of their peers, as revealed in their conformity to the previous group-decided aspiration level, when external pressures opposed their usual inclinations either to raise the aspiration after a group success or to lower it after a group failure. Unfitting or unexpected influences from outside the group apparently caused greater conformity among members.

It is also plausible, although the matter has not been directly studied, that circumstances which generate greater uniformity of belief among members will likewise influence their aspirations for the group, thus a group with a higher degree of cohesiveness or one with more firmly established interdependence among participants may more easily arrive at a similar belief about the most appropriate aspiration level. Research relevant to such issues has been reviewed elsewhere (12).

The level of aspiration was earlier said to be a resolution of a conflict among perceived levels of probability and related incentives. In some situations this conflict is probably simpler to resolve than in others and the most appropriate aspiration level is then more readily apparent. The more it is obvious which level of aspiration is most suitable, the less members should differ when they privately select aspirations for their group. It is interesting therefore that the degree of discrepancy among members' aspirations for their group was less as the difficulty of their group's task was greater ($r = -.31$, $p < .001$). In groups that succeeded more often than they failed, this correlation was $-.45$ ($p < .001$), but in groups that failed more often than they succeeded it was $-.15$ (n.s.). It appears that there was more similarity among members about the appropriate aspiration for their group as the task attempted by the group was more difficult and the group was more successful; both are properties that make a task more attractive.

Members seemingly will have greater similarity in their aspiration estimates when the task is a more challenging one and the likelihood of success is stronger. Rosenthal and Cofer (61) have reported results that fit this conclusion. They compared the process in selecting aspirations for the group when one of its members (an assistant of the experimenter who pretended to be a regular subject) was indifferent and neglectful, on the one hand, and when the same member behaved as a good teammate should. The members took a longer time in selecting a group aspiration when they had an unreliable member whose presence, apparently, reduced their perceived probability of success.

SUMMARY

We have considered the behavior of members when their group repeatedly chose a level of aspiration. The group was as uncomplicated as possible so that we might assume that their behavior was in behalf of that unit and not due to some unique group property.

Does a group choose its aspirations on the same grounds as an individual? An experimental demonstration to examine this issue found no difference in the aspiration-selecting behavior of groups and of soloists. These results, and the choices of members described throughout the chapter, lend credibility to the belief that concepts and assumptions in aspiration theory can reasonably be employed in interpreting the aspiration choices members make in behalf of their group. Explanations commonly offered in writings on the level of aspiration, when stated in terms of group behavior, suitably accounted for specific findings such as the following:

1. A group level of aspiration tends to be located somewhat higher than the group's past level of performance.

2. Members perceive participation by their group on a difficult task to be more satisfying than participation on an easy task.

3. A group level of aspiration is apparently chosen so that it represents a balance between what would be the most satisfying outcome and what would be an achievable outcome.

4. When members receive no feedback on the score of their group during a series of trials, they select more difficult aspirations trial by trial than they do when they regularly learn the score of their group.

5. The direction of changes in group aspiration levels from trial to trial adhere to the rule: succeed, raise; fail, lower.

6. Members more often raise their group's aspiration and raise it by a greater amount after a success than they lower it after a failure.

7. When attainment of a group goal is more important to persons outside the group as in United Fund campaigns, the members are less inclined to lower their goals after a failure.

8. The discrepancy between a future goal and an immediately past level of performance (the d value) is greater after a group fails than after it succeeds.

The generality of the results in this chapter would be greater if better evidence were available that real-life groups, when they perform the same task repeatedly, regularly set group asipirations. One cannot, however, take the present evidence as an indication that social units typically establish such goals since the groups studied (including the United Funds) were asked to set a goal for each trial, and they complied with that request.

If the data were available, an observation would probably be that a majority of organized groups find it worthwhile to set goals. In a study of 197 business firms, McBurney (52) observed that about 90% established future objectives; the more competitive the business, the more they were likely to do so.

CHAPTER 3

**External Social Pressures
on a Group's Aspirations**

On that little-known planet, the "real world," the members of a working group seldom remain solely involved in the internal life of their unit. They become sensitive as well to the actions of persons or organizations in their group's environment, develop feelings of responsibility for nonmembers, or recognize that the group is accountable to particular others. As a result, when they choose an aspiration for their group, their decision may reflect the influence of these external sources. In order to make this abstract assertion more concrete, let us consider several instances of such an influence.

   a.   A group may receive requests from people in other units. Within a United Fund, for example, the annual campaign goal is a decision that interests many persons, inside and outside its board of directors. When establishing its goal, the board considers petitions from social agencies supported by the Fund. It follows that a primary source of satisfaction for board members, is in providing satisfaction for those who ask to have their needs considered.

   b.   Strong pressures may be placed upon a group to favor the attainment of certain objectives rather than others. Anderson and Cockcroft (*1*) report that the major political party in Mexico influences the efforts of the five remaining parties so that the five give priority to particular achievements. The dominant party uses rewards as long as these seem to work, but if this approach fails, they use repressive measures.

   c.   A subgroup in a large organization must coordinate its output with the output of other units. The fender-making department of the Dasher Automobile Company ought not provide fewer or more mudguards than the body-making department wants, and the latter two units must suit their rates of productivity to divisions that provide other parts for the car.

   d.   A group may be influenced because the members themselves decide to imitate another unit. A local United Fund, for example, often compares its goal

29

and its performance with those in similar communities. To facilitate this comparison process, the national headquarters of the United Fund provides a printed manual containing instructions for board members to use in selecting the towns they wish to emulate.

e. A working group must offer enough of what is desirable to those who have contacts with it if the unit is to survive for any period of time. Thompson (70), in advancing a proposition similar to this, states that a group must decide upon certain activities, the population to be served, and the amount of services to be rendered—a set of decisions he designates as the group's claim to a *domain* of effort. The establishment of a domain, he believes, cannot be a unilateral action since the domain can become operational only if the group's claim is recognized by those who might provide the necessary support or approval.

f. Finally, participants in a group may realize that others are watching how well it functions and are urging the unit to improve its performance without specifying any particular output as a goal. To illustrate, in a study of the purposes espoused by 300 national associations, Zander (93) observed that the induction most often placed upon local chapters and member groups by the larger organization was intended to have the units improve their procedures and methods. The next most frequent induction was to foster uniformity in behavior across all groups. In many other ways associations were clearly a source of pressure upon subunits to improve their processes, and a source of expert help in expediting this improvement—doubtless, such implicit pressures affected the goals selected by members.

A change in a group's goal because of new conditions in the environment is of course a decision made by the members themselves. Thus, a given external situation may be ignored by some groups and be a stimulation for change in others, also certain members within the same group may react to its milieu while the remainder are unaffected. There is no empirical evidence we know about that traces the occurrence of such environmental influences or that elucidates the reasons for them. In this chapter we examine the impact of external agents upon the aspirations members choose for their group, observe several conditions that moderate the strength of that influence, and consider why a group's aspirations can be affected by pressures from its surroundings.

AWARENESS OF SOCIAL PRESSURES

The survey of opinions among board members of United Fund organizations was briefly mentioned earlier (89). That study was made because we had previously noted that local Funds often did not lower their goal after a failure. We wanted to know why this happened. Did board members feel pressures against lowering the goal?

In the questionnaire respondents were asked whether their Fund had had a failing campaign during their tenure on the decision-making committee. Those who said this had happened were then asked: "Concerning the most recent failing campaign, why was the goal set so high? What reasons determined where the goal was set?" They were provided a number of alternative answers and invited to indicate which ones were likely to account for the selection of the difficult goal. The reasons most often chosen were: social agencies (dependent on the Fund for their support) needed increases in budgets; lowering the goal might make it necessary for separate agencies to solicit their own funds outside the United Fund campaign; and if the goals were lowered, the Fund would not meet the needs of the community. Clearly, the needs of local welfare agencies provided restraints on board members against lowering the campaign goal.

Half of the respondents on each board were officers or exofficers (central persons) and the other half were peripheral members. The central persons were more aware than the peripheral members of the pressures arising in the community. In a failing Fund, but not in a succeeding one, central persons perceived greater difficulty in lowering the Fund's goal ($p < .05$), and saw less value in doing so ($p < .05$). In a succeeding Fund, but not in a failing one, central persons said that lowering the goal would result in their "receiving pressures from the community" ($p < .05$). And regardless of their Fund's history of success or failure, central persons were more alert than peripheral ones to the need for help and support from influential citizens in the town if the next campaign was to be a success ($p < .05$).

These results indicate that the decision makers in a United Fund are cognizant of the needs of the agencies who depend on the Fund and are aware that these desires as well as the overt pressures from citizens have an impact upon their selection of a campaign goal.

THE EFFECTS OF SOCIAL COMPARISON

In many institutions, as in the United Funds, groups exist in multiples, each a duplicate of the rest. Examples are sales offices in separate regions of a company, Army tank crews, hospital wards, and sports teams. If the performance of each replicated unit is known to all, it seems probable that the groups would compare their actions. This process of comparison is known to occur among solo individuals and to result in modification of their aspirations (18, 24). Do groups indulge in these comparisons with the same effect? An answer was sought in the first ball-propelling experiment (80).

Results were presented earlier from the Control condition of this study. In two experimental conditions the procedures were exactly the same as those already described except that now the experimenter gave the subjects information about the "average score obtained by other teams in their school." Prior to each trial, before subjects selected a group aspiration, the experimenter stated this average (a fictitious one) and wrote it on the blackboard in such a position that comparisons were possible, trial by trial, among the experimental group's scores, its aspirations, and the alleged scores of others. The reason he gave for doing this was stated in a friendly way: "We thought you might be intersted in how well other groups in this school have been doing thus far on this test."

In a *Favorable* comparison condition the scores of the other groups were set at a level easy enough to be exceeded most of the time (mean = 32.5). In an *Unfavorable* comparison condition these scores were set at a level of difficulty which teams would miss most of the time (mean = 40.4).

The mean number of points performing groups earned on the test in each of the three conditions, Control, Favorable, and Unfavorable, was almost exactly the same. We are interested then in the size of the d value in these contrasting situations, expecting it to be larger in the Unfavorable, and smaller in the Favorable, than it is in the Control condition. The Unfavorable comparison in short will create a tendency to select more difficult aspirations and the Favorable comparison a tendency to select easier aspirations. The d values are shown in Table 3-1.

Note first, in Table 3-1, the d value for the initial trial on the test. This is the discrepancy between the beginning group aspiration and the score the group had just attained on its last of three practice trials. The aspiration was chosen by the group immediately after members had been given the first comparison score, either Favorable or Unfavorable, and while members were not wholly sure of their group's ability. The Favorable condition, it can be seen, caused members to set a group aspiration below their last score, thus generating a negative d value.

TABLE 3-1   MEAN d VALUES PRIOR TO FIRST TRIAL
AND FOR ALL TRIALS

	d Value	
Condition	Before first test trial	All trials
Favorable	−2.70	+1.04
Control	+ .31	+1.92
Unfavorable	+ 2.94	+2.99
t of difference, Favorable vs. Control	2.73**	1.83
t of difference, Unfavorable vs. Control	1.85*	2.23**

*$p < .05$.   **$p < .01$.

The Unfavorable condition in contrast caused groups to set their aspirations well above their past score, thus creating a positive d value. In the Control condition there was a small positive d value, as is typical of a group without external sources of influence.

Observe the effect of these conditions throughout the test, after members had presumably developed a somewhat more certain belief about the ability of their group. In the Favorable condition the negative d value disappears and is replaced by a small positive one. In the Unfavorable condition, however, the d value remains positive and large; in the Control condition the d value is between the above two. It appears that both the Favorable and Unfavorable comparisons had effects on the d values, were equally strong sources of influence at the outset, and that the Unfavorable retained its strength while the Favorable did not. The Favorable condition overall was not significantly different from the Control, raising the suspicion that a harder goal may have been chosen in that case, as was true in the Control condition, simply because a harder goal is more attractive and not because of the influence of the Favorable comparison.

Let us examine the changes in group aspirations during the test within each of the three conditions. These results are displayed in Table 3-2.

The groups in the Unfavorable condition, compared to those in the other conditions, raised their goals more often after a success and lowered them less often (or kept them at the same level) after a failure, thus generating the larger d values just noted in Table 3-l. An interesting consequence of these shifts, reminiscent of results we have seen in the United Funds, was that groups in the Unfavorable condition failed in 61% of their trials and succeeded in 39%. Within the Favorable and Control conditions, in contrast, the proportions of success and failure were closer to 50–50.

TABLE 3-2   DIRECTION OF CHANGE IN ASPIRATION LEVEL AND SOCIAL COMPARISONS[a]

Performance on trial k	N of trials	Goal for trial $k + 1$ (%)		
		Raised	Lowered	Kept same
Favorable				
Success	112	79	1	20
Fail	106	6	66	28
Control				
Success	103	78	2	20
Fail	118	8	69	23
Unfavorable				
Success	85	89	—	11
Fail	136	15	51	34

[a] After Zander and Medow (80).

Before each trial a member gave his private judgment (on a 7-point scale) in response to the question: "How sure are you that your team will actually get the score decided on?" In the Control condition the mean rating was 5.4, in the Favorable comparison it was 5.7, and in the Unfavorable comparison it was 5.0. Confidence in attaining the chosen aspiration was reliably lower in the Unfavorable than in the other two conditions ($p < .02$). In an Unfavorable comparison therefore members knew that their chosen aspirations were difficult and in a Favorable comparison that they were easy. Diggory (17, p. 270) has reported similar data for solitary individuals.

All in all, the subjects considered the scores of the referent groups as well as their own group's scores when selecting a group aspiration. In the Unfavorable comparison particularly, the groups selected unreasonably hard levels and stayed with them, even after failing to reach them. Seemingly, the Unfavorable comparisons were more influential than the Favorable ones. That is, members more readily raised their aspirations than they lowered them. Before we ponder over the reasons for this last difference, it will be useful to examine another form of external information.

EVALUATIVE PREDICTIONS BY OBSERVERS

For many groups a source of external pressure is a visible entity that makes its views known and members are aware that ideas from that source are a reaction to the group's quality of work, not merely a general standard of comparison. Because the outsiders are observing their group in action, the members may believe that the observers' information is in some degree evaluative, revealing how they appraise the group. How do such external stimuli influence a group's aspirations?

An investigation developed to examine these matters has already been mentioned briefly (85). A team of *performers* took the ball-rolling test while a team of *observers* sat at one side. Prior to their group's decision about a level of aspiration, the performers received a message indicating what score the observers "believe the group will be able to attain on the next trial." The messages they received did not contain the actual values selected by the observers but instead were preplanned scores substituted by the experimenter and arranged to be at either High or Low levels exactly the same on each trial as those earlier described for the Unfavorable and Favorable conditions, respectively.

The primary supposition was a simple one. Given that the subjects know the observers are watching and discussing among themselves how well the group will be able to do in the future, a High expectation implies that the observers believe the group can make better scores than it is presently earning and a Low expectation implies that the observers believe the performers are playing over their heads, soon their scores will not be as good as they have been. High expectations then are congratulatory and Low expectations are derogatory in the eyes of the performers. Will the social approval implied in the High expectations generate unusually large d values, or will this approval be so satisfying in itself that the members need no longer strive for higher goals? Will Low expectations be viewed as insults and thus to be ignored, or will they generate a tendency to expect their group will fail?

There were 48 groups of performers, 16 in each of the High, Low, and Control conditions. The d values for each condition are given in Table 3-3.

One can see that High expectations invoked reliably larger d values than did Low expectations. These results are similar to those previously noted in the Unfavorable and Favorable conditions, respectively. The d value in the High expectations condition is not significantly different from the d value in the Control condition, once more suggesting that the High level is not due to the influence exerted by the external agent but simply to the greater attractiveness of a higher goal. The d value in the Low expectations condition is however significantly different from the d value in the Control condition, indicating that the derogatory messages from observers might have been influential ones.

The actual difficulty of the group's chosen aspirations can be judged by noting how often groups failed to achieve them. In the High expectation condition they failed on 57% of the trials; in the Control condition, on 53%; and in the Low expectations condition, on 38%. The goals selected in the Low condition were obviously easier than those chosen in the other two. The observers' prediction apparently affected the changes in aspirations from trial to trial. Furthermore, when observers provided Low expectations, performers were less likely to raise their aspirations after a success; when observers provided High expectations, performers were less likely to lower their aspirations after a failure $(p < .05)$.

It should be noted in Table 3-3 that groups receiving Low expectations had an extremely small d value, which means that they tended to stick with the same goal rather than moving to a harder one, even though they succeeded on most of their trials. Apparently the receipt of Low expectations made members willing

TABLE 3-3   MEAN d VALUES OF PERFORMING GROUPS[a]

Observers' level of expectation	d Value	t diff.
Low	+ .13	
None (Control)	+1.50	None vs. Low = 1.85*
High	+2.05	High vs. Low = 2.47**

[a]After Zander et al. (85).
*$p < .05$.   **$p < .01$.

to be satisfied with a success at easy levels, at levels they had in fact attained two thirds of the time. This is a rare phenomenon.

On the basis of the data in Table 3-3 one cannot say with confidence that a High expectation was really a stronger or weaker source of influence than a Low expectation. But it is again clear, as in the former experiment, that the external influence pressing toward a high level of performance generated more failures (than successes) and yet relatively little lowering of the aspiration level. In contrast to the previous study, however, external influences pressing toward an easier level of performance caused more successes (than failures) yet almost no raising of the aspiration level. Perhaps the low expectations by observers did arouse an awareness of the likelihood, and a desire to avoid, failure.

Expectations from observers ought to have more significance to performers if the observers have a stake in the accomplishment of the group than if they have no obvious reason for wanting the group to perform at a particular level. In this experiment, accordingly, half of the observers in each of the three conditions were made to be dependent on the group and half were not. The dependent condition was created by telling subjects (both performers and observers) that they were all parts of a single operating unit and that all would share a prize to be given to the upper one-fifth of the teams taking part in the study. To create low dependency, subjects were told that the observers were not eligible for prizes but would be later on when they became performers.

The separate dependency conditions had no differential effect upon the d values or on any other aspects of the group's aspirations even though the effects of the contrasting degrees of dependency were interesting in many ways reported in other pages. Thus, a prediction from a dependent observing group was not more influential than the same prediction from a nondependent one. Although further study of this finding is needed, it suggests that predictions from observers have an effect on a groups's aspirations regardless of the observers' degree of interest in the group's outcome. Surely this cannot always be so.

THE COMPARATIVE IMPACT OF SEPARATE TYPES
OF SOCIAL PRESSURE

A group aspiration chosen under the impact of outside pressures, especially a level set so high that the group cannot achieve it, is similar to the goal set by some of the United Funds. In those organizations, it will be recalled, a Fund that fails to achieve its campaign goal in one year seldom lowers the goal in planning for the next year, and more often than not fails again. Both in the laboratory and in society then there are conditions that seem to inhibit lowering of a group's aspiration level.

In a United Fund it is not surprising that decision makers dislike to lower their goal after a failure and are willing to raise it whenever they can. Members mention a variety of social pressures we have seen that affect their selection of a campaign goal; these pressures are most often directed upward toward attainment of ever harder goals. Could it be that one kind of pressure is more potent than another in determining where the goal is placed? If this question were answered in the affirmative, we might develop some insight into the reasons that members are influenced by an external agent's acts. Continuing with the United Fund as the case in point, three sources of social pressure appeared to be most plausible and worthy of comparative study:

1. The board members of a given Fund become aware that their Fund's level of performance is better or worse than it is in other towns like their own. Thus, they set their own goal to match the level of performance in comparable cities.

2. The budgetary need of social welfare agencies supported by the Fund is taken to be the most reasonable goal. Thus, board members simply match their goal in dollars with the stated financial need.

3. Various agents in the community, for whatever reasons, exert pressures on the Fund to raise its goal to an unreasonably high level (a variable that had already been investigated in an experiment yet to be described).

Thus, the selection of a goal is a reaction to such pressures. Is one of these sources of influence stronger than the other? Is there some form of interaction among them that might illuminate the source of the larger d values among failing Funds?

It is not feasible to study the effect of these conditions in the United Funds themselves. Instead, Forward and Zander (29) tried to simulate them in the laboratory. Sixty-four high school boys were randomly assigned to four-man groups. They performed the team coding capacity task described more fully in the next chapter. It required that they decide how many units of work they aspired to accomplish within a standard period of time. Three experimental conditions were created to test each of the reasons mentioned above:

1. The members learned the performance of their own group and that of other groups. This information, as in the previous Favorable and Unfavorable comparisons, revealed that their team was doing either better or poorer than other teams.

2. The members were informed that their group's score was important because it contributed points to the sum that their school required. In one case it was made evident that their school had a High need for points, in the other case a Low need for points. This operation was to duplicate the degree of need in the wider community.

3. Members received a direct request for a given level of performance from a Standards Committee as described in later pages. In the present instance these requests were either to have the group attain a specific and impossibly difficult level or a request for members to work hard but not recommending a particular goal. The experimental design for these variables is shown in Table 3-4.

The d values for individual member's aspirations for the group are displayed in Table 3-4. Members of teams that were doing better than other teams who were in a school that had a Low need for output, and who had no specific pressures on them to improve their score, selected group aspirations that were very close to the mean improvement in performance (i.e., they had smaller d values). At the other extreme, members of teams that were doing less well than others, who were in schools with a high need for points, and who had pressures on them to attain a higher score, selected group goals that exceeded the mean improvement in performance by a factor of 3 (i.e., they had larger d values).

As can be seen by the ordering of means, and by the results of the analysis of variance in Table 3-5, each of the three experimental conditions had a wholly

TABLE 3-4 MEAN d VALUE PER TRIAL[a,b]

| Comparison with performance of other teams | School need | | | |
| | High | | Low | |
	Strong pressures	Weak pressures	Strong pressures	Weak pressures
Unfavorable	1.90	1.53	1.35	0.98
Favorable	1.23	1.03	1.20	0.60

[a] After Forward and Zander (29).
[b] As a basis of comparison, the average increment improvement of performance is 0.60.

TABLE 3-5 ANALYSIS OF VARIANCE FOR MEAN SIZE OF d VALUES[a]

Source	df	MS	F
Social comparison (A)	1	2.89	5.16*
School need (B)	1	2.40	4.29*
External pressures (C)	1	2.40	4.29*
A X B	1	0.01	<1
A X C	1	0.43	<1
B X C	1	0.17	<1
A X B X C	1	0.14	<1
Error	56	0.56	—

[a] After Forward and Zander (29).
* $p < .05$.

independent and additive effect on the tendency to raise the goals above levels that were reasonably attainable in the light of past levels of performance. All three main effects were significant and there were no significant interactions. There was no evidence that one condition was stronger than the other.

If these results have any generality to the United Funds, they mean that such an organization may be effectively influenced by several different sources when it selects a campaign goal, and more influenced, the greater the number of pressures at work on the group. There is no simple explanation for the size of the Fund's d value and one source of influence does not modify or interfere with another. A failing Fund, in short, has many pressures not just one that may prevent it from lowering its goal to a more attainable level.

As for the original intention in planning this study, there is no new insight provided here suggesting that members have stronger proclivities to respond more readily to one source of pressures than another. A social pressure it appears is a social pressure.

GROUP SUCCESS OR FAILURE VERSUS EXTERNAL SOCIAL PRESSURES: INDEPENDENT EVENTS

Thus far there is promising but not convincing evidence that external pressures directed toward a higher level of performance are more potent in determining a group's level of aspiration than are pressures toward a poorer, or an unimproved, performance. The precise nature of the influence exerted by harder or easier standards is not entirely clear however as it is recalled that influence attempts directed toward an ever better performance trial after trial typically generate more failures than successes, and the aspiration is not regularly lowered after each failure, whereas repeated pressures toward a lower output generate more successes than failures, and the level of aspiration is usually raised somewhat after each success. To some unknown degree, then, a more difficult external standard may be more influential (or appear to be so) in determining a group's aspiration level because members ordinarily dislike to lower their group's aspiration after a failure, and an easier standard may be less influential (apparently) because members prefer to raise the group's aspiration after a success.

Clearly, the members' responses to their group's success or failure and their responses to fixed external social pressures are each likely to affect the other in such a way that the contribution of one may simply be an artifact of the other. What is wanted is an experimental procedure in which the occurrence of success or failure is largely independent of the level advocated by the external source, so that one is not consistently accompanied by the other. Such a procedure was employed in an experiment by Zander and Ulberg (92).

The experimental design allowed an equal probability of each of four treatments to occur for each group: a group success followed by a hard external standard, a group success followed by an easy external standard, a group failure followed by a hard external standard, and a group failure followed by an easy external standard. The following procedure was used. Twenty-four teams (four members in each) took part in a "team information processing test." It required them to count the number of holes in electronic data cards as rapidly and accurately as they could. Each participant worked on part of each card in a set of cards and passed it to his neighbor. The group aspiration was publicly computed and was the average among the members' separate and privately recorded aspirations for the group.

At the end of each trial the experimenter reported the "time" taken by the team. This was not the exact number of seconds consumed but instead was a preplanned value. Each group had a unique program, previously established, that indicated how much was to be added to the group's level of aspiration for the trial just finished (thus creating a failure to achieve the aspiration level), or how much was to be substracted from the prior aspiration (thus creating a success). Every group had four successes and four failures scattered randomly throughout the eight trials; the average amount of success as well as the average amount of failure was the same for every group by the end of the eight trials.

The *external standard* was said to be the score the given group should contribute to the overall score of their school "in order that the school have a good chance to beat other schools." To make the standard appear to be a custom-made response to the performance of the specific group, and not an arbitrary demand, the participants were told that a panel of local teachers together with the experimenter had used a computer to develop a table of standards. With the help of this table it was possible to tell members exactly what time their group should attain on its next trial, taking into account its recent times and recent aspirations. On half of the trials a group received a *hard* external standard and on the other half an *easy* standard, randomly distributed, regardless of the group's immediately prior speed. A hard standard was 4–8 sec more difficult than the group's aspiration level on its prior trial and an easy standard was 4–8 sec easier. Whether a standard for a given trial was to be hard or easy was predetermined and programmed in such a way that each group had the same average discrepancy between prior aspiration and external standard by the end of the experimental session.

With this procedure it was not possible to use the d value as the indicator of outsiders' influence upon the group's aspiration level. Instead, the mean absolute discrepancy between an external standard and the group aspiration chosen immediately thereafter was taken as the sign that the external standard had had an influence upon the level of aspiration; the smaller the discrepancy between external standard and aspiration (i.e., the greater the congruency between these two) the greater the likelihood that the standard had influenced the members' choice of aspiration. The hypothesis is that congruence between members' aspiration for their group and an external standard is larger when the standard is difficult than when it is easy. The experimental procedure makes it possible to examine whether congruence with a harder external standard is a manifestation of the standard's influence or merely a preference for harder aspirations.

Results. The average amount of shift in members' aspiration for the group from trial to trial was toward a more difficult level after a success (mean 4.44) and likewise after a failure (mean 1.43); there was thus a typical raise in aspiration level after a success, but an atypical raise after a failure. Also, the mean shift in aspiration level was upward after being exposed to a hard external standard (mean 4.68), as well as an easy standard (mean 1.22). The net result is that the level of aspiration generally shifted upward in all conditions, as has often been found in prior studies where external pressures were at work on the group.

The hypothesis that congruence between the external standard and members' aspirations will be stronger when the standard is difficult than when it is easy, was supported: when the standard was easy the mean discrepancy between the external standard and aspiration was 8.16, and when the standard was hard, the mean was 4.62 ($p < .001$). The difference between these two means was largely generated by a very large discrepancy when an easy standard followed a success.

The tendency for members to shift the group aspiration toward a harder level after either a success or a failure, and after either a hard or an easy standard (noted above), suggests however that the congruence may very well be the result of a preference for harder goals rather than an indicator of a stronger influence by a harder standard. It was necessary therefore to adjust the measure of congruence by ruling out any effects that might be due to the preference for selecting harder aspirations trial by trial

In order to normalize the shifts in aspiration, the average shift made by all subjects was subtracted from the aspiration level proposed by each subject within each trial; in effect the mean shift in aspiration over all trials (both successful and unsuccessful) was made to equal zero. When this correction was applied, the hard standard generated no more congruence than the easy one—the mean discrepancy for each was about 5.70. It is evident then that the support for the hypothesis, mentioned above, was in large part an artifact of the greater preference for harder aspiration levels. Support for the hypothesis cannot be taken to mean that hard and easy external standards differed in their influence upon the aspirations members favored for their group.

The comparative effect of a harder or easier standard and a group's success or failure can be observed by examining the mean shift in aspiration level within each of the four experimental conditions, while the control on the preference for harder aspirations, as was just applied, is again in force. These results are displayed in Fig. 3-1.

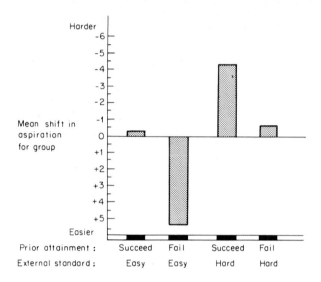

Fig. 3-1   Shift in aspiration for group after controlling on preference for higher levels.

It is evident there that a greater upward shift in aspiration occurs after a success when a hard standard is proposed than when an easy one is offered, and a larger downward shift occurs after a failure when an easy standard is provided than when a hard one occurs. The pressures arising from these separate events are clearly additive when in the same direction; they virtually cancel the effects of one another when the pressures are in opposing directions. We conclude that, under the conditions employed, a reaction to a success or failure was no stronger than a reaction to an easy or difficult external standard.

The results in Fig. 3-1 suggest that it is useful to look more closely at the sources of congruence by eliminating not only the upward drift of aspiration levels but by controlling on the differential shifts in aspiration level generated by either the group's success or its failure. To do this, the average shift upward by all subjects after a success was subtracted from each subject's aspiration for the group after a success, and the average shift downward by all subjects after a failure was added to each subject's aspiration for the group after a failure. The amount of congruence between external standard and aspirations was then examined in each of the four treatments. The results are summarized in Table 3-6. They reveal a source of influence that had not been apparent in previous studies.

In Table 3-6 the discrepancy is greatest (congruence is least) when the level of the external standard is (presumably) unexpected, that is, when an easy

TABLE 3-6   MEAN DISCREPANCY BETWEEN MEMBER'S
ASPIRATION FOR GROUP AND THE
EXTERNAL STANDARD[a]

	Easy standard	Hard standard
Sucess	6.11	5.09
Failure	4.91	5.50

$$F = 3.85, p < .05$$

[a]After Zander and Ulberg (92).

standard follows a success or a hard standard follows a failure. In such a dissonant treatment, it appears, the aspiration choice is based on information other than that implied in the external standard. The discrepancy is least (congruence is greatest) when the level of that standard suits the direction that might be expected, that is, when a hard standard follows a success or an easy standard a failure. Seemingly, then, the attention given to an external standard depends in part upon whether it is, cognitively, what is perceived to be an appropriately directed pressure on the group, after it has experienced either a success or a failure. These results, it should be emphasized, are not at all a product of the preferred reactions to success or failure since the latter have been wholly eliminated; the findings can reasonably be conceived as evidence of the influence created by an external standard. Other results from this study presented toward the end of Chapter 2 show, moreover, that members conform most often to the views of teammates when the external standard is unfitting.

In this investigation then the difficulty of the external standard as such did not determine its ability to influence the aspiration choice, instead the standard's impact was apparently determined by its appropriateness to the member's desires at the moment. As in previous studies, it was found that members placed their level of aspiration closer to a hard external standard than to an easy one, but the experimental procedures made it possible to ascertain, with a degree of certainty that could not be achieved in earlier research, that the closer similarity between a level of aspiration and a more difficult standard was largely due to the preference for attempting harder tasks, and not to the greater influence of a harder external standard.

One cannot conclude, even so, that willingness to conform to harder demands is always an artifact of the members' preference for harder aspirations. The procedures that were necessary in this investigation to create independence among variables also serve to limit the generality of the findings. The tight controls and the independent status of the variables made them isolated events unlike the repeatedly similar external pressures a group usually experiences. Each standard may have had little logic in the eyes of the subjects, despite the stated reasons for the standards given by the experimenter. Each standard was chosen in relation to the prior level of aspiration set by the group and was not modified in the light of the group's performance; probably a standard is seldom set elsewhere on such grounds. Each standard had little implicit evaluation inherent in it. A low standard was not likely to be seen as derogatory in this experiment, whereas such a standard may often be taken as a comment on the potential ability of the group in other settings. This point is worth noting because members who give their group a low evaluation because its score is repeatedly worse than others, or because observers keep predicting that the group will perform poorly, may become uncertain about what aspiration level to choose, harder or easier, and as a consequence, may be considerably more susceptible to pressures arising outside the group. Such a situation could not develop in the present study.

In summary, members may place their group's aspiration closer to a difficult standard than to an easy one. In some cases this congruence is doubtless the result of the members' preference for harder tasks. In other cases this congruence may be the result of the greater susceptibility to influence aroused in members by the presence of such a standard. We cannot yet say what conditions make it likely that congruence with a harder standard is merely a happenstance of the preference for harder aspirations or is truly a result of influence. It is quite clear, however, that an external standard, regardless of its level, is given less attention when it is unexpected or unsuited to the member's experience.

INTENTIONAL SOCIAL PRESSURES ON A GROUP'S ASPIRATIONS

It often happens that external agents directly request a group to establish a particular goal, and, they offer rewards to ensure that the group does as asked, or threaten punishments to deter the group from unwanted ways. When an outside source overtly attempts to influence a group's performance and makes it known that he will reward a good score and punish a bad one, his comments tap motives relevant to attaining the potential reward or to avoiding the potential punishment. Because the members are simultaneously engaged in competition against a standard of excellence, motives are also aroused in them to achieve a satisfying success and to avoid a dissatisfying failure. Does the external agent's arousal of a motive to gain a reward or avoid a punishment strengthen the members' concern about group achievement? Will one who intends to influence the aspiration of a group be more effective if he offers punishments or rewards than if he offers neither? These are questions that we (Zander, Medow, and Dustin) attempted to answer in an unpublished experiment.

The subjects were 48 groups of high school boys. Each group (of three members) was placed in one of four conditions: Control, Request, Reward, or Coercion while they worked on the ball-propelling test. In the Control condition they performed the test and set new goals for each trial in the way that is familiar. In the remaining conditions the members received before each trial a request from a committee of students in their school to attain a particular level of performance. The subjects were told that their teachers and athletic coaches had selected three students to supervise the testing program. The names of these students, who constituted what was called the *Standards Committee,* could not be made public until later, it was said. The three had been chosen not on the basis of their ability on the test, but on the basis of their good judgment, their leadership among students, and their popularity in school. These comments were to establish that the members of the committee were not highly skilled in the test at hand but were attractive persons in the school community who might readily be accepted as referents.

Subjects in the *Request* condition were told that the Standards Committee had asked the experimenter to deliver their request before the team attempted each trial. The Standards Committee furthermore hoped each team would do as well on the test as their own group had done. In this condition, and the following ones, the mean score of the Standards Committee was 41.4, similar trial by trial to the levels proposed in the Unfavorable comparison condition of the earlier study. All groups in the experimental conditions received these unattainably high scores, there was no contrasting condition in which groups learned that the committee requested easily achievable low scores.

Subjects in the *Coercion* condition were given the same information as those in the Request condition; in addition they were told that the Standards Committee would list the member's names and the scores of all teams, along with the scores of the Standards Committee, in the school's newspaper. Subjects in the *Reward* condition were also given the same information as those in the Request condition; in addition they were told that the Standards Committee would publish only the members' names and the scores of teams that performed *better* than the Standards Committee. Subjects in the *Control* condition were not told the scores obtained by the Committee. They were informed that the Committee would receive a list of the members and the scores of all the teams but nothing was said about the use to be made of this list or the level of performance to be expected of them. In all experimental treatments, but not the Control, the members received direct pressures to perform at levels higher than they were attaining.

Because the three conditions were orally established at the beginning of the experiment and not reinforced during later activities, it is useful to know whether the participants had these instructions in mind as was intended. Queries for this purpose were included in a questionnaire given near the end of the experimental session. In each condition the subjects perceived that the Standards Committee contained persons they wished to be like, but attraction to these persons was significantly higher (than Control subjects) only when the external agents offered rewards. The subjects correctly viewed the committee as offering an attractive incentive in the Reward condition and an unattractive one in the Coercion condition. It is clear then that the participants, by the end of the experiment, remembered what they had been told. How did these separate conditions affect the d values of the groups? These are shown in Table 3-7.

In the Reward and Coercion conditions the d values were significantly larger than in the Control; moreover, in the Reward situation they were larger than in the Request condition. It appears therefore that a direct request from an attractive source was more influential in determining a group aspiration level than was no request, but only if a sanction was mentioned when making the request, especially a reward. It is not certain from these data just what effect a potential punishment had since it generated results that were no more or less reliable than those in the Request or Reward conditions.

The sizes of the d values in Table 3-7 suggest where failures would have occurred most often. In the Control and Request conditions groups failed, on the average, in 66% of the trials; in the Reward condition, on 77%; and in the Coercion condition, on 74%. Examination of the aspiration shifts revealed that in the Reward and Coercion conditions members were considerably less willing to lower their group's goal after a failure than they were in the Request and Control conditions. The aspiration was raised after almost every single success in all conditions of the study.

It is concluded that a potential reward (and perhaps a potential punishment) increased the perceived satisfaction from attempting a more difficult task. The attractiveness of receiving a reward and the attractiveness of a satisfying success summate, in short, to provide a stronger tendency to choose a more difficult goal than either of these incentives alone.

Finally, it is interesting to note, a direct request (without sanctions) generated a larger d value and more failures than did an Unfavorable comparison, or a High expectation from observers, in the prior studies.

TABLE 3-7 MEAN d VALUES UNDER OVERT SOCIAL PRESSURE

Condition	d value
Control (no request, no sanction)	+2.16
Request (request only, no sanction)	+3.06
Coercion (request made, coercion threatened)	+3.55
Reward (request made, reward offered)	+3.75
Significant t tests	t
Reward > Control	3.73**
Coercion > Control	3.28**
Reward > Request	2.85*

*$p < .05$. **$p < .01$.

THE OBSERVERS AS ASPIRATION SETTERS

Because the expectations actually selected by observers were never in fact delivered to the performing teams and because observers did not know the aspirations that performers set for themselves, the observers' expectations can be considered as a topic of interest in its own right. The observers' aspirations for the performers are analogous to the goals a committee of standard setters might establish for the rest of an organization to meet.

In United Funds, board members often appeared to follow the psychology of the "asking price" when setting their official goals. They assumed that they would never get more money than their goal but they might very well get less; thus, they often set the goal high, especially in failing towns, in order to be sure that the intake would be reasonably adequate even though the goal is not achieved. Among observers, therefore, the experimenters were prepared to find that those who were dependent on the performers would set higher aspirations for the group than observers who were not dependent. This did not happen. The mean d values for observers' expectations (the amount the observers placed their own aspiration for the performing group above the most recent score obtained by that group) was 1.01. The d values of observers who were dependent and those who were not dependent differed very little. Indeed, the d values of observers and those of performers did not differ significantly in any condition in which they could be compared.

The observers did not know that they were the source of High expectations or Low expectations; so we cannot examine the effects of those two conditions upon their levels of expectation, but part of the observers were given information (which performers could not hear) about how well teams usually do on this test. What they were told was strictly comparable to the Unfavorable comparison condition in the prior experiment. The rest of the observers received no such information. The expectations stated by observers were not at all different in these two conditions—thus, an Unfavorable comparison had little impact on observers, in contrast to what has been previously noted about performers. Also, some of the observers were led to believe that their predictions were being reported to performers and part to believe that this reporting did not occur. Again, this variable had no contrasting effects. In sum, it appears that the observers selected aspirations for the group much as a performing team does for itself; they considered both the probability and attractiveness of the performer's attaining a given level, but, unlike the performers, they ignored any pressures that the experimenters brought to bear on the observers' choices.

Regardless of the experimental condition, the observers changed their expectations in accord with the rule: succeed, raise; fail, lower ($p < .001$), where success or failure was denoted by the group's performance in reference to the observers' expectations.

The observers and performers were different in one respect. This was within the control conditions for both—when performers received no expectations from observers and when observers received no comparative data from the experimenter. In this instance, observers followed the succeed-raise part of the rule more than did performers, after the performers' score equalled or exceeded the performers' aspiration (for performers' shifts of goals) or the observers' expectations (for observers' shifts of goals) ($p < .05$). But performers and observers were not different in their adherence to the fail-lower part of the rule.

Although this brief foray into the aspirations selected by the observers has shown only that observers did not differ much from performers, this fact itself is important. It intimates that a committee charged with setting goals for others will set the same goals as workers set for themselves, all else equal. The results also suggest that such a committee may be less influenced by social comparisons or by their own vested interests than are those who work on the task. There is a need for more study of the psychology of those who set standards for a group.

One finding (or rather, lack of a difference) in the behavior of observers has interesting implications: the observers themselves did not differ when they were dependent on the performers and when they were not. The dependent condition, let us assume, generated an awareness that they were members of a group along with the performers, although only the latter at the moment were working on the group's task; both the observers and the performers would gain or lose as a result of the team's score. The nondependent condition, in contrast, created an awareness that the observers were in a group entirely separate from the performers and they therefore could not be affected by the performers' score. The interesting point is that the observers did not differ when they were "members" (i.e., in the dependent condition) and when they were "outsiders" (i.e., in the nondependent condition). In neither of these conditions, furthermore, were they greatly different from the performers themselves.

The implication of these results is that the reactions to events in a group need not always be viewed as the reactions of one who is a part of that group. In this and later chapters we may wonder if a member is responding to outcomes for the group as such or is responding only to his own outcomes. The results just cited indicate that it is possible for an individual to react to consequences in a group, even though they cannot directly affect him because he is not a member.

SUMMARY

In this chapter, it has been observed that conditions in a group's environment cause members to change their group's aspirations and that goal-choosers are influenced by information that suggests that their group's performance level might be changed. Several findings are noteworthy.

1. Board members in a United Fund were quite conscious of the social pressures toward selecting an ever higher goal for their financial campaigns; this was particularly so after a failing campaign and among more central members of the board.

2. When subjects had an opportunity to compare the performance of their own group with the scores of other groups, they weighed the referent scores as well as their own unit's performance in selecting a future aspiration level. When this comparison was Unfavorable to their own group, they tended to establish unreasonably difficult aspirations for their unit and to stay with those hard aspirations trial after trial even though each trial was a failure. The Unfavorable comparison appeared to be more potent than the Favorable one in determining a group's aspiration level.

3. When members of a group received predictions about their future attainment levels from observers who were sitting in the same room and watching the group perform, the receipt of Low expectations generated no increase in levels of aspiration (and repeated successes), while the receipt of High expectations generated high levels of aspiration (and repeated failures).

4. The opportunity to compare the performance of own group with that of other groups (Favorable or Unfavorable comparison), the awareness of need in an organization of which the group is a part (High need or Low need), and the presence or absence of pressures to raise the group's goal, apparently operated quite independently as social pressures and generated additive effects upon the size of a group's d value.

5. When an experimental procedure was employed that made hard or easy external standards independent of the group's success or failure, it was possible to control on the greater preference for harder levels of aspiration. The application of this control made it evident that a harder external standard was no more influential than an easier one in affecting the group's level of aspiration. The apparent impact of a success and a hard external standard, or a failure and an easy external standard, were more or less equal in determining members' amount of shift in their group's aspiration trial after trial.

6. If the direction of an external pressure was unexpected in the light of the group's prior experience of success or failure, members paid less attention to the outside influence and more attention to the views of teammates in selecting an aspiration for the group, holding constant the shifts in aspiration level after a success and after a failure. If the direction of the external pressure was fitting, members gave it more attention than if it was unexpected.

7. When members of a group received a request to perform at a higher level than they had been attaining and this request was accompanied by an offer of a reward for doing so, the attractiveness of the reward and the attractiveness of attaining a satisfying success apparently summated to provide a stronger tendency to choose a more difficult aspiration level than either of these incentives generated alone.

8.   The goals set by observers were not at all different from those set by the workers themselves. The observers, furthermore, were less influenced by Unfavorable comparisons than were the workers in the previous experiments.

It seems reasonable in these studies that an Unfavorable comparison or a Low prediction from observers may have aroused an uneasiness about the consequences of performing poorly, whereas a Favorable comparison or a High prediction from observers may have invoked a sense of pride in success. In the former type of situation subjects may have been more susceptible to outside influence, than in the latter type of situation, because in the former case they were uncertain whether a hard or an easy aspiration would be the wiser choice. The data, however, do not neatly support such an interpretation. It is worthy of further study; other relevant results will be seen in Chapter 6. The findings do suggest that members behave differently if they seek to avoid group failure than if they seek to approach group success. Such matters are discussed in Chapter 4.

The Desire for Group Achievement

There has been a long standing interest in explaining why a member attends to the goodness of his group's effort. With few exceptions, as was noted in the first chapter, these explanations have been based on the assumption that he personally will benefit if his group performs well. Many studies therefore have attempted to identify conditions that facilitate individual gains for a member or make him believe these gains will occur. Investigators have observed that a member becomes more involved in his group's fate if: rewards for the group's success will be equally shared, the flow of work requires that each member do a part of the total task, more valued outcomes are attainable in that group than in any other, the group's purpose is to satisfy individual needs, or participants are approved for devoting their energies to the success of the group. The variety of satisfactions that can be provided through full-fledged membership suggest, moreover, that most members view their group's success as a means for attaining personal rewards. Individuals are more likely to join a group and remain a member if it provides outcomes they themselves value (11).

It is assumed then that a member's initial and continuing concern is in the benefits he will receive in an organization and that this self-oriented interest fosters a stake in the success of the group. Yet, it is easy to think of instances in which a person works hard for his group when there is not the slightest possibility of personal gain and even, in the extreme case, when such effort may reduce or eliminate rewards he might have received. It is difficult to understand the intentions of such members without assuming some form of motivation that is primarily focused on the outcomes of the group—a more or less selfless concern with the achievement of the group as a unit.

In order to examine more closely the nature of a member's interest in his group's achievement, it is useful to make a distinction between two types of motivation, group oriented and person oriented. In this chapter a conception of group-oriented motivation, the desires to achieve group success and to avoid group failure, is offered. In the following chapter the interaction between individual motives and these two desires is discussed.

EARLY APPROACHES

Helen Lewis was one of the first to comment on the limitations of person-oriented motives when studying behavior in groups. She said (47):

> It seems clear that theories which make use of personal needs as exclusive causal factors . . . cannot account for the causal dynamics in the social environment except in a vague and categorical way . . . . Neither direct social inductions nor personal needs, separately or conjointly, appear to be able to handle behavior which is based on the perception of various requirements of the situation including social structure, activity structure, etc.

Later she adds:

> Motivation in work need not necessarily be egotistical . . . on the contrary, the person is frequently motivated directly by the demands of the objective situation, including the requirements of another person. . . .On still other occasions, man enters upon and pursues tasks in order to help others achieve an ideal. In such cases, the person's aims are not restricted by his own self-demands, which are often pushed aside.

Two investigations, both inspired by the work of Lewis, illustrate the effect of group-oriented motivations. The first was done by Horwitz (37), and the second by Pepitone (57).

Horwitz concerned himself with members' involvement in the needs of their group. He assumed that no one person can achieve a group's goal and therefore studied the tensions that arise in all participants for completion of a group's task. He raised the questions: "Can an individual develop a tension system coordinated to a group's attaining its goal? Can movement by the group reduce this tension?" His subjects were small groups of volunteers from college sororities who believed they were competing with other sororities. He had them collaborate in solving each of a number of jumbo-sized jigsaw puzzles through voting on where the experimenter should place the separate pieces. The girls could not see one another and did not know the votes made by colleagues except as the experimenter informed them of these. They were told that it was not necessary to finish each of the puzzles in order for their group to get a basic score. Accordingly, the experimenter asked them part way through a puzzle whether they wished to continue or stop. If they stopped, they got the basic score; if they continued and did well, they got a bonus set of points; but, if they continued and did poorly, they lost points. With these instructions it was possible for him to contrive three situations: the announced vote was to continue the task and they did so; the announced vote was to continue but the experimenter stopped anyway; and the announced vote was to stop and they stopped. At the end of the experiment Horwitz asked the girls to recall and describe each of the puzzles on which they had worked. These data measured the tension of members—it was expected that they would best recall the tasks on which they did not have a reduction in tension, that is, those the group did not get a chance to finish.

Horwitz presumed that the group goal was "getting as many points as possible," and that each participant had a goal of seeing her team attain the best possible score. Within the three conditions described above, however, a person's own vote could agree or disagree with what the rest of the members wanted. Through an analysis of the situations in which the votes of members and those of the group agreed or disagreed, Horwitz showed that motivational tensions of members depended in a systematic way upon the position of the group relative to its preferred location, not upon the member's personal preferences.

Pepitone was interested in the origin of the responsibility members develop toward their group. To study this problem, in contrast with prior research, she precluded direct inductions of one member upon another and assumed that a member's perception of what his group requires is in itself a motivating condition. The strength of this requirement was based, in her view, on the extent to which the performance of a personal task was perceived as essential in order for the group to succeed. Thus, the perception that a task is important to the group in enabling it to reach its goal gives rise to a force, she assumed, the strength of which corresponds to the degree of its importance (57).

A motive which derives from the importance of the task to the group may correspond to the phenomena which are often observed and referred to as a sense of responsibility to the group, or a sense of duty. Although these motivations are undoubtedly related to own need satisfactions, our assumption is that their effects may be discerned when own motivations are constant, thus constituting additional motivating forces in performance.

Her central hypothesis went as follows:

The speed of locomotion of a member toward the group goal is a function of the strength of a force which originates in the importance of the task for the group's locomotion.

In four-person groups, each participant sorted and matched abstract symbols while out of sight of the remaining members. A subject was led to believe that two of his teammates were doing tasks other than sorting. In one condition, members were told that their role was *necessary* for achievement of the group's goal and for progress in that effort. In another condition, they were told that their job was *not important* in either of those respects. In a final condition, they were informed their activity was *as important as the other tasks* in the group. It was observed that members felt more responsibility toward the whole group when performing the necessary role than when performing either of the other two. Moreover, members who believed that they had the more important task sorted significantly more pieces than those who believed they had the less important one.

The experiments by Horwitz and Pepitone suggest that members become motivated to have their group achieve its goal and are satisfied when it does so. The success of the group rather than any private gain is taken to be the major source of this satisfaction.

THE DESIRE TO ACHIEVE GROUP SUCCESS AND THE DESIRE TO AVOID GROUP FAILURE

Our conception of the desire for achievement of group success resembles the theory and assumptions advanced by Atkinson and Feather (4) in their studies of individual achievement motivation. The present research was not initiated with that similarity in mind and had progressed through several of the experiments described below before it became evident that the findings in many ways resembled those that Atkinson and Feather had reported. When this similarity became evident, it was convenient to speak informally about a need for group achievement. Later, after becoming more familiar with the work of Atkinson and Feather, it was decided to use their concepts more explicitly and to seek further similarities and dissimilarities in theory and results. Atkinson and Feather, like their predecessor McClelland (53), did research on personal levels of aspiration when testing their theory of achievement motivation. The similarity between their research methods and ones used here fostered a congruence between the present approach and theirs.

It will be best to begin with a brief review of the major concepts in the theory of individual achievement motivation because the comparison between the group-oriented terms and those of Atkinson and Feather thus can be made most visible. This review is in large part a paraphrase of a statement provided for this purpose by Forward (27).

Individual Achievement Motivation

When an individual is faced with an activity that can be performed at any of a number of levels of difficulty and when he expects that his skill in performing the task will be evaluated against some standard of excellence, the particular level of task difficulty he will prefer to attempt (his level of aspiration) will be a function of the relative strength of two conflicting tendencies: the tendency to approach success and the tendency to avoid failure. (The word tendency is now used by Atkinson and Feather, in place of their earlier term motivation, to denote this disposition to act.)

The *tendency to approach success* (Ts) is assumed to be a multiplicative function of the motive to achieve success (Ms), the perceived probability of success (Ps) and the incentive value of success (Is). The *motive to achieve success* is conceived as a person's capacity to experience satisfaction from the successful accomplishment of challenging tasks. It is taken to be a more or less enduring disposition which is aroused whenever the individual becomes aware that certain actions will lead to consequences he perceives to be favorable.

The degree of difficulty inherent in a given task is represented psychologically for the individual by the *subjective probability of success* he associates with each of the different tasks. Stated levels of aspiration represent path choices in terms of the subjective probability that performance will lead to success and its favorable consequences.

The class of *incentives* which constitute the aim or end state of performance for persons in whom Ms is strong is restricted to the intrinsic satisfaction from achievement or pride in accomplishment which these persons experience as a consequence of successful performance. The special assumption is made that the degree of achievement satisfaction is greater following success on a difficult task than after success on an easy task. That is, the incentive value of success is assumed to be a linear inverse function of the subjective probability of success.

Given that Ts is a multiplicative function of Ms $\times$ Ps $\times$ Is, and that Is is an inverse function of Ps, it turns out that Ts is weaker for easier and harder tasks than for those of intermediate difficulty. To illustrate, suppose that Ms = 1, that Ps = .90 (easy level), and that Is = .10 (success not very attractive). The product of these values (the Ts) then is .09. Suppose that Ms = 1, that Ps = .10 (very hard level), and Is = .90 (success is very attractive). The Ts of these values is again .09. Suppose, now, that Ms = 1, that Ps = .50 (intermediate level of difficulty), and Is = .50 (success is moderately attractive). The Ts here is .25, larger than the amounts given above. Thus, intermediately difficult tasks tend to create stronger Ts and to be more arousing than easier or·harder ones.

Consider now the effects of increasing the strength of Ms. If Ms = 3, the easy task would have a Ts of 3 $\times$ .09 = .27, the difficult task a Ts of .27, and the intermediate task a Ts of .75. If Ms = 5, the amounts would once more increase accordingly. Thus, the greater the Ms, the more Ts increases for all tasks, but more so for those in the intermediate range of difficulty. When choosing a level of aspiration, therefore, persons with greater Ms will more often select an aspiration in the intermediate range. This prediction has been supported in a variety of investigations. We assume that the tendency to choose intermediate tasks is a convenient indicator of the strength of Ms.

Any situation which arouses the expectation that performance will lead to success arouses at the same time the prospect that the performance may lead to failure. The *tendency to avoid failure* (Taf) is assumed to be a multiplicative function of the motive to avoid failure (Maf), the subjective probability of failure (Pf), and the incentive value of failure (If). The *motive to avoid failure* is conceived as a personal capacity to experience dissatisfaction when faced with potential failure and the embarrassment that follows an experience of failure. Again it is assumed to be a more or less enduring disposition of an individual that is aroused when he perceives that certain actions will lead to failure and its repulsive consequences. Since a person in whom Maf is strong is more sensitive to the consequences of failure, it is. presumed that task difficulty levels are represented psychologically for him in terms of the *subjective probability of failure* he associates with different tasks. It is further supposed that the negative consequences are stronger following failure on an easy task than following failure on a more difficult one.

When making predictions for persons in whom Maf is stronger than Ms, Atkinson and Feather assume that the resultant tendency is such that they would prefer not to engage in the task at all. When they are required to engage in the activity, however, the inhibition against engaging due to the tendency to avoid failure is strongest for tasks where the probability of failure is .50 since this is where the expected negative value of failure is greatest. Persons in whom Maf is greater than Ms thus will prefer a level of aspiration that is away from the intermediate range of task difficulty—either an easy task where failure may be avoided altogether or a difficult task where the expected negative value of failure is minimized. Several studies have supported these predictions and examined conditions under which they hold for aspiration choices (4).

Group Achievement Motivation

Suppose next that an individual is a member of a group working on a task requiring interdependent effort among members and that all participants expect that the score of the group will be judged according to some standard of excellence. Imagine that the members must decide upon a single level of aspiration for the group (as in previous chapters) and that the members are told only the score for the group after each trial, not the quality of their individual contributions. What are the determinants of a member's preferences when selecting an aspiration level for his group?

The level of aspiration a member prefers is assumed to be a function of the relative strength of two group-oriented tendencies: the tendency to approach group success and the tendency to avoid group failure.

The *tendency to approach group success* (Tgs) is taken to be a function of the desire to achieve group success (Dgs), the perceived probability of group success (Pgs), and the incentive value of group success (Igs). The *desire to achieve group success* is a disposition to experience pride in and satisfaction with a group when it successfully accomplishes a challenging group task. The assumption concerning the inverse relationship between Ps and Is made by Atkinson and Feather (that Is is greater for harder tasks) also applies to the relationship between Pgs and Igs in a group achievement situation.

The *tendency to avoid group failure* (Tgaf) is a function of the desire to avoid group failure (Dgaf), the perceived probability of group failure (Pgf) and the incentive value of group failure (Igf). The *desire to avoid group failure* is a disposition to experience embarrassment for or loss of pride in the group following failure. Again, it is assumed that the expected negative consequences of group failure are stronger as the perceived chances of group success are greater.

When Dgs is stronger than Dgaf, it is expected that members will prefer aspirations for their group in the intermediate range of difficulty for group tasks. Among members in whom Dgaf is stronger than Dgs, when the group is constrained to perform the task even though they would prefer to avoid it, the contrasting prediction is that these members will prefer group aspirations away from the middle range of difficulty, either very hard ones or very easy ones. Thus, it may be assumed that Dgs is present in a group to the extent that group aspirations are in the intermediate range and that Dgaf is present to the extent that group aspirations are away from the intermediate range.

An obvious difference between the ideas of Atkinson and Feather and those proposed for group achievement lies in the assumptions made about the nature of the individual motives Ms and Maf and the group-oriented dispositions Dgs and Dgaf. Atkinson and Feather believe that the individual motives to achieve success and to avoid failure are stable and enduring personality dispositions which are susceptible to independent measurement. It is not clear, however, whether the desires to approach group success and to avoid group failure are stable dispositions or are wholly dependent on the nature of the relationship a member has with his colleagues, the objective demands of the group and the state of the group's properties. Until there is evidence to the contrary, it shall be assumed that member's Dgs and Dgaf are dispositions which are unique to the one group under consideration at the moment, and are not necessarily relevant to the member's relationship with any other group. Later, in this chapter and in Chapter 5, this question will be reconsidered and several attempts to determine under what conditions individuals are disposed to prefer either group achievement (in any group) or to prefer individual achievement will be examined.

EXPERIMENTAL VARIATION IN DESIRE FOR GROUP SUCCESS

An initial attempt to arouse different degrees of enthusiasm for the group's outcome was based on grounds that now seem inappropriate. It was assumed that members would become increasingly interested in the fate of their group as they had more communication with one another. The information conveyed in such a circumstance would emphasize the desirability of doing well as occurs in a sports team when players "talk it up" and the content as well as the tone of the messages would result in an increased desire for group success. In groups where there was little opportunity for communication, in contrast, members would become less involved in the work of the group. Personal experiences in teams rather than theory or controlled observations was the source of this hypothesis.

To test such notions, the subjects who received requests from a Standards Committee (described in the previous chapter) were invited to write their views, after every other trial, about how things were going. Participants in half of the teams were asked to pass their comments to one another, those in the remaining half were not to pass their notes but to keep them for a later, unstated, private purpose. Members were not allowed to talk in either of these conditions.

When the notes were a form of communication, they were more concerned with suggestions about ways of improving the performance of the group and various forms of catharsis. When the notes were private ruminations, they largely contained evaluative remarks about how well the team was doing. There was no difference in the pass and no-pass conditions, however, in the urging of greater effort or otherwise expressing the importance of trying hard—if anything those who did not pass their notes more often expressed such desires than those who did pass them.

The experimenters looked to see if the note passers preferred intermediate tasks rather than easier or harder ones, an indication of stronger motivation. The note passers and nonpassers were not significantly different. A further check on this last relationship under conditions that allowed for two-way, oral communication was later made by Dustin (*19, 20*). The results again were negative. Thus, interaction among members as such is not an arouser of desire for group success under the conditions employed. We shall see in Chapter 6, however, that group discussion can modify the strength of members' beliefs that are relevant to motivation.

Clearly, an experimental operation was needed that would more certainly stimulate a member's desire for his group to perform well. The findings by Pepitone, mentioned earlier, suggested a relevant approach. Accordingly, a plan was made to vary experimentally the degree of responsibility for the outcome of a group, focusing upon a participant's own aspiration for his group rather than the group-decided level of aspiration (Medow & Zander, *55*). The latter emphasis seemed warranted because in no instance in previous studies had the mean of privately chosen aspirations for the group differed from the group-chosen aspiration level.

Effects of Central and Peripheral Positions in a Group

Three-person groups were used and two social positions were created within each: *central* and *peripheral*. In the central position the occupant was most responsible for facilitating completion of the group's task; unless he did his part well, the group could make little progress. A person in a central position was expected to perceive therefore that the success or failure of his group was primarily due to his own effort. In a peripheral post the above requirements and perceptions were very weak or absent for its occupant.

The subjects were 180 boys who were invited to participate in a testing program on Organized Work Aptitude, described as the ability to work in a team relationship. They were seated at a single table but concealed from one another by wooden screens. They were told that each was to construct on the table before him within a limited time, an exact duplicate of a domino design, that each would work individually to construct the same design, that all must work in accord with particular rules, and that the score of the team was determined by the length of time taken for all members to complete their design.

On the wall, placed so that subjects could easily see them, were 14 large poster cards, each displaying a pattern made of dominos. The designs regularly increased in complexity. On each card there was also a large number in red with a percentage sign; these values were larger for simpler designs and smaller for more difficult ones. The subjects were told that the numbers denoted the proportion of teams like their own that had been able to complete the pattern within the allotted time. The series, therefore, constituted a 14-point scale of difficulty from very easy to very difficult levels.

Each boy was furnished a bucket of dominos sufficient to complete the chosen pattern plus a number of extra pieces intended to increase the difficulty of the task. He was instructed to draw dominos from his bucket, five at a time, as rapidly as he could, and to build his design in numerical order. That is, he could not begin until he found a domino with one dot (Number 1) and put it in place, after which he sought a domino with two dots (Number 2) and put it in place, and so on.

In order to determine who would be the central and peripheral persons, the boys drew lots. Degree of centrality was created by a restriction on the way the work was to proceed. All participants were told that the two peripheral persons could not put a given domino in place until the central person had done so and had stated that fact aloud. The central person therefore announced each piece as he put it in his pattern. His actions were more central in the structure of the task since he led the way and set the pace, even though all three members performed exactly the same physical movements in the same order.

The assumption in the foregoing was similar to that made by Pepitone: a member's perception of what his group requires is in itself a motivating condition, the strength of this requirement being based on the extent that performance of his role is perceived as essential for the group to succeed. Central persons would perceive that their task was more important for the group's success and they therefore would have a greater desire for their group to succeed.

An additional condition was introduced in order to create greater variation in the degree of responsibility the central person might attribute to himself. A subject was given greater or lesser say in selecting the aspiration level for the group, called his degree of decision centrality. In a *centralized decision* condition, members learned that the unit's aspiration level would be decided by the person occupying the central position on the task; he was to make this choice alone without any advice from his teammates. Although all members would state their aspiration for the group on a private ballot, the central person's vote was to be the group's aspiration. In a *decentralized decision* condition, subjects were told that each would privately vote for the design he preferred for the group and that majority rule would decide. The announced majority was in fact a fabricated one chosen to match a design level selected in one of the centralized decision groups so that pairs of centralized and decentralized teams would work on tasks with similar degrees of difficulty. The time limit was the same regardless of the difficulty of the task. A group's time was not reported to the members. Instead, half of the groups were told that they did not finish fast enough and the other half were told they had beat the limit.

Results. It was intended that one team member (central) perceive himself as having a more responsible position than the other members, thus it was necessary to determine if the subjects were aware of this distinction. Queries on these matters were contained in a questionnaire given as an interruption in the testing. The responses reveal that central subjects, compared to peripheral ones, perceived they had a larger part in the group's task, that peripheral persons were more dependent on the central ones, and the central persons were more responsible for the quality of the group's product (all three differences with p values better than .001). It is interesting that the central members believed they were more responsible for the performance of the group when it had failed than when it had succeeded ($F = 14.72$, $p < .001$).

The major prediction was that central persons, more than peripheral ones, would choose tasks in the intermediate range of difficulty. To test this hypothesis, the variance among the aspirations that members selected for their group were first compared after all groups had worked on exactly the same task. Prior to the initial trial, they were asked to begin on task level Number 7. After they had finished task 7, they chose an aspiration for the group. The variance among the aspiration levels chosen by central members after this first trial was smaller than the variance among the levels chosen by peripheral members ($p < .025$). But this was true only within the centralized decision groups; in the noncentralized groups the central and peripheral persons were not significantly different.

Another way to test the above prediction is to compare the variances in the average amount that members shifted their aspirations for the group from trial to trial regardless of the difficulty of the task attempted. Again, this variance was smaller for the central persons than for the peripheral ones ($p < .01$) and once more this difference existed only in the centralized decision condition and not in the decentralized one.

These results provide support for the hypothesis that central members more than peripheral ones prefer aspirations for their group in the intermediate range of difficulty, but the hypothesis is supported only if the central member also chooses the official aspiration level and thus is truly the most responsible group member.

Apparently a more important role makes a member more concerned about the success of his group and because of this he prefers aspiration levels which are neither too difficult nor too easy. The behavior of the central member in choosing aspirations for the group is not unlike that of individuals who have a stronger motive to approach success on a solo task. But questions come to mind. Was the central person more affected by his task position or his decision responsibility? Were the personal motives of members the same in the two positions? Were these results perhaps due to the differences between subjects in the separate roles? These uncertainties suggested that it would be wise to have a better control over the nature of the persons in the C and P positions and to reduce the likelihood of confounded variables in several other respects. Thus, the effects of centrality and peripherality were studied once more with an approach that was designed to eliminate such ambiguities.

In this new plan (Zander & Forward, 88), the procedure was the same as above in that three subjects were again used in each group, two were placed in a peripheral position and one was in a central position, the trio worked on domino designs and no conversation was allowed among subjects. The method was different in several ways. The patterns to be constructed now consisted of precisely nine pieces on every trial, to be laid in a designated numerical order, a different order for each trial. This task was less likely to generate mistakes. The man in the central position was the only one who was given a description of the test pattern and he was the only one who put pieces together from dominos he had on hand and those provided by occupants of peripheral positions. He had a standard set of message cards and requested the dominos he needed by sliding the appropriate messages under the partitions to his teammates. The peripheral member who had the needed piece then slid it to the central person under the screen. This procedure made it crystal clear that completion of the group's task was largely due to the effort and deftness of the central man. The individual motives of members to approach success (Ms) or to avoid failure (Maf) were measured (as described in the next chapter) and the participants in the experiment were selected and assigned positions so that these motives were appropriately balanced throughout the design. At the end of the first five trials the one in the central place changed roles with one in a peripheral position. A second block of five trials was then run. In this way the personal characteristics of the occupants in each position were equalized for two of the members, the responses of the third person were not used in analyzing the data.

Because the difficulty of this new task was approximately equal for each trial, levels of aspiration were now determined by asking members to select a team goal "in terms of the time limit you would like to see your team try for in the next trial." In order to give some awareness of the difficulty level for each potential time interval, the experimenter displayed a chart showing a range of time intervals and designating the period that would be easy, average, or difficult to attain (from previously established norms) with this test. This chart provided the standard of excellence against which members could compare their group's performance and aspiration levels.

Before each trial the members privately recorded the time they believed their team should try to attain in the next trial and gave this to the experimenter. Immediately thereafter, without knowing the choices of other members, the central person in one-half of the groups was asked to set an "official" level of aspiration for the group. He announced his choice aloud and the experimenter posted it on the chart. In the other half of the groups a person in a peripheral position made this choice for the group. This last contrast was to permit a comparison of task centrality and decision centrality in determining the members' concern about group success.

After each trial the experimenter gave an accurate report of the time taken to complete the design and recorded this on the chart next to the team's level of aspiration for that trial, thus enabling the members to see how well their performance matched their expectations.

Upon completing each of the two sets of five trials, the participants answered a brief questionnaire. Their responses revealed that they perceived themselves to be more "responsible for the success or failure of the group" in the central position than in the peripheral one ($F = 13.31$, $p < .01$).

The primary hypothesis again is that a member will more often select intermediate aspirations for his group in the central position than in the peripheral one. Our attention is limited for the moment to the aspirations selected by a person who is in the central position on the group task and who also chooses the official goal for the group compared with those chosen by a person who is in a peripheral role and not responsible for the group's aspiration.

In analysis of the data the intermediate range of difficulty for each trial was determined, rather than assumed, on the basis of members' responses. An empirical estimate was made by computing the mean of the aspirations privately selected by the subjects in all conditions. A deviation index (a Z score) was then obtained for each member by dividing the discrepancy between the above mean and the member's own aspiration by the standard deviation of the mean. The smaller the value of this index, the more a member's aspiration for the group is intermediate in difficulty. The mean deviation index for the first trial and the next four trials is shown in Table 4-1. It is evident that a member made more intermediate choices when he was in a central position than when he was in a

TABLE 4-1   MEAN DEVIATION SCORES, ASPIRATIONS FOR GROUP

| | Position in group | | |
	Central	Peripheral	F
First trial	.61	.82	3.26*
Trials 2—5	.65	1.02	6.66**

*$p < .10$.   **$p < .05$.

peripheral post and that this contrast increased during the five trials. The source of this difference in the effect of the two positions, we note in passing, is that a member, when in a peripheral post, significantly more often raised his aspirations for the group after it had succeeded, and lowered them after it had failed (and made larger shifts in doing so), than he did when in the central position ($p < .05$). In sum, occupying the central position generated a moderate tendency in shifting the group's aspirations.

Which was more potent task centrality or decision centrality in determining the location of aspiration choices? To consider this question, we now turn to results from members who were in the central position on the task (but did not set the official goal) and from members who set the official goal (but had a peripheral position on the task).

The data reveal that participants felt considerably more responsible for success or failure of the team when in the task-central position (with no say about the goal) than when in the decision-central position (with no important part in completing the task) ($p < .05$); they also felt more tense in the former situation than in the latter ($p < .05$). When setting aspirations for the group, members in the decision-central position chose more intermediate goals than they did when in the task-central position, but only on the first trial ($p < .05$). On subsequent trials this difference faded away.

Therefore, there is no unequivocal answer to the question posed. The results suggest that having a more important role in the work of the group may arouse a greater sense of responsibility than having control over the group's aspiration level. Doubtless, the strongest concern about the success of a group is aroused when a person is in a central post both in working on the group's task and in choosing the group's goal. There will be more said about the comparative effects of central and peripheral positions several times in later chapters.

Strength of Group

If a member is to be concerned about the achievement of a group that faces a challenging task he must perceive the presence of at least three conditions: (a) that a social unit exists, (b) that he is within that unit rather than outside it, and

(c) that events in the group are likely to be relevant to his satisfaction with that group. If these three are present for a person, one may assume that he will be more interested in the outcome of the collective's effort than when they are absent. When these conditions exist for members, the group is said to be *strong*, one that has unity, certain inclusion of members, and is relevant to their satisfactions. When these conditions are absent for members, the group is *weak*, with little unity, uncertain inclusion of members, and little relevance to their satisfactions. A strong group is more meaningful to members, for both cognitive and affective reasons, than is a weak group.

In a previous study, Zander, Stotland, and Wolfe (*78*) had observed that individuals in a group with high unity were personally more affected by the success or failure of their organization than those in a group with low unity. It seemed reasonable to suppose, therefore, that members in a strong group might be more eager to have their group do well than would those in a weak group. This was the general hypothesis in an experiment conducted by Zander and Medow (*83*).

The subjects were 216 high school boys invited to participate in a testing program on Communication Coding Capacity. They arrived in the laboratory in groups of three, one pupil from each of the 10th, 11th, and 12th grades. Boys from three grade levels were used so that previous acquaintance among them might be minimized.

After appropriately introducing himself and the reasons for the test, the experimenter began:

> In setting up groups to take part in this testing program we try to put together people who are well matched and who will get along well while they are working together. To do this we use certain school records and ratings of the students.

To create a *strong* group, the experimenter gave this comment to the participants while they were seated at a table, facing one another, with complete freedom to talk. The experimenter consistently addressed the boys as "this team" or "this group." He asked the laboratory assistant to look up the records on this set of persons, which was done by examining pages in a thick black notebook. After a private conversation between experimenter and assistant, the experimenter went on:

> We've been particularly lucky with this group because we've put together three of you who will probably fit together well and get along well together as a group.

Following this statement and the pleased grins it caused among participants, they were asked to pick a name for their team. This was done in order to give them an opportunity to talk on a matter of mutual interest and to create the sense that they were a distinct social unit, with a unique designation. When their name was decided, it was carefully lettered on a large card and hung on the wall, and the subjects were allowed several more minutes to sit in formation and to converse as they wished. Following this, they were asked to move to a table where screens separated them one from another. Thereafter, they had no opportunity for oral interaction.

To create a *weak* group, the participants heard the first statement while seated behind the screens. The experimenter addressed the subjects as "you," not "this group." At no time did they have an opportunity to talk with one another and they did not choose a name for their team. After consultation of the record book, as described above, the experimenter commented:

> Unfortunately, we have had some scheduling problems and didn't do too well in creating a good fit among you. We couldn't manage to schedule three people for this hour whose characteristics would go together well. The three of you may find that you don't get along as well with each other as you might if you were with some other people.

The experimental task has already been mentioned in Chapter 2. It required that each subject circle, in a particular sequence, sets of numerals printed on specially prepared cards. The cards contained 20 fields of numbers, each field having four columns with numbers from 1 to 12. During the test, subject A was to circle the 1's, B the 2's, and C the 3's. After each subject circled his number in a given field, he passed the card to his right; a card was circulated around the group once for each separate field. When the appropriate marks had been made, the card was tossed into a box in the center of the table. A subject began each trial with six cards, the time limit was the same for each trial—"just under three minutes." The level of aspiration for the group was the number of fields the members believed they could complete within the time interval. There were 13 fields on the card so that this level could be anywhere from 1 to 13. Each group completed two practice trials and five test trials.

The specific prediction, in terms of these operations, is that members of strong groups, more than those in weak groups, will prefer tasks in the intermediate range of difficulty. This prediction was tested in several ways. First, the variance among each member's own aspirations for his group over all trials was determined, and these means were compared by t tests. The strong condition had a mean variance of 1.92 and the weak condition a mean of 2.75 ($t = 2.03$, $p < .05$). Second, it was assumed that the task level a member states as his aspiration for the group represents approximately the .50 level of subjective probability for him on that trial. Thus, the mean amount that a member shifted his aspiration for the group from trial to trial was determined. In the strong condition this mean was .34 and in the weak it was .68 ($F = 1.97$, $p < .001$). These results support the prediction.

The results from the last three studies suggest that members can develop a motive-like desire that is primarily concerned with success of the group and which generates (as Ms does for an individual) a tendency to make challenging choices when selecting group aspirations. It is plausible that certain conditions in a group create a greater amount of this group-oriented desire. The minimal requirements probably are that a person perceives he is a member of a group and that the group faces a challenging task in which its score will be compared to some standard of excellence. Thus, simply setting a group aspiration, as a result of repeated experiences on the same task, probably arouses the desire. Other conditions help to strengthen it. Among these, one can guess, is an awareness that group mates are concerned about group success, that the group has frequently experienced success, that the group is attractive to members, that the member has an important role in the work of the unit, or that external agents will provide rewards for success. Although we are not yet prepared to be more precise about the origins of Dgs than the bald listing of such variables, there is a common denominator among these that suggests a direction for future research. It appears, in brief, that the more members are committed to membership in the group or are responsible for its fate, the more they will develop a desire for its success. We return to this issue in Chapters 6 and 9.

Desire to Avoid Group Failure (Dgaf)

Often, a social unit is constrained to continue performing a task its members would like to avoid. Rather than revealing a lethargy or a tendency to quit, the members engage in an active process of evasion. In a committee for example they may participate in interminable listing of items on the blackboard without evaluating the wisdom of any of them, may indulge in tangential discussions unrelated to the primary issue, may compete with one another, may agree to a plan but not intend to abide by the agreement, may select impossibly difficult assignments, choose absurdly easy tasks, and the like. One is impressed in such a group by the tendency of members to avoid the consequences that might occur when the task is completed. Apparently these consequences are perceived as likely to be unfavorable for the organization.

There is good evidence that an individual may develop a way of life in which he is dominated by a motive, denoted as Maf, to avoid the consequences of personal failure. An individual who is strongly inclined to avoid failure, as already seen, tends to prefer either very difficult solo tasks or very easy ones instead of those with a medium degree of difficulty. The apparent reason for choosing such aspirations is that the negative consequences of failure are perceived to be less likely to occur at either of the extremes. He is less worried about failure on an easy task because the chances are good that he will in fact succeed on such a goal. He is less uncomfortable about failure on a very difficult task because the likelihood is strong that he will suffer less embarrassment or loss of pride should he fail. In groups whose members are dominated by a desire to avoid the unfavorable consequences of group failure, we may similarly expect that the members will prefer group aspirations at either the more difficult or the easier extremes of difficulty rather than those in the intermediate area, but, as was observed in Chapter 3, be uncertain which level to choose.

Persons in peripheral positions and those in weak groups, as noted above, tend to prefer group aspirations away from the middle of the tasks arrayed along a scale of difficulty. These results might be taken to mean that members in peripheral posts or in weak groups have developed stronger Dgaf than Dgs. This conjecture does not sit well however when we recall the procedures used to create a peripheral position or a weak group; specifically, there was nothing in the experimental treatments one could point to as a probable source of Dgaf. Rather, it seems more sensible to assume that weak Dgs was created in one set of conditions (peripheral position and weak group) and strong Dgs was created in the contrasting set of conditions. In the former case, any aroused Dgaf might then have been relatively stronger than in the latter case.

What is wanted is an experimental treatment that on its face can be accepted as an appropriate operation for arousing Dgaf. Such a situation is not easy to invent in a pure form since it must have the following properties: (a) the members must be more sensitive to the effects of failure by the group than to the effects of success; (b) the consequences of failure must be perceived to be undesirable; and (c) the undesirable consequences must be greater for failing on an easy task than for failing on a difficult one. This last property (c) is necessary in order to reproduce the theoretically assumed inverse relationship between the repulsiveness of failure and the difficulty of the task.

As an additional aspect of the experiment on weak and strong groups (83), an effort was made to develop a condition in which the above properties would be present and one in which they would be absent. These two conditions are designated as *cost* and *reward*, respectively. In the cost condition Dgaf is presumed to be stronger than Dgs; in the reward condition Dgs is presumed to be stronger than Dgaf. Half of the strong groups were given the cost condition and the other half the reward, likewise for the two halves of the weak groups.

To create the *cost* condition, the experimenter, prior to the first trial on the card-marking test, gave each member 33 poker chips with the understanding that each chip counted one point toward the team's final score. He stated that throughout the test he would penalize the team (take chips away from each member alike) any time that the team *failed* to complete the chosen number of fields within the time allowed. The penalties would be carried out in accordance with a chart posted in each subject's booth. If the team chose to do one field and failed, 13 chips would be deducted, two fields, 12 chips, three fields, 11 chips, and so on. A failure at the most difficult level would cause a loss of only one chip. They were told that there would be no change in the group's chip total whenever it succeeded. Thus, in the cost condition, when the group performs poorly, the consequences are negative and the easier the task on which they fail, the worse are the consequences.

To create the *reward* condition, the experimenter said that the team would earn points each time the team *succeeded* in completing its selected number of fields within the time limit. The points (chips) would be paid out in accord with the chart posted in their booth. In this instance if the group attempted one field and succeeded, each member was to receive one chip; if it tried two fields, each member won two chips; three fields three chips, and so on. They were told that they would receive no payment if they did not succeed. Thus, in the reward condition, when the group performs well, the consequences are favorable and the more difficult the task on which it succeeds, the more favorable are the consequences. The number of successes and failures were controlled and were alike within the cost and reward conditions. The hypothesis is that members in the cost condition, compared to those in the reward condition, will prefer group tasks away from the intermediate range of difficulty.

The mean of the variances among the aspirations each member chose for his group was indeed larger in the cost condition (2.88) than in the reward condition (1.79) and these were significantly different ($t = 2.69, p < .01$). In a later experiment conducted by Forward (*28*), to be described in the next chapter, essentially the same experimental procedures were used. He again observed that members in the cost condition more often preferred levels of difficulty away from the middle range. The hypothesis is supported.

In summary, the conception that members may develop a stronger Dgaf than Dgs, or vice versa, seems to be a reasonable one. This desire can be generated in the laboratory and develops the results one might expect; further studies without the use of sanctions (gains or losses) are needed. In a later chapter it will be seen that executive boards in United Funds that failed year after year acted as though they had a greater desire to avoid group failure and those that succeeded year after year apparently had a greater desire to achieve success.

We have separately considered the tendency to approach group success and the tendency to avoid group failure even though these occur simultaneously in a group. The general tendency of members to select a given level of aspiration for their unit is a function of the strength of the members' desire to attain group success and their desire to avoid group failure, the perceived probability that engaging in the task will provide preferred outcomes, and the value placed upon those outcomes. The *resultant tendency* to engage in any given group task, then, is determined by the strength of the members' tendency to approach that task minus their tendency to avoid it.

Mean Group Aspirations

The existence of group-oriented achievement desires, Dgs and Dgaf, is premised thus far on the general finding, in accord with the theoretical prediction, that the presence of the former leads to choices of intermediate difficulty (by the persons involved), whereas the presence of the latter leads to choices that are not in the middle range. If these findings are correct, it can be foreseen what persons with higher Dgs will do when choosing a group aspiration level, but it cannot be stated with certainty what those with Dgaf will do, only what they will not do. Ideally, one should like to predict precisely what strength of motivation leads to what level of aspiration. Given the complexities of interaction among the variables included up to this point and the paucity of available information about them, any possibility of making such neat forecasts lies in the future.

A small step toward that possibility can be made by noting the mean group aspiration levels associated with different degrees of desire for group achievement. A repeated but not wholly consistent result is that members of groups with stronger Dgs tend to select higher group aspirations than those with weaker Dgs. Horwitz and colleagues (36), in a study to be given more attention in Chapter 8, created conditions that can be interpreted here as several degrees of desire for achievement of group success. It was observed that subjects anticipated their group would attain higher scores as more of the presumed Dgs was present ($p < .01$). Zander and Forward created varied amounts of Dgs by reporting to subjects the results of a test of "the concern among them for doing well." The higher the reported score on this test, the more difficult were the goals chosen by participants ($p < .01$); Zander and Ulberg had a similar result (92). On the United Fund boards central members proposed higher goals than peripheral members ($p < .01$), presumably the former were more concerned than the latter about the Fund's success. In several laboratory experiments consistent successes (assumed to foster more Dgs) generated higher average goals than consistent failures, and this was also true among the United Funds.

Yet, a central member of a laboratory group did not choose a higher goal than a peripheral member, a strong group did not select a higher aspiration than a weak group, and groups in the cost condition (contrary to expectation) chose higher aspirations than those in the reward condition ($p < .005$). In the latter experiments it is likely that the experimental controls on success and failure confounded in some way the subjects' estimates about what their group could truly achieve.

If further study provides better support for the generalization that greater Dgs leads to higher goals, why would this occur? A plausible reason is that greater Dgs causes a member to place greater value on the favorable consequences for his group that will follow its success—thus, he favors goals that will provide greater satisfaction, harder ones. There is a possibility that he also attaches more incentive value to any given level of difficulty than does a member with less Dgs. As a result, he is more strongly attracted to more difficult group aspirations, as his Dgs increases. Findings in an exploratory survey of 276 company managers who were asked to rate separately the incentive value and the probability of success on a particular task by the group they supervise revealed that these men gave higher ratings to incentive than to probability and men who were believed on other grounds to be more concerned with group success were more likely to make this distinction (91).

Group Aspiration and Group Goal

In Chapter 1, the several functions of a group level of aspiration were postponed for later consideration. It is appropriate now to examine this matter. This examination is wholly conjectural as there are no data directly relevant to the following ideas.

A *group performance goal*, it is assumed, is an end toward which the joint effort of members is directed. A group level of aspiration is not necessarily a goal or the same as a goal, it functions as a criterion for evaluating a group's performance and in a fashion similar to a goal under conditions that make attainment of success particularly important to members—a matter to be discussed below. Moreover, a performance goal is not the same as a level of aspiration, even though attainment of the goal level may often be a source of satisfaction or dissatisfaction for the members. In the latter case it is better to say that the goal happens to be at the same location as the aspiration level; attainment of the goal in such an instance means that the level of of aspiration has also been attained. A decision designated as a performance goal may often, but not always, be determined by the same conditions as those involved in selecting a level of aspiration. When it is determined by those matters, it is placed at the same level as the aspiration. If it is determined by other matters, it will be at a different location. A goal level and a level of aspiration may not be similar because the former is so vaguely stated, for example, that its exact location is not known. Even when precisely defined, a goal may be put forward at a level different from the aspiration in order to indicate a general direction of effort, to state a policy, to describe a need, to encourage the effort of members, or to state a forecast without any intention that it be used as a criterion for judging a future performance as a success or a failure. A goal that is imposed upon a group by another unit is often different from its level of aspiration and is often relevant to motives other than group achievement.

The central assumption, in short, appears to be this: a group performance goal and a group level of aspiration may be based on quite similar determinants or quite different ones; as the determinants of the goal and the aspiration increase in similarity, the two become congruent in location and function.

Although this assumption has not been tested, something like it is needed to account for the observation that a criterion that has the function of determining the satisfaction or dissatisfaction in a group's performance (a level of aspiration) often is at the same level as a group's goal, to account for a goal that apparently arouses satisfaction from success or dissatisfaction from failure, and to account for a goal that seems to arouse little satisfaction or dissatisfaction whatever the group's performance, that is, a goal that does not arouse the effort of members to attain it. The assumption reminds one in brief that a given goal level may or may not invoke the incentives Igs or Igf and a given level of aspiration may or may not serve to guide the work of members. To illustrate, members may not realistically expect to attain a level of aspiration that is placed at a very difficult level.

If members choose a group aspiration while they have a strong *tendency* to seek success (high Tgs), one may presume that the members will be likely to work (put out effort) toward that level because the strong Tgs implies that the aspiration setters have made a choice that is largely influenced by their *impulse to act.* Attainment of the chosen level is important, so important that *the aspiration level has the same function as a goal.* The presence of strong Tgs is a reasonable guarantee that members will have set an aspiration level that functions as a goal does.

If strong Tgaf has been aroused among members, one cannot be certain that the level of aspiration a group chooses will function as a goal since a group level of aspiration for such persons has been largely influenced by an impulse to minimize the undesirable consequences of failure and to avoid the task if possible.

WHICH OCCURS MORE OFTEN: TGS OR TGAF?

When a group faces a challenging task, is it more likely to approach success or to avoid failure? Although this question cannot confidently be answered with available data, we are inclined to believe that, all else equal, the members of a group are more likely to develop Tgs than Tgaf. There are findings from scattered sources that support this view and suggest that it is worthy of further study.

1. When the members of a group know their unit is in competition with other units but have no reliable evidence on how well their own group or the other ones are actually doing, they typically judge their own group to be better than the others. This observation has been reported often (*8, 23, 90*). If it is assumed that an experience of success fosters desire for future success, members of competing groups will more often develop this desire.

2. When members of a group know their group's score as well as its aspiration level, they are more likely to deny their group's score after it has failed than after it has succeeded; thus, group members seek to see their group as successful and thereby generate greater Dgs (Chapter 6).

3. When members of a group are asked to comment upon the behavior of individual members, there is more restraint against discussing inadequate behavior than against discussing favorable behavior (59). Thus, members become more aware of and informed about favorable actions than about negative actions and anticipate that this favorable behavior will be repeated in the future.

4. When members develop pressures toward uniformity within a group, these pressures are likely to be stronger for tasks in the middle range of difficulty than for easier or harder ones; such pressures are more typical of groups with stronger Dgs. Cartwright and Zander (12) assert that the strength of the pressures toward uniformity within a group is a function of the incentive value attributed to performing as one is being pressed to do and the perceived probability that such behavior will result in attainment of that incentive. Thus, adherence to the standard is greater as the product of incentive times probability is greater. Because tasks of medium difficulty are also assumed to have a larger product of value times probability, it follows that pressures toward uniformity will usually be stronger for such tasks than for those away from intermediate levels. Because groups with Tgs exceeding Tgaf tend to choose intermediate tasks more often, such groups will also develop stronger pressures toward uniformity with intermediate choices.

5. When members of a group face a challenging task, each is concerned to ensure that members favor goals in the intermediate range of difficulty (those which result from Tgs > Tgaf) than easier or more difficult tasks, and each member places pressures on others to favor such goals. Evidence in support of this assertion was obtained by Emerson (21) in a study of the American team engaged in climbing Mount Everest. During this effort in which a strong desire for group success was extremely important, Emerson observed that the climbers repeatedly communicated to one another in such a way that they fostered uncertainty about the outcome, that is, the odds on probability of success were 50-50, thereby maintaining maximal group motivation.

6. When the members of a group working on a challenging task run into stress, Korten (43) proposes, those who have greater interest in the attainment of the group become even more involved, while those who have little interest in the group's achievement become even less so. This is particularly true among the leaders of the group.

Korten adds several conjectures, however, that are not wholly in accord with earlier statements. He believes that the leaders, when pressing for sure attainment of the group's goals, become increasingly authoritarian in their behavior, suggesting that members may end up working for the leader rather than for the group. No doubt, the officials of any organization are more deeply interested in the success of their group than the rest of the members; officers in United Funds, for example, are more involved in the group's success than are nonofficers. Yet there are also indications that supervisors tend to favor difficult goals rather than medium level ones. Likert (48), for example, emphasizes that the managers of more successful organizations tend to set high goals and to press for their attainment. Does this mean that an overly enthusiastic administrator may press his group into a failure, may thus unwittingly arouse a fear of failure and make it difficult for his group to have an experience of success? Gross (34) thinks so; he states that managers "try to respond promptly to crises that emerge. They may even try to create crises by setting high aspirations and accentuating fears of failure." Likert reports that the more effective manager usually allows his subordinates to have some say in determining their goals—perhaps such actions modify the leader's tendency to press for higher levels of attainment and simultaneously arouse stronger Tgs in the group.

One problem remains. It was noticed earlier that groups on the average fail more often than they succeed. Might not the predominance of failure generate stronger Tgaf than Tgs?

Outcomes Preferred: For Self or Group?

We have seen the results from several attempts to arouse, experimentally, the desire for achievement of group success. There will be other efforts of this kind in coming chapters. Such an approach provides no evidence about the generality of this disposition and there is no evidence from other sources indicating that some people may be more inclined to work for the achievement of a group than to work for their own personal achievement. We all know persons who seem to prefer group tasks, who always are in meetings, or who choose to call a committee together when others might prefer to work alone at their desk on the same topic. If there is any merit in the notion that a member can have more or less desire for group success when conditions are appropriate, it is important to determine whether some individuals are more disposed to work for a group, any group, any time, while others prefer to work for themselves. For the sake of argument, it is now proposed that the desire for group success may not be wholly situation bound; some persons may perhaps prefer to meet their challenges in a group and thus may be more susceptible to the development of this group-oriented desire. In line with this approach, and to anticipate issues to be raised in the next chapter, attempts were made to measure in several ways the strength of comparative preferences for group outcomes versus personal outcomes, and to study the effects of certain motives and conditions on these preferences.

There have been several investigations relevant to this purpose. Schachter (63) has reported that individuals prefer to join a group rather than remain alone while waiting their turn to take part in an anxiety arousing activity. These people need people, Schachter believed, in order to learn how the others were reacting to the upcoming unpleasantries. He based this interpretation on a theory, proposed by Festinger (24) that a person who wishes to evaluate his opinions or abilities will have a stronger desire to be in the presence of others the more he perceives the others to be a reliable basis of social comparison. If, however, an individual does not need the presence of others in order to evaluate his competence because he can get this information directly from his own performance, he should then prefer to work alone since he will learn more about his personal ability when he does the task privately than when he shares the load with others. The latter hypothesis received support in a study by Willerman *et al.* (73). They report that individuals strongly disposed to achieve success (high Ms motive) were more inclined to work alone than individuals who were strongly disposed to avoid failure (high Maf motive).

Two different approaches were used by us in examining whether a person preferred to work on a task alone or with others. The first was a survey employing a paper and pencil measure of the respondent's preference in this respect, called the *Personal Preference Inventory* (PPI). The second was a laboratory experiment in which participants were given an opportunity to choose, over several trials under different conditions, whether they preferred to work for their own outcomes or for those of a group.

The Field Study. In some of the experiments described in this volume it was necessary to get measures of various personal motives such as need for achievement, or need for affiliation. The method for obtaining these measures, described in the next chapter, required that a number of high school students be given paper-and-pencil tests prior to the beginning of research. From the original pool of potential participants, subjects were then chosen who had the characteristics needed for a given study. At the time these tests were administered, the Personal Preference Inventory was also included. The findings to be presented now were gathered in this way; the availability of scores on the personality tests allowed us to examine how well different personal dispositions were related to the PPI.

Three separate forms of the PPI were used, each about three months apart. Each was supposed to be an improvement over previous versions. But because the results were quite similar for all three, we need not pause over the efforts to refine the instrument. The final version is presented in Fig. 4-1. All three variations had high face validity so that subjects were probably aware of the purpose of each question. It can be seen that the questionnaire asks the respondent to state whether he prefers to perform each of a number of activities alone or with others. Each group choice counts one point. The higher the score, the more the respondent favors working for a group.

In the following questions you are asked to choose between two things on the basis of your own personal preference. Answer each question by putting a *check mark in the box* beside the alternative which you most prefer. There are no right or wrong answers, so give the answer that suits you best.

1. If I had an important project to do for class and had a choice, I would rather. . .

   * ☐ work on it with a few others as a group project
   ☐ work on it on my own

2. I prefer to . . .

   ☐ do things on my own
   * ☐ do things while working with others

3. I think I generally am most efficient when . . .

   * ☐ I work with a group
   ☐ I work by myself

4. If I had to choose between them, I would prefer to be . . .

   ☐ the pilot of a single seater military plane
   * ☐ the pilot of a military plane with a crew on board

5. If I were on the track team, I would rather . . .

   * ☐ run as a member of the relay team
   ☐ run in an individual race

6. I prefer to do my homework . . .

   ☐ alone in a room
   * ☐ in a room with others present

7. If I wanted to learn to play the guitar, I would rather . . .

   * ☐ join a combo of beginners
   ☐ practice at home in my room

8. If I were a medical research worker looking for the cause of a disease, I would like to . . .

   * ☐ be a part of a team that makes an important discovery
   ☐ make an important discovery on my own

9. When I play tennis or ping-pong I like . . .

   ☐ to play against another boy in a singles match
   * ☐ to join another boy in playing against two others

10. In sports, I like to take part in . . .

   * ☐ team games like football, basketball, baseball, etc.
   ☐ individual sports like wrestling, golf, swimming, or track

11. When there is a job to do, I get more satisfaction out of . . .

   ☐ getting my share done on my own
   * ☐ doing my share while working with a bunch of people

12. I find that I learn more . . .

   * ☐ when I am a member of a student group planning a report for the class
   ☐ when I plan my own report for class

* Group preferred.

Fig. 4-1 Items contained in the Personal Preference Inventory.

The significant findings from this simple survey ($p < .05$ or better) can be briefly summarized.

1. In the total sample, 65% had scores (six or less) indicating that they would rather work for personal outcomes, and 35% had scores suggesting they would rather work for group outcomes.

2. Subjects with high need for achievement and low test anxiety, that is, those who had stronger motivation to approach success than to avoid failure (Ms > Maf), were more interested in working alone than in working for a group.

3. Subjects with low need for achievement and high test anxiety, that is, those who had a stronger motive to avoid failure than to approach success (Maf > Ms), were more interested in working for a group score than alone.

4. In the first of the three PPI forms an effort was also made to determine the relative preference for working in a central role or a peripheral role within a group. Persons with greater need for achievement had more interest in the peripheral role than in the central role.

5. Subjects who differed in their strength of need for affiliation did not differ in their preferences for group versus alone.

6. College students ($N = 125$), given the form in Fig. 4-1, had somewhat different responses. Among males, 55% would rather work alone and 45% for a group. Among females, 33% would rather work alone and 66% *work for a group*. These were students in a course in group dynamics and thus were probably unusually interested in group membership.

All in all, with this method of measurement and this population of subjects, there is greater preference for a personal score than a group score. This tendency seems to be stronger among individuals who have a stronger motive to achieve success. Those who choose to work for a group rather than themselves are characterized by a motive to avoid failure.

The Laboratory Experiment. Although the PPI contains questions about a variety of activities in a number of settings, it is essentially a free-floating measure with little specification of time, difficulty of task, or nature of participant's competence. It seemed useful then to determine the nature of the choices by similar subjects under more controlled conditions.

A total of 138 boys volunteered to complete the PPI, a measure of need for achievement, and the test anxiety questionnaire. From this sample, fourteen groups were created with four members in each, two being persons with Ms > Maf and the other two with Maf > Ms. A conference room in the school served as a laboratory. The opening instructions to the subjects were as follows:

Today you will be taking part in a study which is designed to investigate certain aspects of group or individual performance. Each of you will work for a series of trials on what is called a Perceptual Motor Skills Test. This test gives us accurate measures of such basic skills as eye-hand coordination, speed and accuracy of movement, and the ability for concentrated and sustained attention. While working on this test, you will be asked to make a choice as to whether you would like your performance to be combined with the others here as a group score, which can be compared with the scores of other groups we have tested, or whether you would like your performance to count as an individual score, which will be compared with other individuals we have tested.

Now, the choice of whether to work together for a group score or to work for yourself on your own individual score is not a choice between good or bad. If you think about it both choices are acceptable. Many important tasks today require several people to work as a group, to pool their efforts to achieve something important. On the other hand, there are jobs which require a person to work by himself apart from others. So either choice, to work for the group or alone is of interest to us and is acceptable; it is a matter of your own particular preference.

The subjects were seated at the end of a large table and separated from one another by screens; they were not allowed to converse during the experiment. There were eight trials on the task, two for practice and six for the actual test. For each trial a subject was given an essay-type paragraph containing exactly ten lines of print. At the left-hand margin of each line a letter of the alphabet was displayed. The participant was instructed to cross out each appearance of that letter; it appeared exactly five times in that line. Thus, a perfect score (crossing out all letters correctly and omitting none) would be fifty, for one trial. When explaining the task, the experimenter stressed that both speed and accuracy were important for a good score.

After they had had several practice trials, the subjects were asked to choose whether they preferred to work for a group or an individual score in the next three trials (Block 1). This choice was made on a private ballot and each participant subsequently learned (via a written message from the experimenter) that the majority in his group had chosen whatever he had selected, group or individual. In addition, each subject indicated on his ballot (on a 5-point scale) how strongly he felt about his preference. At the end of this Block the subjects made another choice for group or self in anticipation of the second set of three trials (Block 2).

After each trial a subject received from the experimenter a report of his own, or his group's, score (according to his choice), an alleged average score of all individuals (or groups) previously tested on this trial, and a rating on 5-point scale indicating how his (or his group's) score compared to that of others: well above average to well below average. Regardless of their choice of work setting, half of the subjects were informed that their performance was above average and the other half below average.

A subject completed a brief progress questionnaire after each of the two Blocks of trials and a short set of additional questions after the second Block.

Results. On the first Block of trials 66% chose to work for an individual score and 34% for a group score, almost exactly the same as the results obtained with the use of the PPI. These proportions were the same regardless of previous scores on the PPI; therefore, the PPI did not reliably predict what subjects would do when they made a "live" choice. The proportions were also the same, regardless of the subjects' personal motives to approach success (Ms > Maf) or to avoid failure (Maf > Ms).

Because the boys also rated the strength of their preference for working with a group or alone, it was possible to create a more differentiated measure of their preference. The subject's strength of preference was combined with his choice (group versus alone) in such a way that a 10-point scale resulted: very strong preference for individual work (scale point 1); weak preference for individual work (scale point 5); weak preference for group work (scale point 6); very strong preference for group work (scale point 10). The higher the score on this scale, the greater is the strength of preference for working in a group. The average score on this scale was 4.45, showing a weak preference to work for self. There was a correlation of .24 ($p < .05$) between score on PPI and this measure of choice strength. Thus, the PPI is a better predictor of the strength of a particular choice than of mere preference for self or alone. The relative degree of Ms or Maf, however, was not significantly related to the scores obtained on the 10-point scale.

In stating their preferences for the second block of trials there were a number of shifts, but even so 68% of the choices were again in favor of working alone and 32% were for working in a group. As can be seen in Table 4-2, individuals who originally chose to work for themselves were more likely to stay with that choice on Block two than persons who had previously chosen to work for the group ($p < .05$). Neither the previous scores on the PPI or the levels of Ms or Maf affected this choice. The mean strength of preference on the 10-point scale for Block two was 4.04, a slightly stronger preference for working alone than at the outset.

We see in Table 4-3 that persons with stronger Ms than Maf and who were above average in their performance on Block 1 (either group or individual task) most strongly preferred solo work in Block 2. The boys in all other conditions also preferred to work for themselves, but to a weaker degree ($p < .10$).

TABLE 4-2   CHANGES IN INDIVIDUAL VERSUS GROUP
CHOICE IN BLOCK 2

Choice for Block 1	Choice for Block 2	
	No change	Change
Individual	26 (70%)	11 (30%)
Group	7 (37%)	12 (63%)

TABLE 4-3   MEAN STRENGTH OF GROUP VERSUS
INDIVIDUAL CHOICE IN BLOCK 2^a

| | Performance in Block 1 | |
	Above average	Below average
Ms > Maf	1.92	4.92
Maf > Ms	4.55	4.59

a 1 = very strong preference for working alone; 5 = very weak
preference for working alone.

It was anticipated that changes for Block 2 might follow the rule: succeed, stay; fail, change. About 55% followed this rule and 45% did not; the initial preference for working alone and later shifts in that direction outweighed the effects of success or failure.

The quality of performance during the first block of trials can be taken as a sign of motive strength. The major determinant of performance was the personal achievement motive of the member. Persons with stronger Ms than Maf worked faster ($p < .05$) and had better overall scores ($p < .05$) than those in whom Maf was stronger than Ms, whether they worked for the group or themselves.

The results obtained from the use of the PPI suggested that subjects preferred to work in a group if their motive to avoid failure (Maf) was stronger than their motive to achieve success (Ms). Perhaps membership allowed them to avoid responsibility for a poor personal performance. Accordingly, we included a number of items in the post experimental questionnaire to measure their involvement in the task, their feelings of responsibility for the group's score, their attraction to the task, and the like. The results provided no evidence that persons who chose to work for the group rather than for self (said that they) did so in order to evade blame for the outcome. There was some indication that those with greater Maf preferred to have their score count for the group because they could take it easy and did not have to work as hard than when their personal score was clearly visible.

In summary, the results of this experiment match most of the major results from the paper and pencil measure. In the ratio of about two to one the participants prefer to work for their own score rather than a group score. This tendency persists regardless of success or failure. Persons with greater desire to approach success (Ms) are more likely to prefer to work for themselves especially after they have been successful as individual performers in a previous set of trials.

It is quite clear, within the conditions studied, that the majority prefer to work for themselves rather than a group, among high school students, an age group that is often said to be highly concerned with group activities. For whatever reasons—the type of measure, the lack of overt interaction available in the group (making it a rather dull club), the emphasis upon individual enterprise in the suburban communities where these subjects lived, the chance to evaluate oneself more accurately, or the inability to trust the skill of other participants— the greater number prefer to be in charge of their own fate. Perhaps there is a greater interest in group participation in a more mature sample of subjects. Results from college students and those in Chapter 5 suggest that this is so.

The available evidence implies that an individual choice is favored because the boys may be more certain about the chances of satisfying their motive to achieve success when they work alone than when they work for a group. It appears likely, as earlier proposed by Willerman *et al.* (73), that the boys were more interested in working for their own score because the unambiguous feedback available in that case gave them more reliable information about themselves than could be obtained from a group's score. Individual information was more desirable than the type available in a group score, even when the individual score was an unfavorable one. There is the additional and provocative possibility, however, that a person in the nature of things cannot assign as strong a probability to successful effort by groupmates as he can (or will) assign to himself, human beings are unpredictable things and a group of them who must collaborate to accomplish a task may be seen as even more unlikely to succeed. An improbable group situation may be less attractive than a more probable solo one. There is more to say on this matter later.

SUMMARY

In this chapter we have considered several unorthodox forms of "motivation" in which a person is concerned about the achievement of his group. The first, called the desire for achievement of group success (Dgs), is a disposition of a member to experience pride in and satisfaction with his group when it successfully accomplishes a task. The second, called the desire to avoid group failure (Dgaf), is a disposition of a member to experience embarrassment for or loss of pride in the group following failure. Both dispositions are conceived as being uniquely relevant to the group in hand and not necessarily to any other.

Evidence was offered from several investigations to show that the disposition Dgs can apparently be generated among members by enhancing their responsibility in a group or their degree of membership commitment to it. Under conditions in which their strength of Dgs was supposedly increased, members became more inclined to select group aspirations in the intermediate range of difficulty, rather than easier or harder ones. Evidence concerning the arousal of Dgaf, thinner than that available about Dgs, suggested that this group-oriented disposition will occur when the effects of group failure are undesirable and failure has become more salient to members than success. As its strength presumably increased, members became more inclined to select group aspirations away from the intermediate range.

It was conjectured that a group goal and a group level of aspiration become more similar in location and function as tendency to act and to seek success (Tgs) increases.

A number of findings from various sources were cited to support the hunch that members in working groups are "naturally" more likely to develop Dgs than to develop Dgaf. This hypothesis needs better verification than is now available; it merits such study, however, because it has obvious implications for groups in practical situations.

Several field studies and a laboratory investigation into the basic preferences of high school boys when they choose either to work in behalf of a group or for themselves alone, revealed a surprisingly consistent result. About 65% preferred to work for themselves and 35% to work for a group. Thus, if there is an enduring personal disposition toward Dgs, Dgaf, or both, which we doubt, it cannot be very strong in much of the high school population. Individuals who have a strong personal motive to approach success are especially likely to favor working for their own outcomes rather than those of the group. There is some, not strong, indication that persons with greater uneasiness about working on challenging tasks prefer to work for a group. Data similar to these are needed from more mature persons.

By now we have enough evidence, in this or previous chapters, to merit the assumption that members may develop a disposition oriented toward the success of their group. A member, however, is part of his group. His interest in the group's performance may be largely grounded in what this tells him about his own output, or in gains that come to himself if the group does well, even though this success is confounded with the output of others and diluted by his fractional part in its productivity. How does a member's individual motive for his own personal achievement affect his reactions to the group's score? These matters require attention in Chapter 5.

**Personal Motives
of Members
and the Desire
for Group Achievement**

A variety of approaches has been used in studying the effect of personal motives on group life. Some investigators have identified the motives persons bring with them and how these dispositions cause people to enter different roles in a group. Others have examined how separate needs affect the interactions among members of a social unit, their participation in the organization, their tenure, or their effort at work. Students of administrative behavior in business firms have paid particular attention to the compromises of managers when they select goals for their company; these decisions are believed to define the personal motives a manager can legitimately seek to satisfy in that organization.

Advisors who write for leaders of groups often suggest that managers should help members to fulfill their personal needs, whatever these may be. Administrators often have difficulty however in acting upon such advice because they assume that a member should work primarily for the good of the institution and ought to pay little attention to his personal purposes. Bennis, in summarizing ten different theories of managerial behavior (7), observes that in each theory there is a preoccupation with the conflict between the demands of the organization and the personal needs of members. Hughes (38) states this issue concisely in an admonition that "every manager must understand how to harmonize individual and organizational goals if he is to ensure the future well-being of his company."

There is no question, as noted earlier, that a working group provides personal satisfaction or dissatisfaction for a member, although there is much to be learned about the effects of such satisfactions in a social setting. There is no question, furthermore, that the satisfaction of personal dispositions may either be enhanced or attenuated by the demands that a group places upon a member.

In this chapter interest centers mainly on a person's motives for achievement of individual success and how they modify his aspiration for his group: Does a member with a stronger need for personal achievement react differently to a challenging group task than one who has a weaker need? Is a member's concern about his group's attainment largely determined by his desire to obtain satisfaction for himself? Is his Dgs or Dgaf modified by his individual motives?

It is useful at the outset to determine whether the members of a group are more often interested in their own achievements, in those of the group, or both. Accordingly, an attempt to determine if such separate emphases can be identified was made in several questionnaire studies of groups outside the laboratory. In these projects, in contrast to those described at the end of the previous chapter, the subject already is a full-fledged member, and is not deciding if he will become one.

CRITERIA OF SATISFACTION
IN WORKING GROUPS

As a part of the educational activity in a classroom, it often happens that a teacher directs a committee of students to investigate a particular issue and to prepare a report of its findings. He subsequently grades all members of the committee alike in accord with the value he attributes to the group's report. Participants in a group who expect such a unitary form of appraisal develop an awareness of the interdependent relationship among them and a strong desire for the group to do well on its assignment, as Deutsch (15), Thomas (68), and others have shown. In such a situation a member who strives to help his group is simultaneously working for his own satisfaction. In what sense then is he concerned with the fate of his group? Is this concern any different from his self-interest?

In a course on the dynamics of groups the students were asked to form committees of five to seven members. Each group was to select and study an established organization in the local community and to write a report about that organization in accord with a mimeographed set of instructions. Each was required in addition to prepare a report of its own group's procedures while accomplishing the assignment. The grade given to the written report and that each member received for the joint project, was one-fourth of his grade for the course. Thirteen groups were created; on the average each had two men and four women.

These groups have certain advantages for the present purposes. The members are similar: juniors, seniors, and some graduate students, most in their early twenties. Each group has the same task and a common set of rules. They are alike in size and exist for the same period of time, about ten weeks. Each unit is in a state of competition with the others, each works hard, and the reports are uniformly well done, making it difficult to differentiate among them when assigning grades. The written histories of the committees are remarkably alike, showing an early phase of confusion and strain, an increase in confidence as data collection begins, and a strong increase in interest as the final report is being prepared. During the project the members have no reliable evidence about the quality of their group's work compared to that of other groups.

A brief questionnaire was given to all students at three separate times, each administration about three weeks apart. All responses were anonymous since the students were being asked to make evaluative ratings of themselves and their groups as a part of their regular course work. The items in the questionnaire were Likert-type rating scales under several categories: ratings of quality of group performance, personal participation in the work of the group, satisfaction with personal performance, satisfaction with group performance, tendency to approach success in the group task, and attractiveness of the group. The repeated administration of this instrument made it possible to examine changes in these ratings over time and to identify possible causal links among these changes by a cross-lag method of correlational analysis advanced by Pelz and Andrews (56). Because the detailed findings of this study are available elsewhere (90) and since the tabulations consume much space, comment will be limited to a summary of the significant results relevant to the questions posed above.

1. The mean ratings of group performance at each time of measurement revealed a general trend toward favorable perceptions of their group's performance. In ranking their own group, 75% placed it in one of the six better ranks (out of 13 possible ranks) at the time of the first measurement and 90% among the top six at the final measurement. Virtually everyone, therefore, perceived his own group to be above the average. The men gave their group a significantly better ranking than did the women.

2. The men believed their group's product was more likely to receive a top grade than did the women.

3. The men perceived their own personal participation and influence as increasing toward the end of the project while the women perceived their own participation and influence as not increasing during that period.

4. Among men, the attractiveness of their group was heightened if they approved the quality of its work; among women, the attractiveness of their group was greater if they had more favorable perceptions of their own personal performance as members.

5. Men were more satisfied with their personal performance when they were more favorable toward the group's performance; women were more satisfied with their personal performance when they felt they had greater influence in the group.

Correlations among ratings made by respondents at an earlier and a later time (examined by the method of cross-lag correlations) allowed us to identify certain variables as precursors of others. Noteworthy relationships occurred only in the responses made by men. Among these are the following:

6. Men gave a higher evaluation of their group's performance if they previously had a stronger desire for an A on the group's report.

7. They said they participated more actively and influentially in the group if they previously perceived their group to be performing well.

8. They rated their own personal performance better if they previously rated their group's performance higher.

9. They said they participated more actively and attributed greater influence to themselves if they previously had expressed a stronger desire for their group to succeed.

An interesting finding in this study was the gradual change over time toward more favorable ratings on most measures. Apparently, members who work on a joint task, and have no objective evidence about the quality of their group's performance, are more likely to develop approving opinions than disapproving ones about the group's and their own personal performance. As noted in Chapter 2, no feedback is good feedback.

The differences between the men and the women were not expected. It appears that the men were more concerned about the fate of the group while the women were more interested in their own personal outcomes. The contrasting sources of satisfaction for men and women occurred under conditions where a good performance by a member helped the group and a good performance by the group helped the member. This fact provides a controlled setting for the separate criteria of satisfaction.

In other results it appeared that the men became the dominant members, even though they were a minority in numbers, at a time when the groups were in a crisis created by the need to finish the report on time. Thus, the women's concern about their personal performance and influence may have been stirred by an awareness that they were not effectively competing with the men on these matters. The men, when they became dominant, may have felt this status was a more satisfactory position vis-a-vis the women and they thereafter could devote full attention to the quality of the group's effort since their own role was no longer an issue. The men behaved in much the same way as members have done in previous experiments when they are in central roles while the women behaved like members do when they are in peripheral roles. Perhaps the men viewed the group task primarily as an opportunity for group achievement while the women saw it as an opportunity for personal affiliation. Thus, the males were largely oriented to the task and the females primarily oriented to personal relationships with others in the group.

Although these results must be viewed as tentative because of the crudeness of the measures, they support the notion that a member may be interested in the outcome of his group while giving less attention to his own personal gains, or be interested in his personal needs without paying much attention to the group's fate. The fact that these major differences occurred between men and women is unfortunate because few other studies on purposive behavior in groups have had females as subjects. Certainly the differential tendencies among men and women in their strivings for achievement should be a focus of future studies into group motivational processes.

An opportunity to satisfy personal motives in an organization does not mean that members will necessarily be indifferent to the performance of their group. This was evident in an unpublished study of managerial workers ($N = 185$) in one department of a large chemical firm. The respondents were asked to describe the most satisfying features of their jobs. The most frequent answer, given by 52% indicated that they valued the autonomy available to them for developing and attaining their personal objectives in their managerial careers. Yet, when they were asked what were the most dissatisfying aspects of these same positions, the most frequent answer (given by 42%) was that they had no clear conception of how well they were contributing to the company's achievement, if at all. It is interesting that the respondents who were more concerned about the advancement of their own careers (as indicated by a separate measure) were less concerned about the firm's progress and those who were least concerned about their own careers were more interested in the achievement of the firm.

In the questionnaire sent to the board members of United Funds it was possible to get some idea of the comparative strength, as the respondents saw these matters, among the motives they had for participating in the Fund. Each respondent was asked: "If, or when, your community raises enough money, reaches its goal, and has a success, what might contribute most to your sense of satisfaction from such an event?" He was to rank order five alternatives. These are listed in Table 5-1.

TABLE 5-1   BOARD MEMBERS' SOURCES OF SATISFACTION FROM SUCCESSFUL UNITED FUND CAMPAIGNS[a]

	Mean rank order, all respondents
Welfare needs of community can be met	1.38
Knowing that our UF is a successful organization	2.39
Community will be approved for doing a good job	3.09
Personally working hard on my part to achieve goal	3.46
The community will approve of my personal efforts	4.64

[a]After Zander et al. (89).

We observe in Table 5-1 that satisfaction from meeting the welfare needs of the community is given the highest ranking by respondents, having the Fund be successful as an organization is next most satisfying, and personal gain from the Fund's success is least satisfying. Practically all of the respondents, it should be added, were males. The source of satisfaction ranking first, meeting the needs of the community, was significantly more important to central members of the boards than to peripheral ones ($p < .05$). The source ranking second, successful performance of the organization, was more important among those central members who perceived themselves to be more active in behalf of the Fund (as shown by a response on a later question) than for peripheral members who were most inactive in the Fund ($p < .05$), and the source of satisfaction ranking fourth, satisfaction with own efforts, was more important to highly active central persons in successful towns than in failing ones ($p < .05$). No doubt these answers are biased to some degree by the desire to make socially acceptable responses.

The reactions of these board members are probably not typical of those in many other settings. The men are volunteer citizens who work for the Fund because they strongly believe in the value of the community service it provides. Thus, their interest in the performance of the Fund is not unexpected—they joined it in order to help it do a good job. It seemed wise then to study the views of men in a different kind of institution, preferably a company. It was possible to do so in a brewery firm located in a Western European nation the author was visiting at the time (91). The way of doing business and the values of the managers in that country are similar to those in the United States; thus, there is no obvious reason to make anything of the cross-national contrast. One may reasonably assume, however, that a brewery has a different function in a community than a United Fund.

The company is fairly large with over 6000 employees. It has been unusually successful in recent years, owning about half of the national market in their liquid line. It sells in 23 geographical districts, each of which has a supervisor who administers the activities of 6 to 12 foremen, who in turn direct groups of salesmen.

A brief questionnaire was mailed early in the calendar year to one-half of all foremen in the sales, production, and accounting departments and to all managers above that level. Of these, 81% were returned in time to be used, a total of 276, from men occupying six different status levels in the company hierarchy.

The fact that these respondents were participants in a complex social structure made it possible to observe the kinds and strengths of satisfaction they might have with three entities: the company as whole, the group they supervise, and themselves as individuals. Because of a need to keep the questionnaire brief and fairly simple, questions were asked about only three criteria of satisfaction: quantity of output, quality of output, and pride in performance. The procedure was as follows.

A set of questions first sought to measure the *incentive value* of the three criteria. To do this, as was learned in pilot interviews, it was necessary to refer to them as "goals"; other terms did not make sense to the respondents. The introductory statement therefore went: "Men who work in the same company often differ in the importance they attach to certain goals, for the company, their work group, or themselves. Regardless of how well the following goals have been attained in the past year or so, how important is it to you that these goals be *reasonably well achieved* during this year?"

Following this opening question, a respondent rated the importance (on a 10-point scale) of each of the following:

    a.   The company as a whole achieves its sales goals.
    b.   The company as a whole achieves its profit goals.
    c.   People who work for this company have pride in its achievements.
    d.   The company gets the *amount* of production needed from your work group.
    e.   The company gets the *quality* of work needed from your work group.
    f.   The members of your group have pride in its performance.
    g.   Co-workers get the *amount* of production needed from you.
    h.   Co-workers get the *quality* of work needed from you.
    i.   You have pride in your performance at work.

The reader will note that the same three questions were asked about company, group, and self. The discrepancies in wording of questions were necessary in order that the respondent understand the query. No doubt, in the future a better scheme than this could be devised for measuring potential satisfactions in differently sized entities.

Next, the respondent read: "Most men notice that some goals are more difficult to reach than are others. We need to know what you think the chances are that each of the following goals will be reasonably well achieved during this year." Thereafter, he rated the same nine items on a 10-point scale running from "cannot possibly happen" to "will certainly happen." This is taken to be a measure of their *perceived probability* that the event will occur.

The product of the rating for incentive value times the rating for perceived probability is the strength of the *desire for attainment of favorable consequences.* Because of limitations in machine data analysis procedures, these scores were reduced to 9-point scales (no one marked scale point 1 anyway); thus, the maximum value possible is $9 \times 9 = 81$, not 100. The mean values for this scale for company, group, and self are shown in Table 5-2. The scores for each of the means nad a good normal distribution.

It is plain first, that the mean desire (average of quantity, quality, and pride)

TABLE 5-2 MEAN SCORES ON DESIRE FOR ATTAINMENT
OF FAVORABLE CONSEQUENCES[a]

	Quantity	Quality	Pride	Mean
For company	54.0	52.5	41.6	49.4
For group	57.7	60.7	51.8	56.7
For self	57.8	60.0	51.8	56.5
Mean	56.5	57.7	48.4	

[a] After Zander (91).

for group and self is very similar and both are reliably higher than the mean for the company ($p < .001$). Thus, a respondent was as eager for his group to obtain satisfactory consequences as that he himself do so. The outcome for the company was, on the average, less important.

The desire for pride in work is given a lower rating than is the desire for satisfactory quality and quantity. The score for pride is particularly low for the company. The highest values are given to quality of performance by group and self. This interest in quality implies that a standard of work has been satisfactorily met and that meeting this standard is more important than amount of output or pride in what is attained.

The responses at all status levels were fairly similar to those in Table 5-2, which was not what was expected. It seemed reasonable that the higher-status men might be more involved with the fate of the company. They were not. One unusual set of respondents were the supervisors of the districts in the sales department (a middle-management level) who gave scores of 62.7 and 62.1 to their group and selves, respectively. Further inquiry revealed that these men receive more complete and frequent feedback on their units's performance than any other personnel and had recently adopted a practice of having the men in each district establish their own sales goals. The availability of goals and feedback data created more involvement in group and self than did level of status.

Here then is an instance in which men have a stronger desire that their work group attain favorable consequences of performance than that the larger organization do so. They are as much concerned about the consequences for their work group as they are about their own achievements. The respondents are of course supervisors of these groups, and thus, no doubt, believe that they personally are judged at least in part by how well the group under their leadership performs. Thus, in one sense, the interest in their group is not surprising. It is noteworthy, nevertheless, that in other data, the men often showed greater involvement in their group than in their own career or the company. The following briefly listed significant differences illustrate that involvement. They report that:

1. They discuss their group with their superior more than they discuss the company or their own performance.

2. They wish to discuss their group more than the company or self.

3. They evaluate the performance of the group higher than the performance of company or self.

4. They are more concerned about the consequences for their group if its past production record has been better; previous production of company is not related to this desire (no data on individual productivity).

Whatever the reason for a manager's interest in the performance of his group, whether it be to help the company, to help the group itself, or to make sure that he wins approval from his superiors by appearing to be a good leader, there can be no doubt that it is a real and lively involvement, certainly stronger than his interest in the fate of the larger entity, to which he also belongs, the company.

In some settings it is obvious that the behavior of members is intended to satisfy their own personal wishes regardless of whether it is helpful to the group in accomplishing its task. Such behavior is particularly important and perhaps detrimental when it occurs in a decision-making body. Fouriezos *et al.* (30) observed meetings of 72 committees in government and industry and counted the frequency of behavior they believed to be primarily directed toward the satisfaction of what they called self-oriented needs. The more these behaviors occurred in a meeting, it was observed, the less the group was effective in its work and the less members were involved in the success of their meetings.

In the light of the several field studies just described, there is merit in questioning the assumption that members work only for the satisfaction of their person-oriented motives. Some at least become heavily interested in the fate of their unit. Yet it is also clear, particularly in a group that requires interdependent effort, that members may be concerned with the group's outcome in order to obtain personal satisfaction. We need better data on this issue, which would allow us to determine what leads to what. In the following pages two approaches are described to meet that need. First, an experiment is presented which attempts to determine if person-oriented motives of members have important effects upon their interest in group success. Second, several experiments are offered to examine the interaction between person-oriented and group-oriented motives.

PERSON-ORIENTED MOTIVES
AND ASPIRATIONS FOR THE GROUP

If one wishes to know what effect personal motivation has on desire for group success, it is necessary, in contrast to the methods used in the immediately prior studies, to be certain that the members have a given strength of motive and then to observe the purposive behavior of those who differ in that respect. The strategy adopted in the following study was accordingly one in which the strength of a particular personal motive was first measured in a number of individuals; groups were then composed of people who had strong motives and other groups were composed of people who had weak motives; the groups took the ball-propelling test.

The most relevant personal disposition is the members' motive to achieve success. At the time the plans for this experiment were made, it did not seem feasible to measure the strength of this motive reliably by having subjects write stories about Thematic Apperception Test pictures, the method most often employed (2). A previous attempt to use such pictures by showing them on a screen in a darkened room had taught us that this procedure invites a high proportion of absurd stories and much jocular behavior from high school boys.

On the basis of advice provided by students of the achievement motive, a form of the Test Anxiety Questionnaire (TAQ) prepared by Cowen (14) for high school pupils was used. This instrument is brief, easy to administer, and simple to score. The relation of the TAQ scores with other measures discussed by Mandler and Cowen (51) and Atkinson and Litwin (3) reveals that it is an appropriate indicator of the motive to avoid failure (Maf).

Because the motive to avoid failure and the motive to approach success (Ms) appear to be independent (Atkinson, 2), it was assumed that, in a set of students selected because they are known to be high in Test Anxiety, the average strength of the motive to avoid failure would be higher than the average strength of the motive to approach success; among a set of students selected because they are known to be low in Test Anxiety, on the other hand, the average motive to avoid failure would be lower than the average motive to approach success. The resultant motivation in a group composed of persons with Low Test Anxiety, then, would be to approach success, while in a group with High Test Anxiety it would be to avoid failure. In later studies, following the encouragement obtained from this one, more appropriate measures were developed for determining the strength of Ms and Maf.

Prior to the experiment a pilot study was made to determine if scores on the TAQ were related in any way to members' attitudes about events in their groups. In this instance all subjects completed the TAQ prior to an experiment being conducted for another purpose. There was no selection of subjects on the basis of these scores. Contrasts in their behavior during the experiment and in their responses to the post experimental questionnaire were sought between the half of the subjects who had higher scores on the TAQ and the half who had lower scores. The results revealed that members with greater Test Anxiety did indeed differ from those with less Test Anxiety. Boys who apparently were uneasy when facing challenging tasks, worried more about how well they had performed in the group task, worried more about the evaluation their group would receive, were less interested in changing their group's procedures so that they might obtain a better score, and were more doubtful about the validity of the group task than subjects who were not uneasy when working on a challenging task. These results were stronger, moreover, if the group had more often failed to achieve its goals than if it had more often succeeded in doing so. In general, then, there was reason to expect that members with more test anxiety might become less involved in a group's task and might have less interest in having the group do well.

The participants in the experiment (Zander & Wulff, *86*) were 144 11th grade boys who were invited to take part in a testing program of team-muscle control. A total of 36 teams were formed with four members in each; as already remarked, half of these teams were composed of boys with higher scores on the TAQ, and the other half of boys with lower scores. The experimenters were uncertain that subjects who are uneasy about taking a paper and pencil test (which is what the TAQ measures) are also uncomfortable when faced with a test of motor ability. Thus, the subjects were asked to complete a brief ten-item questionnaire immediately after they had tried the ball-propelling task several times. This last questionnaire requested self-ratings of personal competence in individual motor tasks. A typical question: If I took a test of ability in physical coordination, I would probably score (Very low—Very high). Persons with high TAQ scores rated themselves as likely to be more inept in a physical task than did those with low TAQ scores ($t = 3.31$, $p < .01$). It appeared therefore that a person's score in the TAQ is a reasonable indicator of his hope for success or his fear of failure in a motor task.

Each four-member group performed the ball-propelling test exactly as described in Chapter 2; a member voted privately on his preferred aspiration for the group, and all members then met in conference to select the group's level of aspiration. The task was modified so that an additional variable could be introduced: the degree of *competence* each person had in the work he performed as a member. Before describing this modification, let us consider the possible effects of variations in individual competence.

Suppose that a member is told that he is either the most competent or the least competent person in his group but has no knowledge about the ability of specific others. In such an instance, it may be assumed that a member who is high in competence (HiComp) will develop confidence in himself and a readiness to seek personal success, whereas one who is low in competence (LoComp) will develop low confidence in himself and a tendency to avoid personal failure. If both HiComp and LoComp persons attain these personal characteristics while working in the same group and experiencing alike the score obtained by that group and all members perform exactly the same task at precisely the same moment, it follows that a member's motivation to approach or to avoid can be satisfied only through the performance of his group. Thus, HiComp members can be expected to have more desire for group success than LoComp members and their greater Dgs will be revealed in their tendency to favor aspirations of intermediate difficulty for the group.

HiComp members and LoComp members can differ in another respect beyond their tendency to develop Dgs or Dgaf; they may differ in their interest in the group's success versus their personal success. A HiComp person is likely to be less uneasy about his personal achievement than a LoComp person, and therefore will be relatively more free to develop an interest in the performance of the group; he is already taking adequate care of himself. The LoComp member, in contrast, is likely to be more displeased by his personal achievement so that the group's performance may have relatively less salience for him than his own achievement; the group can take care of itself. HiComp persons then might feel more comfortable about their group membership, be more engrossed in the achievement of the group's task, and be more concerned about the group's aspiration than LoComp persons. This seemed to be the case among males, compared to females, in the previously described study of classroom committees and in the survey of workers in the chemical firm.

Variations in the competence of members were introduced in the following fashion. Four rubber grips were attached at equal intervals to the aluminum pole members used to propel the ball and a large wire cable was extended from its trailing end. This cable led to several black boxes with dials, dancing indicator hands, and small lights. Each participant was asked to pick up the pole with his right hand (carefully, since it was said to contain electronic equipment) at the grip labeled with the letter randomly assigned to him when he arrived in the room. In addition, he was asked to hold another grip in his left hand, similarly festooned with wire cable.

These pieces of equipment made it credible for the experimenter to allege that we were measuring electrical skin conductance, speed of movement, and strength of swing, so that we would know how well each was performing as an individual on the group's task. Before each trial, the experimenter turned on the lights and activiated a quiet buzzer—ostensible parts of the measuring machinery. After each trial, he read the results from the dials and presumably calculated a score for each member. These scores were privately reported to them in three ways: a numerical score (from zero to 100), a letter grade ("A" through "E"), and a numerical rank ("1" through "4"). The person in the HiComp condition was given scores in the 90's, a grade of "A," and a rank of "1" for each trial. The person in the LoComp condition received scores in the 60's, a grade of D+ and a rank of "four." The MidComp person was given scores between those two. One member was told that his dial was not working and that he could not yet be given information about his performance. This is the *control* condition. The participants were requested not to show or tell their competence ratings to others.

After the group level of aspiration had been selected for the sixth trial, the routine was interrupted and the participants were asked to complete an appraisal questionnaire introduced as an effort to obtain their advice for improving the procedures on this test in the future.

Results. The results due to scores on the TAQ and to differences in individual competence will be discussed separately as there was little interaction between these two variables among the results relevant for this chapter. Individuals with higher scores on the TAQ are denoted as having a stronger disposition to avoid failure than to approach success (Maf > Ms) while those with low scores on the TAQ are denoted as having a stronger disposition to approach success than to avoid failure (Ms > Maf).

If the separate motives of members do in fact have different consequences for their group-oriented desires, one should find that groups whose members are more strongly disposed to approach success will have less variance in their aspirations for their group as a unit than do groups whose members are more strongly disposed to avoid failure. The results shown in Table 5-3 support this prediction. In both the individually chosen aspirations and the group-decided ones the variances on each trial moreover were closely similar to those in Table 5-3. The variances here were based on the choices among members within a given condition. Several other methods of calculating the variances, described in earlier pages, provided similar results. It is concluded that persons who differ in their personal motives have these motives aroused in a challenging group task and that their chosen aspirations for the group reflect these motives.

The results in Table 5-3 suggest that members with Maf exceeding Ms placed their group aspirations a greater distance from their group's previous level of aspiration than did members with Ms exceeding Maf. A measure of the size of this tendency was taken to be the number of instances in which subjects moved their aspiration for the group by two standard deviations or more (toward either easier or harder levels) from the level they had preferred in the trial immediately preceding. In the Maf > Ms groups there were 90 such jumps and in the Ms > Maf groups there were 65, rather equally distributed among success and

TABLE 5-3   MEAN VARIANCE IN ASPIRATION LEVELS
AMONG MEMBERS AND GROUPS DIFFERING
IN Ms AND Maf

	Member's aspiration for group	Group-decided aspiration
Ms > Maf	13.23	8.71
Maf > Ms	53.82	47.09

failure trials. The difference is statistically significant ($\chi^2 = 9.9$, $p < .01$). Groups in which the members were more disposed to avoid failure than to approach success made larger shifts in group aspirations.

It was expected that competent members more than incompetent ones would prefer intermediate group aspirations. This prediction was not supported.

Several results suggest that the more competent members had greater interest in the fate of the group while the less competent members had stronger interest in their own outcomes. In Table 5-4 are shown the correlations between a member's changes in his aspiration for the group and the changes made by the group when selecting its level of aspiration. It is notable that the HiComp members gradually developed a closer relationship between the changes in their aspiration levels for the group and the group's changes in its aspiration levels, while the opposite proved true for members with other degrees of competence during the series of trials. These results are due to either of two circumstances. The HiComp member may have become more aggressive and thus influential in determining the group's level of aspiration during the experimental session, which implies that he expressed more concern about what the appropriate group aspiration level should be or the HiComp person may have been more influenced by the group aspirations over time and moved his preferred level to match that of the others, which also implies a concern with what the appropriate goal should be. Because no member knew the competence level of specific teammates, it is not likely that members were consciously more willing to be influenced by or defer to the person they thought was most competent.

In the postexperimental questionnaire members were asked about their degree of interest in the group's performance versus interest in their own performance. The participants with separate levels of competence did not differ in their mean responses on this question. When the Ms or Maf of the members

TABLE 5-4 CORRELATIONS BETWEEN CHANGES IN MEMBER'S
ASPIRATION FOR GROUP AND CHANGES IN GROUP
ASPIRATION (N = 36 IN EACH COLUMN)[a]

	Member's competence			
Changes during	Control r[b]	High r[b]	Mid r[b]	Lo r[b]
Trial 1–2	.72	.43	.81	.51
Trial 2–3	.82	.42	.79	.58
Trial 3–4	.76	.68	.77	.51
Trial 4–5	.61	.76	.61	.42
Trial 5–6	.60	.75	.34	.42

[a]After Zander and Wulff (86).
[b]All rs have p values of < .025 or better.

was also taken into consideration, it was evident, however, that persons in the LoComp condition were more concerned about their own *personal* output if they had a stronger disposition toward Maf while persons in the HiComp condition were more concerned with their *group's* output if they had a stronger disposition toward Maf. Specifically, in correlations between score on TAQ and the following questions, the higher the score on TAQ, the more the LoComp member perceived it to be important to do well personally on the test (LoComp $r = .33$, HiComp $r = -.10$), the more satisfaction he had in his personal performance (LoComp $r = .44$, HiComp $r = -.23$), and the less he was satisfied with the team's performance (LoComp $r = .24$, HiComp $r = .40$). A correlation of .32 is significant at the .05 level here. Thus, the degree of Maf helped to determine a participant's sensitivity to his competence in the group. Finally, the LoComp member believed, less than a person in another level of competence, that he had a smaller part in the work of the group ($p < .05$) and that it was unimportant for the group to do well on the test of teamwork in muscle control ($p < .01$) (see also Table 6-4).

In summary, the degree of his Ms or Maf can affect a member's desire for his group to be successful, as shown in the aspirations he selects for his group, regardless of his personal competence on the task. The competence of the member appears to make him more concerned about the group's fate if his ability is high but more concerned with his own personal performance if his ability is low. The fact that personal competence and motivation did not show much statistical interaction indicates that they are quite different variables. Apparently Ms and Maf, when aroused, determine the amount of effort to be devoted to challenging tasks, whereas awareness of personal competence determines the direction of that effort in behalf of the group or in behalf of oneself. It is easier to be concerned about the fate of one's group if one is pleased with his own personal performance within that unit. The behavior of the HiComp member resembles that of the males in the classroom committees described earlier, whereas the behavior of the LoComp members resembles that shown by females.

THE RELATION BETWEEN PERSON-ORIENTED AND GROUP-ORIENTED MOTIVES

We now have evidence suggesting that a personal disposition can govern in some degree a member's desires for his group. This result, however, makes the earlier question more imperative: might not a member's personal motivation primarily determine his degree of Dgs or Dgaf? It is to this question that our interest now turns. Two experiments were conducted in attempting to answer this question, the second to overcome deficiencies in the first.

To review, there are two different sets of motives concerned with achievement. One set, group oriented, includes Dgs and Dgaf. The other set, person oriented, includes Ms and Maf. Any of these may be aroused within a group facing a challenging task. The issue is, how will members who differ in their degrees of Ms or Maf react when they are placed in a condition which demands more or less concern with the outcome of the group?

In the first approach to this question, Zander and Forward (88) worked only with variations in Dgs, setting aside variations in Dgaf. In order to create differences in the strength of Dgs, a member was placed for half of an experimental session in the central role of a group and for the other half in a peripheral role. This procedure, as already observed, required that the central person be largely responsible for the score obtained by the group and to choose the group's level of aspiration as well; in the peripheral role he assisted the central person. To create variations in person-oriented motives, one member was more disposed personally to seek success than to avoid failure (Ms > Ms), one was more disposed to avoid failure than to seek success (Maf > Ms), and the third person had a disposition between those two. This third person remained in the peripheral position throughout the experiment and is not included in the results reported here. Thus, there were persons with Ms exceeding Maf in the central role part of the time and in the peripheral role part of the time, and likewise persons with Maf exceeding Ms in each of these two roles for part of the time.

The major interest is again in the intermediacy of the choices made by members of the group. It was seen earlier that members in the central role make more intermediate choices than those in the peripheral role, and that members with Ms exceeding Maf select more intermediate choices than members with Maf exceeding Ms. In respect to the interaction between these two sets of variables, two different outcomes, with quite different implications, are possible:

1. Members with contrasting personal motives will be more dissimilar in the central position than in the peripheral one in their expressed levels of aspiration for the group, and members in whom Ms is stronger than Maf will more often prefer group aspirations in the intermediate range when they are in the central role than when they are in the peripheral role. If such results occur, they would mean that a central position in the group does not in fact arouse greater Dgs than Dgaf but instead provides the cues necessary for the arousal of stronger Ms or Maf. The personal motive would be doing the work attributed heretofore to the group-oriented desires.

2. Members with Ms exceeding Maf and those with Maf exceeding Ms will develop fairly similar preferences for intermediate group aspirations when occupying the central position but quite different preferences when occupying the peripheral position. If these results occur, this would mean that group-ori-

ented achievement tendencies have sources and effects which are independent of the sources and effects of personal motives, moreover, a group-oriented achievement tendency (induced by the occupancy of a central position) and an individual-oriented achievement tendency (aroused by the challenging task) will summate in determining a member's resultant tendency and his ultimate preference for a group aspiration.

To illustrate the latter outcome, when occupying the peripheral position, only the effects due to members' differences in Ms and Maf will appear; members in whom Ms is stronger than Maf will show greater preference for intermediate group aspirations. While occupying the central position in which members develop a considerably stronger Dgs, a member whose Ms exceeds Maf will have his individual tendency to approach group success supplemented by the stronger Dgs and as a result will favor group aspirations in the intermediate range. In that same position a member in whom Maf exceeds Ms, in contrast, will have his personal tendency to avoid failure opposed by the induced tendency to approach group success. If the group-oriented tendency for success is sufficiently strong, it will overcome the tendency to choose extremes (due to Maf) and will instead generate preferences for group aspirations in the intermediate range.

Somewhat more reliable procedures than those used in the previous study were developed for determining the strength of Ms and Maf. Two measuring instruments provided a resultant score. The first instrument, a modified version of the common method for eliciting the fantasies of subjects, required them to write brief stories, Instead of being given the usual Thematic Apperception Pictures as stimuli, however, they were given very brief verbal descriptions of the four scenes most commonly used in measuring need for Achievement. The stories from this procedure closely resemble those obtained from the pictures and are coded in the same way (Atkinson, 2). The second instrument was the TAQ created by Cowen for high school students (14).

Forty-eight high school boys were selected from a pool of 120 11th graders. Hereafter, those described as Ms > Maf are the 16 who scored highest in the amount of achievement imagery on the story-writing measure and lowest on the TAQ. Subjects described as Maf > Ms are the 16 who scored lowest on the first measure and highest on the second. Each group again had three members.

The task (creating sequences of dominoes to duplicate a specified order) and the procedure for this experiment have been described in the previous chapter.

Results. The major concern is the aspiration chosen for the group, as revealed in a deviation index. A smaller score on that index indicates that a member's aspiration for his group is more intermediate in difficulty. The mean deviation-index scores within each experimental condition are revealed in Table 5-5. The summary of the analysis of variance for these results is contained in Table 5-6.

TABLE 5-5   MEAN DEVIATION SCORES, ASPIRATIONS
FOR GROUP, FIVE TRIALS IN EACH
POSITION (CELL N = 8)[a]

	Group position		
	Central	Peripheral	Mean
Ms > Maf	.56	.61	.58
Maf > Ms	.62	1.14	.88
Mean	.59	.87	

[a] After Zander and Forward (88).

TABLE 5-6   SUMMARY OF ANALYSIS OF VARIANCE FOR TABLE 5-5[a]

Source	df	SS	MS	F	P
Between subjects	15	5.76	—	—	—
Ach motives	1	0.69	0.69	1.92	—
Ss within groups	14	5.07	0.36	—	—
Within subjects	15	2.57	—	—	—
Group position	1	0.65	0.65	6.05	<.05
Motive X Group position	1	0.41	0.41	3.86	<.10
Position X Ss within groups	14	1.51	0.10	—	—
Simple main effects					
P: Ms > Maf vs. Maf > Ms				4.65	<.05
C: Ms > Maf vs. Maf > Ms				<1	—
Ms > Maf: C vs. P				<1	—
Maf > Ms: C vs. P				9.79	<.01

[a] After Zander and Forward (88).

It is evident that members occupying the central position choose aspirations for the group which are more intermediate in difficulty than members occupying the peripheral position. Members with stronger Ms do not choose significantly more intermediate aspirations for the group than those with stronger Maf, although the results are in the predicted direction. The absence of this difference is due to the contrasting reactions in the central and peripheral positions, as follows.

When subjects with different person-oriented motives occupy the central position, they do not differ at all in their aspirations for the group. However, when they occupy the peripheral position, members with stronger Maf have much larger deviation indexes than members with stronger Ms. The typical contrasts due to Ms and Maf are therefore present in the peripheral position but not in the central one. These results suggest that the central position not only provided the cues necessary to arouse stronger Ms or Maf, as the tendency may have been in the subjects, but stronger Dgs, aroused in the central position, caused members in whom Maf was greater to reduce their tendency to choose aspirations for the group away from the intermediate range. The central position served, in effect, to cancel the tendency of Maf > Ms members to select aspirations for the group away from the intermediate area of difficulty.

If the Dgs aroused in the central position did in fact summate with the person-oriented motives, why did not the people with Ms exceeding Maf have smaller deviation indexes when they were in the central position than when they were in the peripheral one? It seems likely that there is a limit to the amount of intermediacy possible in aspiration choices. Persons with stronger Ms perhaps set intermediate choices while they were in the P position which they could not exceed when they moved to the C position.

We conclude (but not with confidence) that a member in whom Ms exceeds Maf becomes more concerned about his group's success than does one in whom Maf exceeds Ms, but only when occupying a peripheral position. When occupying a central position, the latter person becomes as much concerned about the group's success as does one in whom Ms exceeds Maf. The central position appears to add an increment to the motivation of members beyond that provided by the person-oriented motives.

The fact that members with stronger Ms did not differ in the central and peripheral positions is puzzling, despite the explanation offered in the last paragraph. This finding means that one cannot rule out the possibility that these persons were responding only in terms of their own motives and that the presumed effects of greater or lesser Dgs created by the central and peripheral positions did not exist for them. Or, the central position may have aroused a greater need for social approval than did the peripheral position, which could have been the reason that persons in whom Maf was stronger than Ms appeared to repress their usual tendency to avoid failure. These dilemmas cannot be resolved from the present data because the person in the central position was indeed more visible, the quality of his effort could not be wholly buried in the score of the group, there was no control on the disposition of members to seek social approval from other members, and the central versus peripheral roles may have differed in meaning for members who had different person-oriented motives. To be more precise on this last point, members who had Maf exceeding Ms faced a conflict of motives in the central position that they did not meet in the peripheral position. The requirement stemming from strong Dgs was opposed to their disposition based on their Maf, when they were in the central role; but Dgs was presumably too weak to create much conflict for Maf > Ms members when they were in the peripheral position. Members who had Ms > Maf, however, faced no conflict in either the central or the peripheral position—the challenging task apparently was enough to arouse them regardless of their post in the group. Presumably they would have met greater conflict if there had been a Dgaf condition. A new experiment, by Forward (27,28), thus was constructed with these problems in mind.

In this study the effects of Dgs and Dgaf were compared. To create these conditions, two operations were used which were similar to those employed in an earlier study by Zander and Medow (83). In a *reward* group incentive condition, members were told that their group was competing with other groups to see how many team points it could accumulate over a series of trials. If the group was successful in attaining its level of aspiration on any trial, it won a number of points proportional to the difficulty of the group aspiration. If the group failed to achieve its level of aspiration, it neither won nor lost points. In a *cost* group incentive condition, a group was given a number of points at the start and was told it would be competing with other groups to see how many of these points it could retain over the series of trials. If the group failed to attain its stated level of aspiration on any trial, it lost a number of points which was inversely proportional to the difficulty of the group aspiration. If the team was successful, it neither lost nor gained additional points. The procedures for creating these conditions were presented in the previous chapter. It was reported there that members of reward groups preferred intermediate aspirations more than did members of cost groups, presumably because the reward condition generated Dgs whereas the cost condition generated Dgaf.

The individual-achievement related motives were measured exactly as in the last study, using a modified form of the story-writing test and a high school form of the Test Anxiety Questionnaire.

In addition, measures were made of the need for affiliation (Atkinson, 2). On the basis of these pretest scores, 64 high school boys were assigned to 16 four-man groups such that half the members in each group were those in whom Ms was stronger than Maf and half were those in whom Maf was stronger than Ms. The subjects were also alike (all four within every group) in their scores on need for affiliation, thus equalizing any individual desires for social approval.

For each trial, each of the four group members received a modified data-processing card which had nine fields with four columns of numbers per field. To complete one field, each member circled a number in field 1, column 1, and passed his card to the member seated on the right. This procedure, circling one column and passing cards, continued until the team had completed the required number of fields for a given trial. Conversation among members was not permitted during the test.

Different levels of task difficulty were created by setting the same standard time limit for each trial and asking members to state aspirations in terms of the number of fields they thought their team could complete within the time limit. A chart was displayed showing the proportion of teams that had been able to complete each level of task difficulty (i.e., from one to nine fields) within that time. The proportion of these successful completions was inversely related to the number of fields attempted. Because all groups were given similar normative data, it was assumed that the members had uniform standards to use in estimating their subjective probability of success at each level of difficulty.

Prior to each trial, each member privately voted on the number of fields he would like his team to attempt—his aspiration for the group. After collecting these votes the experimenter announced an alleged majority group aspiration. Because the aspirations for the group were the major dependent variable in his study and because there was reason to believe that these private votes might reflect in some cases variations due to complex interactions between level of task difficulty and the chosen group aspiration, Forward provided majority votes for each trial in accordance with a standardized sequence of group aspirations. These were administered to all groups alike. Thus, all groups had exactly the same levels of aspiration in the same sequence. In a similar manner, feedback to the group after each trial was standardized for all groups; they succeeded on the first two and the last two trials and failed on the middle three. As the group aspiration levels were controlled by the experimenter, it was possible for him to make the relationship between group aspirations and feedback such that it generally supported that which members might expect if they accepted the normative probabilities for group success described on the chart—that is, groups failed on difficult group aspirations, succeeded on easy ones, and succeeded or failed with equal frequency on tasks of intermediate difficulty.

As in previous studies, and for reasons provided there, Forward predicted that members in the reward condition would choose more intermediate aspiration levels than would those in the cost condition, and also that members with Ms exceeding Maf would favor intermediate group aspirations more than those with Maf exceeding Ms. His major hypothesis, however, was as follows: group-oriented and individual achievement tendencies are independent and additive sources of the overall resultant tendency to engage in achievement activity. The 2×2 factorial design of this study, as shown in Table 5-7, was considered appropriate for testing this hypothesis because, as Forward put it (27):

> For members in whom Ms > Maf, the resultant tendency to engage in the group task under the reward group incentive condition will be an additive function of both the group and individual tendencies to approach success. For these same members in the cost group incentive condition, the group and individual tendencies will be in conflict since the tendency to avoid the negative consequences of group failure will be opposed by the tendency to seek the positive consequences of success based on their personal need for achievement. Likewise, for members in whom Maf > Ms, the group and individual tendencies to avoid failure will summate to produce a strong resultant tendency to avoid failure in the cost group incentive condition, but the personal avoidant tendency will be opposed by the group approach tendency in the group reward condition. Support for the

hypothesis of independence and additivity will be found then only if both the predictions [concerning the effects of reward versus cost and Ms > Maf versus Maf > Ms] are upheld and if no interaction occurs between individual motives and group incentive conditions [p. 21].

Results. The intermediacy of the aspirations members preferred for their group was estimated by a deviation score. This score is similar to the index used by Litwin (49) to assess the degree of preference for aspirations of moderate difficulty by individuals working on solo tasks. It is like the measure of deviation used in previous studies except that in the present instance the deviation was determined in reference to the mean of the aspiration choices made by all subjects with Ms exceeding Maf who were in the reward group-incentive condition. The theoretical justification for using only these members to obtain this estimate is discussed by Atkinson and Feather (4, p. 310), but the main reason for its use is that the resultant tendency to approach group success will be strongest for the members in the reward group condition. An additional estimate of intermediacy of aspiration preference was based on an analysis of d values, described in Chapter 2 as the absolute difference between the performance of a group on trial k and the aspiration level set by a member for the group on trial $k + 1$. It was assumed that smaller values on both these measures represent greater preference for aspirations of intermediate difficulty.

The average deviation scores for each of the experimental conditions are to be seen in Table 5-7 and the summary of the analysis of variance for these results is given in Table 5-8. The first three trials are excluded from this analysis since it was evident that members in the cost condition did not perceive its true nature until after their group had failed and they had lost some points (all groups first failed on trial 3). The mean deviation scores indicate that members of reward groups selected significantly more intermediate aspirations for their group than did members of the cost groups and that members in whom Ms exceeded Maf selected aspirations which were significantly more intermediate than members in whom Maf exceeded Ms. Of most importance, however, is the fact that the interaction in the effects of the group conditions and the individual motives is minimal, which supports the hypothesis of independence and additivity between group and individual scores of achievement motivation.

An analysis of d values produced results similar to those obtained for the deviation scores. Members in the reward condition set aspirations for their group that were significantly closer to prior levels of group performance than did members in the cost condition ($F = 21.33$, $p < .001$) and members in whom Ms exceeded Maf had smaller d values than members in whom Maf exceeded Ms ($F = 5.35$, $p < .05$). The interaction between group incentive conditions and individual motives was not significant ($F = 1.73$). Again the results necessary for support of the hypothesis have been provided.

Two sets of results from the postquestionnaire strengthen the credibility of

TABLE 5-7   MEAN DEVIATION SCORES, MEMBER'S
            ASPIRATIONS FOR GROUP[a]

	Reward group condition (Dgs > Dagf)	Cost group condition (Dagf > Dgs)
Ms > Maf	.61	1.45
Maf > Ms	.95	2.05

[a]After Forward (28).

TABLE 5-8   SUMMARY OF ANALYSIS OF VARIANCE
            FOR TABLE 5-7[a]

Source	MS	df	F	P
Group incentives	15.15	1	15.74	<.001
Motives (Ms, Maf)	3.88	1	4.03	<.05
Group incentives X Motives	.23	1	.24	
Within error	.96	60		

[a]After Forward (28).

the assumptions Forward made concerning the degree of conflict between individual and group aspirations under different experimental conditons. The participants were asked, "Did you feel too tense to give your best performance during the last seven trials?" The members in whom Ms exceeded Maf reported feeling less tension than those in whom Maf exceeded Ms; but when the response of members with these different personal motives were contrasted within the reward and cost conditions, persons in whom Ms was stronger than Maf felt more tense in the cost condition where individual and group tendencies conflicted than in the reward condition where these tendencies were congruent. Similarly, members in whom Maf was stronger than Ms felt greater tension in the reward condition, which was the conflictful condition for them than in the cost condition. These results are reported in Table 5-9.

In another question the subjects were asked to what extent they selected aspirations which they thought would be "best for the group score:" Here the same kind of interaction was found to be significant. Members in whom Ms exceeded Maf reported greater concern for the group score in the reward than in the cost condition while members in whom Maf exceeded Ms reported greater concern for the group score in the cost rather than in the reward condition. These results are also shown in Table 5-9. Forward comments (28):

TABLE 5-9   MEAN FELT TENSION AND RATING OF ASPIRATION PREFERENCE AS "GOOD FOR GROUP"[a,b]

	Reward group condition	Cost group condition
Felt tension		
Ms > Maf	2.44	3.00
Maf > Ms	4.44	2.88
F (group condition $\times$ motives) = 4.65, $p < .05$		
Aspiration Choice good for group		
Ms > Maf	6.07	4.94
Maf > Ms	5.81	4.68
F (group condition $\times$ motives) = 5.01, $p < .05$		

[a]After Forward (28).   [b]Ratings made on 7-point scales.

The results from both the measures of aspiration preference and self-report provide support for the hypothesis that individual and group oriented achievement tendencies are independent sources of motivation for group achievement and that they combine in an additive manner to produce a resultant tendency towards engaging or not engaging in the group task.

When the selection of an intermediate group aspiration serves both to maximize the expected group score and to maximize expected individual achievement satisfaction, members in whom Ms > Maf not only select intermediate group aspirations but they feel relatively free of tension during the performance and consider that they are contributing significantly to a good group score. When the same members are in a cost group condition, where an intermediate group aspiration would continue to maximize individual achievement satisfaction but at the same time maximize potential loss of group points, their aspiration preferences are less intermediate and they report greater felt tension and less concern about obtaining a good group score.

Contrariwise, when an extreme (i.e. very easy or very difficult) group aspiration serves to minimize expected group losses and to minimize the expected negative consequences typically associated with failure for members in whom Maf > Ms in the cost condition, they select the most extreme aspirations of any set of subjects and at the same time feel less tense and more concerned with a good group score than when their individual failure-avoidant tendency is opposed by the need to maximize group points in the reward condition [p. 307].

The results of this study demonstrate quite well that the arousal of action tendencies based on individual achievement motives in a working group has effects which are independent of the effects due to the arousal of group-oriented achievement tendencies. When tendencies based on group or individual achievement motives conflict in determining the choice of a preferred goal, they are found to summate and to produce a resultant tendency to engage or not to engage in the group task. The results of the study do not support the assumption that group achievement motivation is solely a function of the arousal of individual motives which members bring to the group.

OTHER PERSONAL MOTIVES

Members have motives other than achievement of success when they take part in a group endeavor. We noted above that the college women in student committees displayed a somewhat stronger interest in social emotional relations than in achievement even though the group had work to do. French (*37*) has reported that she was able to arouse members' need for affiliation while they were working on a group task by making comments about their skill in getting along with one another and was able, in contrast, to arouse members' need for achievement by commenting upon how well the group was performing. In some units, depending upon their purpose, it is appropriate for members to ignore their achievements and to devote their energies instead to nurturing others, to seeking security, to making friends, to winning approval, to obtaining influence, and so on through a variety of affective interpersonal concerns. Moreover, individuals with such different motives may behave quite differently when they are asked to work with others. In a situation that allowed participants either to cooperate or to compete, Terhune (*67*) observed that those with a stronger motive to seek success were more willing to help others, those with a greater need for affiliation were more defensive and suspicious of their partners (apparently because they had a fear of rejection), and those with a greater need to gain power were more ready to exploit their colleagues. It seems reasonable that some motives may enhance interest in the fate of the group while others may prevent such an interest from developing.

It would be good to know if individual motives not concerned with personal achievement have analogs at the group level, and to determine the relationship, if any, between the person-oriented nonachievement motives and those found to exist in a group. One might expect, for example, that members want their group to provide nurturing, to offer security, to foster friendliness, to generate status differences, or to encourage competition or hostility for those who participate in that unit. Such group-oriented desires quite conceivably are linked at a given time with individual motives. Research on such matters, however, is still to come and must be based on a better knowledge than is now available about the impact of personal motives upon behavior in a group setting.

If one is to move beyond the motive to approach success and the motive to avoid failure, a sensible next candidate is the so-called *need for affiliation*, defined as the desire to establish or maintain friendly relations with others. This motive is suitable because it probably is aroused during the operation of most groups, students of leadership have often asserted that the manager of effective groups must be able to "gratify" this motive under particular conditions (Fiedler, *26*; Likert, *48*), and some of the experiments reported in earlier pages may have aroused the members' need for affiliation or his fear of rejection. If this last is true, what effect might the arousal of such a motive have had? Several attempts were made to obtain empirical data that would help us to understand the nature of this problem.

The Affiliation Motive in Central and Peripheral Roles. When a member occupies a central role, as has been shown, he is more likely to be concerned about the success of his group than when he occupies a peripheral position. The primary difference between the central and peripheral positions in previous investigations was taken to be the amount of responsibility the member had for the score of the group; central members were patently more accountable for the group's performance than peripheral members. But there is a conceivable distinction between the central and peripheral positions which may also have had a differential consequence for the occupant's desire to establish or maintain friendly relations. In the central role the occupant may have felt more open to blame or approval and to acceptance or rejection than in the peripheral role because he is the member who most determines the satisfactions obtained by personnel in the unit.

If a central person is more aware of the possibility that his actions decide whether he is to be accepted or rejected, it is probable that his need for affiliation will be more aroused in a central position than in a peripheral one and that he will act to ensure that he establishes and maintains friendly relations to a greater extent in a central position than in a peripheral one. If he develops such an interest, the central person's preferred aspirations for the group may be affected as much or more by his motive to ensure friendly interpersonal relations as to achieve satisfying consequences in the group.

Assuming for the moment that the need for affiliation might be more aroused among central than among peripheral members, what effects would this arousal have upon his preferred aspirations for the group? Two quite different effects seem equally plausible:

1. A person who is strongly disposed to seek friendly relations will select aspirations that are neither too hard nor too easy and will make such selections more often than one who is weakly disposed; this distinction will be stronger in the central position than in the peripheral position. The above hypothesis is based on the assumption that persons with stronger need for affiliation, who are therefore more eager to maintain favorable and accepting relationships with others, believe that such relationships can be best developed and bolstered if the group has a fully satisfying success.

2. A person who is strongly disposed to seek friendly relations with others will select easier group aspirations than one who is weakly disposed to seek such interpersonal relations and this distinction will be stronger in the central position than in the peripheral one. By the reasoning for this hypothesis, a person with a stronger n affiliation will wish to avoid any occasion for strained relations among members in order that friendliness can be fostered and encouraged. A feasible way for him to do this is to ensure that the group has a successful experience in

its work, regardless of the challenge or the sense of satisfaction inherent in that success; people will get along better in a succeeding group than in a failing one. A success can be more reliably expected if the group attempts easier goals than if it attempts more difficult ones.

An experiment designed to test these hypotheses by Zander, Forward, and Krupat was a close replica of the one described earlier in which subjects who differed in need for achievement were placed in three-person groups to perform tasks in central and peripheral roles. In the present instance the participants were selected because of their scores on a test of the need for Affiliation (2). Each group was composed of one person who was strongly disposed to affiliate with others, another who was weakly disposed to do this, and a third person whose strength of affiliation motive fell between those two. As in the previous experiment, subjects performed in the central role for half of the trials and in the peripheral role for the other half, in a balanced design. The task was different from that used in the previous study, in order to make it possible to have a public and a private condition, but the differences were not important enough to concern us now. In half of the groups an effort was also made to arouse greater need for affiliation among members. This was done by having them stand so that they could easily see one another (they were separated by wooden screens during the task), introducing them all, and informing them that they would have an opportunity at a later point in the experiment to choose a single partner from among other members with whom they would then work on a subsequent task. These procedures were omitted for the other half of the groups. It is interesting to note that this effort to arouse greater need for affiliation among members had no noticeable effects. It either did not create a viable variable in the theoretical sense or it was not a suitable method for arousing the need for affiliation—probably both. All participants in this study (total $N = 24$) had fairly similar scores on the motive to achieve success (Ms) or the motive to avoid failure (Maf) and these scores were near the median ordinarily obtained by such subjects. All other features of this experiment were similar to those followed by Zander and Forward (88).

Each group completed ten trials. After the first five they answered a brief questionnaire, completed five more trials, and answered the same questionnaire again. These questions were a check on the effectiveness of the central and peripheral inductions. The responses revealed that the members perceived they were more responsible for the "success or failure of the group" when they had been in the central position than when they had been in the peripheral one ($p < .01$), felt their job was more important when in the central than when in the peripheral position ($p < .05$), and were more tense in the central position than in the peripheral one ($p < .10$). There is little doubt that the central and peripheral posts were perceived in the manner in which it was intended that they should be.

Turning to the aspirations members chose for their group, there was no indication that subjects with High need for affiliation preferred more intermediate levels than those with Low need for affiliation. Thus, the first alternative hypothesis received no support. It appears then that individuals with a stronger desire to establish and maintain friendly relations do not attempt to ensure a satisfying outcome for the group as a means of ensuring that acceptance of interpersonal relationships will occur.

The results relevant to the second alternative hypothesis were more puzzling than enlightening. The tentative prediction, as we recall, was that persons with stronger need for affiliation will choose easier group tasks than will those with weaker need for affiliation, and this difference will be stronger in the central than in the peripheral role. The mean choices for each experimental condition are shown in Table 5-10. It is evident that persons with High need for affiliation do indeed choose easier levels of aspiration in the central position than in the peripheral one, but persons with High need for affiliation are not inclined to choose easier tasks than are ones with Low need for affiliation, and members with Low need for affiliation act just the opposite of what was predicted. That is, those with Low need for affiliation selected easier aspirations in the peripheral post than in the central one. The marginal differences between members in the central roles and those in the peripheral roles, moreover, are not significant. These results do not support the second hypothesis and it is difficult to know what to make of them. It appears, at the least, that persons in the central and peripheral positions did not act as they did in earlier studies now that their need for affiliation was perhaps aroused. There is no reliable evidence that occupying a central position led to a stronger desire for social approval than occupying a peripheral position. Apparently these two positions invoke more (or less) concern for group achievement than concern for social acceptance.

Even though this effort to examine the effects of need for affiliation contributed little more than blazing confusion, it was sensible to have one more try at the matter in quite a different situation. In this instance, Forward (27), within the study earlier described, examined the effects of need for affiliation while subjects were in either the reward or cost conditions. The subject's scores on Ms and Maf were kept at an intermediate level and were fairly similar. Within

TABLE 5-10 MEAN LEVEL OF ASPIRATION FOR GROUP,
FIRST TRIAL (IN SECONDS)

	Central	Peripheral
High n Affiliation	80.6	70.6
Low n Affiliation	60.6	78.1
Interaction $F = 4.63, p < .05$		

each group of four persons, two were High in need for Affiliation ($N = 32$) and two were Low ($N = 32$). All procedures were exactly the same as in Forward's earlier study.

He observed that subjects with High need for affiliation did not differ from those with Low need for affiliation in the intermediacy of their goals or in the difficulty levels of their goals, thereby relieving us of any further interest in the earlier two hypotheses. He then inquired if members with High need for affiliation were somehow more ready to conform with the beliefs of others than those with Low need for affiliation, assuming that they attempt to foster friendly relations by agreeing with others in the group. In several studies the members have been required to arrive at a single level of aspiration for their group either by discussion or a majority vote. If it is assumed that this decision is seen by the members to be a group standard, and if it is assumed that approval-seeking tendencies may be aroused in a group task, it is plausible that some unknown part of what we have taken to be group achievement motivation is a function of the tendency to seek and obtain social acceptance by conforming to others' preferences for a group aspiration.

In order to measure the tendency toward conformity in these groups, he introduced an additional treatment, already mentioned briefly in Chapter 2. In half of the groups, after receiving the members' private votes for a group aspiration, the experimenter announced a "majority" that was consistently within the intermediate range of aspiration for all trials. This is called a *medium* group aspiration condition. In the other half of the groups he announced a majority aspiration that was either in the very difficult or very easy range of task difficulty for all group trials. This is called an *extreme* group aspiration condition. Forward expected that persons with High need for affiliation would adjust their own votes to fit the apparent will of the majority more than would persons with Low need for affiliation. The results supported this expectation. Members with High need for affiliation cast their private votes on each trial in a way that was strongly in accord with the majority vote that had been announced by the experimenter in the previous trial, regardless of whether that majority was in the medium or the extreme condition ($p < .001$), whereas persons with Low need for affiliation paid little attention to the prior majority vote when selecting their aspirations for the group.

An item in the postquestionnaire produced results which also supported the expectation that High need for affiliation members are more sensitive to the wishes of other group members. In response to the question, "How often did your own private goal choices differ from the majority team goal?", the High need for affiliation members, more than the Low need for affiliation members, reported that their private aspirations differed little from the majority ($p < .01$).

We conclude from these several explorations of the need for affiliation that when this need is aroused it has by itself little effect upon the level of aspiration members prefer for their group. Rather, it appears to determine the readiness of members to accept and conform to the perceived expectations of others in their unit. Conceivably then, members with High need for affiliation may provide a stabilizing influence, serving to establish and fix the group-oriented motivation among the members by their tendency to conform to the group's standard. Further study of the effects of need for affiliation on group motivational processes is warranted.

SUMMARY

In this chapter we have examined the relationship between person and group oriented motives. The answers to several questions were sought: Is a member's desire for group success mainly a reflection of his motive to attain personal success? Is a member's concern about his group's aspiration largely determined by his desire to obtain satisfaction for himself?

The results from several questionnaire studies of "real-life" groups indicated that members can develop either an interest in the success of their group, or an interest in their own personal success while a member, or both. It was noteworthy in one study that men professed to be more concerned with the score obtained by their group while women in the same units were more interested in their own personal quality of performance.

An experiment to examine the effects of the personal motive to achieve success (Ms) and the motive to avoid failure (Maf) employed groups in which all members had either stronger Ms than Maf or stronger Maf than Ms. This investigation revealed that the individual tendency to approach success or to avoid failure is reflected in the intermediacy of their aspiration choices for the group; groups composed of members with stronger Ms, compared to those with stronger Maf, revealed a greater desire to approach group success.

The individual competence of a member in the work he does for a group had no effect upon the aspiration he favored for that unit. More competent members, however, were more concerned with the group's outcome (they said) while less competent members were more concerned with their own personal performance, if they were personally more disposed to avoid failure.

Several investigations into the interactions among Ms or Maf and Dgs or Dgaf were reported. In the first study persons with stronger Ms and ones with stronger Maf each occupied central posts and then moved to peripheral ones or began in peripheral positions and then moved to central ones. The findings suggested that person-oriented motives and group-oriented motives are independent but the results were not wholly convincing because members in whom Ms was stronger did not react differently to the central and peripheral positions, making it impossible to rule out the possibility that their behavior was due to their personal motives rather than their concern with the fate of the group.

The second study was designed to overcome deficiencies in the previous experiment. In this case members differing in personal achievement motives were placed in either a condition that induced Dgs or a condition that induced Dgaf. The data demonstrated quite well that the arousal of action tendencies based on individual achievement motives has effects which are independent of the effects due to the arousal of group-oriented achievement tendencies. There was no support for the assumption that group achievement motivation is solely a function of the arousal of individual motives which members bring to the group.

Several hypotheses were tested concerning the possibility that aspiration choices in a group are due to interests in establishing and maintaining friendly relations among members. Although the results were not as clear as one would like, there was no reliable indication that a member's motivation to affiliate with others determines the level of aspiration he prefers for his group. There was evidence instead that the need for affiliation does affect a member's tendency to go along with whatever he perceives the rest of the members prefer—to conform in effect to the standard set by the other members, in that way, presumably, establishing and maintaining friendly relations with the others.

CHAPTER 6 | Motivated Beliefs of Members

The last several chapters have been based on the assumption that one can detect a member's interest in the achievement of his group through observing the aspirations he favors for it. Ordinarily, however, in daily living, this degree of interest is estimated on grounds of simpler evidence. It is assumed that a teammate has a tendency to approach work on his group's task, for example, if he states that it is important to him, that he is willing to work hard on it, and that he is sure his colleagues feel the same as he does; or, it is observed that he actually works hard. One concludes in contrast that a member has a desire to avoid work on his group's task if he makes derogatory remarks about it, says he is not responsible for the group's performance, or asserts that he personally is better than the group's score might suggest.

Such signs of greater or lesser involvement in a group's achievement may be designated as *motivated behaviors and beliefs.* We limit ourselves in what follows to beliefs because the operations for measuring these reactions have been virtually all verbal. Effort and quality of performance will be discussed in a latter chapter.

The general proposition is as follows. *Events within a group that arouse an anticipation of favorable future consequences generate beliefs among members that reveal their desire to approach the task, while events that arouse an anticipation of unfavorable future consequences generate beliefs that reveal their desire to avoid the task.* There are two interrelated themes in this proposition. One is the emphasis on the meaning of events for members of a group; the other is that members can develop a group-oriented motive during their experience in the group. The reasoning behind the proposition is not new. Yet, the logic merits a brief review, placed in a wider setting, in order to illuminate these two themes.

Let us assume that a person who joins a group brings with him previously developed habits of avoiding unfavorable personal outcomes and of approaching favorable ones. When his group is engaged in a challenging task, he becomes alert to its achievements and to the positive and negative consequences thereof. Such outcomes have a meaning for him as long as he is interested in the group.

Suppose his group has, for any of a variety of reasons, many more successes than failures in a repeated activity. These successes generate in him favorable reactions to conditions in the group, the nature of its task, the score of the group, and the behavior of teammates. Any similarity in his reactions and those shown by others, along with the enthusiastic communication among participants concerning the effort of the group, gives the member faith in the propriety of his responses. Agents outside the unit, moreover, may display their approval, or can be expected to do so. The point is that the consequences following success are viewed as favorable and their favorableness is enhanced by conditions acting upon or within the group itself. Once these consequences are known and valued, a disposition is aroused in a member to seek such outcomes in the future. This inclination is exactly the state needed for the development of a motive, a disposition to be satisfied by a particular outcome.

If the present group has been successful and the consequences are valued by all or most of the members, they develop a similar tendency among them to approach the group's task and to work toward the achievement of just such consequences in the future. This motivation, sooner or later, may be taken to be a property of the group as participants become aware of and agree, in effect, to value such views about their unit. The beliefs members express about the nature of their group will indicate then that the members have developed a group-oriented motivation to achieve success and that each member assumes this to be the case for his teammates. The presence of such a view, we may add, is likely to enhance the cohesiveness and the stability of the group.

Imagine instead that a group has, for whatever reasons, many more failures than successes. These failing events create negative attitudes toward such things as the standard expected of the group, the output of the team, and the actions of members. The member's awareness of such views and the talk among participants concerning their dissatisfaction with its performance confirm his attitudes. Individuals outside the group may also reveal their negative feelings or may be expected to do so and may withhold rewards or provide punishments for the group. The critical fact is that the consequences following a failure are perceived to be unsatisfying and that their unpleasantness is verified by conditions acting upon the group or within it. When it is evident that these consequences have negative value, the members wish to avoid them in the future and may then be said to have a motive to avoid the unfavorable qualities of these outcomes.

Because the group has failed and the consequences of such an event are dissatisfying to members, the beliefs they hold in this circumstance reveal their desire to avoid the consequences of failure, and each participant assumes that others see matters as he does. Furthermore, their beliefs reveal that the participants wish to ensure that unfavorable consequences do not occur in the future.

In sum, members' motivated beliefs indicate that they have developed dispositions to seek particular satisfactions for their unit, or to avoid dissatisfactions for it, and that they intend to act in accord with such desires. These beliefs, it should be emphasized, arise out of experiences in that group alone.

The case thus far has been presented in terms of group success or failure since the contrasting effects of such experiences are intuitively sensible. There is value, however, in stating the major notion in more general terms. Any condition in a group that makes salient either the favorableness or the unfavorableness of potential consequences for that unit will arouse either the desire to approach the group's task or to avoid it, respectively. In accord with this broader view one may expect that such matters as the difficulty of the group's goal, the competence of individual members, the adequacy of the group's procedures, the skill of the unit's manager, the motives he taps in order to influence subordinates, the availability of necessary resources, and the like may make it evident to a participant that certain consequences are likely to occur for the group, just as the success or failure of the group affects his beliefs about the future. The possibility is not excluded moreover, that individual differences may occur among members in their reactions to the group's quality of work because of unique experiences there, in other groups, or in solo tasks.

To return to the twin themes of the proposition then, the consequences experienced in a given group generate motives in members that are unique to that unit, and members' views about the group are useful indicators of their group-oriented motivation.

EXPERIENCE IN A GROUP AS A SOURCE OF MOTIVATED BELIEFS

The data available for evaluating these ideas are not exactly ideal. They are the responses to questions after subjects had had experience in a group, in the laboratory or elsewhere. These questions were the final activity in an experiment but were given to subjects with the explanation that answering them was an interruption in the experimental task and that work would continue after the forms were completed. The timing of this explanation is important since it means that the participants were in the set they had developed up to that point, while they were completing the questionnaire, rather than psychologically removing themselves because they believed the experiment was finished. The responses are taken to indicate the views members hold about the future of their group.

A standard set of nine questions was prepared and used during seven experiments. In some instances this list was shortened in order to make room for queries that were more central to the purposes of a given study. In addition, another eight questions were used when time permitted. It would have been better if the same questions had been consistently employed. At the time the data were collected, however, their function was uncertain; thus, consistency did not have the virtuous quality that hindsight now gives to it.

The most commonly used questions are listed below so that brief reference can be made to them later. Each was answered by ratings on an appropriate 7-point scale.

a. How important is it to you for your team to do well on this test of muscle control?

b. In your opinion, how important is it for your team to be good at teamwork in muscle control?

c. How important is it for your team to do as well as other teams in your school?

d. How hard do you think people usually try on a test like this?

e. How hard do you think other members of the team tried to do their best?

f. How large a part do you feel you played in your team's performance?

g. How responsible do you think you personally were for your team's score?

h. Was the test your team took today a good or a poor measure of teamwork in muscle control?

When the ability being measured was not teamwork in muscle control, these questions were modified to suit the ability said to be under investigation.

Can we be confident that the beliefs of members on such questions do in fact reflect their motives? A straightforward way of determining this is to compare the answers given under conditions intended to arouse differing degrees of desire for achievement of group success. When, for example, participants were placed in a central role or in a peripheral one, on the assumption that the former aroused greater responsibility for the fate of the group than did the latter, there was ample evidence that the central persons believed they had a larger part in the group, that they were more responsible for what happened there, that teammates were dependent on them, and that they wanted the group to be successful. When members were led to believe that the personnel in their group were disposed to have their group be successful, they then indicated that it was important to do well, that other members tried to do well during the test, and that they themselves tried. The strongest and best-controlled evidence on this matter is found in Zander and Ulberg (*92*). When groups were formed of members who had strong personal motives to approach success (Ms > Maf), or, in contrast, to avoid failure (Maf > Ms), the responses were in accord with what one would expect: the approachers demonstrated greater involvement in the consequences of their effort than did the avoiders. The results from other independent variables were similar. One is justified then in assuming that the beliefs of members reveal their motives.

The results we now consider provide illustrations for parts of the earlier statements, offer elaborations on those parts, or are based on derivations from them. They are not from efforts to test previously posed predictions. For lack of a better term the statements describing these data are called *generalizations*.

Generalization 1a. When a group succeeds more often than it fails, members reveal they are more attracted to approach the group's task.

In the first experiment in Chapter 3 (*80*) the members became aware that their group was either performing somewhat better or somewhat worse than groups like their own. The former groups succeeded more often than the latter. After each aspiration level had been chosen (by group discussion), the subjects were asked, trial by trial: "Do you think others will try their best to get the score the team has decided it should be able to get?" Those in more successful units repeatedly anticipated more effort from their colleagues in the future than those in less successful units ($p < .01$).

Later in that experiment when members were asked to reflect on the group's experience during all its trials, those in the successful groups, more than those in the failing ones, judged that it was important to do well on the test ($p < .01$), and that it was important to do as well as other teams in the school had done ($p < .05$). Similar results were obtained in several other studies (*82, 86*). In further investigations when the question concerned how hard teammates had in fact tried to do well (*20, 55*) the members of successful groups perceived that their teammates had exerted greater energy than did the members of failing groups ($p < .001$).

Generalization 1b. When a group fails more often than it succeeds, members reveal a desire to withdraw from the situation and to avoid the consequences of their group's performance.

Individuals in failing groups, more than those in successful units, believed that they had had a smaller part in the group's activity (*55*), perceived themselves as less responsible for the group's score (*55*), saw themselves as less helpful (*86*), believed others were not helpful (*86*), were less attracted to continued membership in that group (*55, 78, 82*), and preferred more often to dispense with the practice of setting goals (*89*).

Participants in failing teams also believed that there was less value for a team to be competent in the ability being measured $(p < .01)$ (80) and they consistently and strongly believed the test to be an invalid tool for measuring the ability it was supposed to measure. With these beliefs the members of failing groups were presumably able to dismiss or reduce the repulsiveness of the consequences from a failure.

In summary, members in a successful group reveal that they are more ready to approach the group's task than do members in a failing group. We will return to further effects of success and failure in the last few generalizations in this chapter.

Generalization 2.   Regardless of their group's success or failure, as the difficulty of the group's aspiration increases, the members' inclination to approach the task (rather than avoid it) increases.

The major implication in this assertion is familiar, namely, that the consequences of a success are perceived to be more favorable and the consequences of a failure to be less repulsive as the difficulty of the task is greater. Thus, members reveal a greater tendency to approach more difficult tasks than easy ones and become more motivated to move in the directions implied after they have worked on such tasks.

The relevant data are from the experiment (82) in which groups were started on either a difficult level of aspiration or an easy one. The findings of interest were reported for another purpose in Table 2-3 (Chapter 2). It can be seen there that as the average difficulty of their groups aspiration level increases (holding constant the frequency of successes and failures), members see more value in tests like this, believe it is more important to do well on such a test, perceive people usually try harder on tests like this, perceive the skill to be an important one for a group to have, and state that they were deeply involved in the test.

Generalization 3.   Face-to-face discussion of their group's experience invokes stronger responses relevant either to approaching or avoiding, than the same persons provide in prior private responses.

If members privately develop their beliefs after a period of participation in a group, discussion of such beliefs will stimulate awareness of the most appropriate view. As a result of the group's discussion participants become more "approaching" if that is their inclination and more "avoiding" if that is their preference than they were before the discussion began.

The last paragraph states an hypothesis tested in the study just described (82). After the subjects had privately completed their ratings on questions such as those noted earlier, they were asked to meet and to reach a unanimous agreement on ratings for three of the items. The three were: the value of tests like this, the validity of the test, and the importance the members attribute to successful performance by their group. During this discussion the experimenter left the room.

TABLE 6-1 MEAN DISCREPANCY BETWEEN INDIVIDUAL
AND GROUP-DECIDED BELIEFS[a]

	Difficult	Easy
Sucess	+.25	−.48
Failure	+1.00	−1.34

[a] Difficult vs. Easy, $F = 6.93$, $p < .025$. Success vs. Fail, n.s.

In their private ballots, members gave higher ratings if they had worked on harder tasks and lower ratings if they had worked on easier tasks; in addition, members who were in more successful groups gave more favorable ratings than those who were in less successful groups. Interest at this point is in the contrast between the private ratings and the ratings made by the group during its discussion. For this purpose it is convenient to treat the scores on the three questions as a single index.

The results in Table 6-l describe the amount of difference between the private responses of members and the group decisions. A negative value indicates that the group decision was lower than the average private rating; a positive value indicates that the group decision was higher. It can be seen that the discussion generated more approaching responses on difficult tasks (and more avoiding on easy tasks) than did the private judgments. Although most of this last difference was due to members who participated in groups that failed more often than they succeeded, the group votes were not significantly more avoiding in the failure groups or more approaching in the successful groups than were the private judgments.

Generalization 4. A supervisor of a subgroup within a large organization has more favorable beliefs about the potential output of persons he supervises than of persons in the larger organization.

The questionnaire in the study of managers in a brewery (91) included four queries asking the degree that: (a) people do their work as well as they can (b) personnel expect one another to do their work as well as they can, (c) people work as hard as is expected of them, and (d) people are competent enough for their jobs. These questions were raised about the company as a whole, the group supervised by the respondent, and the respondent himself. The mean responses are shown in Table 6-2.

In every instance the potential effectiveness of the group is rated higher than the company as a unit. In addition, those who completed the questionnaire rated themselves better than their group. Seemingly, the success of one's own group is

TABLE 6-2   MEAN BELIEFS RELEVANT TO POTENTIAL EFFECTIVENESS IN COMPANY, GROUP, AND SELF[a]

	Company	Group	Self
Try to do work well	3.61	4.32	4.56
Expected to work well	3.32	4.00	4.47
Do work hard	3.00	3.30	3.50
Competence for work assigned	3.28	3.47[b]	3.58[b]

[a]After Zander (91).
[b]All means in each row are significantly different except these two, $p < .05$ or better.

perceived to be more possible in this case than the success of the larger company.

Generalization 5.   A member who wishes his group to select a higher level of aspiration than the group selects for itself reacts more strongly to either a success or a failure of the unit than a member who wishes his group to set a lower level of aspiration.

Within any aspiration-setting group, some members are likely to prefer higher levels than the group chooses while other members are likely to favor lower levels; these people are called *Upward-directed* and *Downward-directed* deviants, respectively. Any contrast in the beliefs of such persons is interesting because they have experienced exactly the same events within their group, yet (their separate views suggest) they have somewhat different motives.

Concerning an Upward deviant, on the basis of earlier evidence, it is taken for granted that such a person, when in a successful group, has a stronger desire to obtain the favorable consequences of success than to avoid the unfavorable consequences of failure. When in a failing group, however, an Upward deviant has a stronger desire to avoid the unfavorable consequences of failure than to seek the favorable consequences of success. Thus, Upward deviancy has a different implication in a successful group than it has in a failing one.

Concerning the Downward deviant, it is assumed that such a person, is less interested than his teammates in the consequences of either success or failure; he is not particularly excited about having a satisfying success as shown in his preference for an easier goal, and he is not bothered by failing on that simpler task if this were to occur. It follows that Upward deviants should reveal a tendency to approach when they are in a successful group and a tendency to avoid when they are in a failing group, while Downward deviants should not have strongly contrasting reactions to their group's success or its failure.

In an experiment by Zander and Medow (80), 51 teams worked on the ball-propelling test and set a group level of aspiration 14 times. Prior to each group discussion held to select their group's aspiration level, each member voted privately on his aspiration for the group. The latter data, when compared with the group's selection, were used to identify those who were the Upward deviants and those who were the Downward deviants. A third person, called a Nondeviant, was one whose aspirations for the group were closest to the level chosen by the team in its discussions. The beliefs of Upward and Downward deviants are shown in Table 6-3.

It is observed that Upward deviants gave responses suggesting that they had a stronger desire to approach the task when they were members of successful groups than when they were members of failing groups. Downward deviants, however, were not significantly different in their reactions to group success or failure. Closer examination reveals that most of the above difference among Upward deviants is due to the low ratings they made in the failing groups. Thus,

TABLE 6-3   MEAN BELIEFS OF UPWARD AND DOWNWARD DEVIANTS

	Quality of group's performance			Significant differences
	Success	Control	Fail	
Important for team to have ability?				
Upward deviant	6.5	6.4	5.3	S>F*, C>F**
Downward deviant	6.2	6.0	5.7	—
Important to do as well as others?				
Upward deviant	6.2	4.1	4.3	S>F**, S>C**
Downward deviant	5.3	4.9	4.4	—
Others will try their best (trial-by-trial predictions)				
Upward deviant	6.8	6.5	6.0	S>F**
Downward deviant	6.6	6.5	6.4	—
How hard others have tried				
Upward deviant	6.1	5.9	4.6	S>F**, C>F*
Downward deviant	5.9	5.8	5.7	—
Contribution of individual teammates (excluding self)				
Upward deviant	5.9	5.5	4.9	S>F**, C>F*
Downward deviant	5.7	5.2	5.2	—
Contribution of respondent (assigned by teammates)				
Upward deviant	5.4	5.2	5.1	—
Downward deviant	5.8	5.7	4.8	S>F**, C>F**

$*p < .05.$ $**p < .01.$

Upward deviants were generally more eager to avoid the unfavorable consequences of a failing performance. The last item in Table 6-3 indicates that Downward deviants were perceived by their peers as having contributed most to the group when it was successful and least when it was unsuccessful. Clearly, it is laudable to propose small increases in goals when the group is succeeding, but it is bad form to suggest lower goals when the group is failing.

Although it is not shown in Table 6-3, the Nondeviants were quite similar to the Downward deviants. Also, the Upward, Downward, and Nondeviants were all alike in stating contrasting evaluations of the group's performance and in expressing opposing degrees of satisfaction with that performance after their group had failed and after it had succeeded. Thus, all three types of subjects equally well accepted the group's level of aspiration as an appropriate criterion for evaluating the success or failure of their group. Additional analyses similar to those in Table 6-3 were done in which the amount of deviancy, regardless of its direction, was considered. This approach produced no noteworthy results.

In summary, the beliefs of these members were appropriate to the motives that apparently were aroused in them. This experiment did not include questions about personal responsibility or the member's own share in the task. If such questions had been included, we perhaps would have found that Upward deviants in failing groups perceived they had little responsibility for the performance of the unit.

Generalization 6. Members who believe they are more competent individuals in their work for the group demonstrate a stronger desire to have their group approach the task than do members who believe they are less competent individuals.

Data in support of this statement have already been noted in Chapter 5. The procedure used to create a perception for a member that he is either very competent or less competent on a task in which all participants performed in exactly the same way and at the same moment, was described there. The relevant results are given in Table 6-4.

It is evident that the more competent persons were more deeply involved in the success of their group than were the less competent persons, that they felt more responsible for the group, and felt more pressure from their teammates to do well. When one examines the significant differences in Table 6-4, one notes that most of them are due to the lower ratings made by less competent members (compared to control subjects) rather than the higher ratings made by more competent members. It is perhaps fair to say that low competence arouses more desire in members to withdraw from the group's task than high competence arouses in them to approach it.

TABLE 6-4   MEAN MOTIVATED BELIEFS OF MEMBERS DIFFERING
            IN COMPETENCE[a]

| | Competence of member | | | |
	Control ($N = 36$)	High ($N = 36$)	Low ($N = 36$)	Significant differences
How large your part in group?	4.47	4.72	4.11	Hi $>$ Lo*
Important to equal other teams?	5.78	5.11	4.89	C $>$ Hi*
				C $>$ Lo**
Importance of ability to group?	5.61	5.44	4.81	C $>$ Lo**
				Hi $>$ Lo*
Value of tests like this?	5.06	5.11	4.06	C $>$ Lo**
				Hi $>$ Lo***
Validity of test?	4.83	5.22	3.86	C $>$ Lo**
				Hi $>$ Lo***
Felt pressure from teammates?	3.58	4.36	3.69	Hi $>$ C*

[a]After Zander and Wulff (86).
*$p < .05$.   **$p < .01$.   ***$p < .001$.

Generalization 7.   A member of a group feels greater tension as conditions in his
                     group more strongly arouse reactions that conflict with his
                     personal dispositions.

A conflictful situation arises when a member prefers to avoid the group's
task yet he cannot do so. Members of failing groups commonly rated themselves
as more tense than did members of successful groups because, apparently, the
desire to avoid, aroused in failing, was countered by the requirement to
continue. And, members who had a stronger personal disposition to avoid
challenging tasks (Maf $>$ Ms) consistently felt greater tension in group activities
than those who had a stronger personal disposition to approach challenging tasks
(Ms $>$ Maf).

Results from the work of Forward (28) provide a more interesting example
of the effect of conflicting motives in a member because in his research, as
opposed to the results just cited, one can better specify the source and direction of the motives. The contrasts, it will be recalled, were between group-
oriented desires to achieve group success or to avoid group failure and individual motives to approach the task (Ms $>$ Maf) or to avoid the task (Maf $>$ Ms).
The results have been reported in Table 5-9. It is clear there that tension is
greater where the conflict is apparently stronger for members. That is, individuals with stronger Ms indicated greater tension when they were in a group
condition that aroused desires to avoid the task than they did when in a condition that aroused desires to approach it, whereas persons with stronger Maf

revealed greater tension when in the group condition that aroused desires to approach the task than they did in the one that aroused desires to avoid it. Contrasting motives, group required versus personally desired, aroused tension in the members.

Results in a similar vein were obtained in quite a different setting by Thomas and Zander (69). In that study, the participants (military officers), who were soon to take part in a test of their ability to survive in a hostile environment, were queried about the strength of their desire to do well in this examination. The test itself lasted four days and demanded that small groups of men move through deep snow, without food, to a predetermined goal. At the end of each day the participants (N = 387) completed brief questionnaires and additional data were provided by observers who accompanied each group. Because this difficult test was required of them and each officer would receive a grade on his personal output (assigned by the observer), a member who had less concern about doing well was more likely to be in a conflict during the exercise than one who wished to do well. Daily ratings made by the participants (perceived difficulty on the day's hike, perceived disturbance during the day), as well as ratings made by the observers, revealed that individuals who had a weaker motive to perform well developed greater tension during the trek ($p < .01$).

It is obvious that the role a member is required to perform may be too heavy for him and thus be a source of felt tension, regardless of his personal motives. Demands on a member appeared to generate greater tension in several markable instances: central members felt greater tension when they were responsible for the group's productivity than when they were responsible for setting the group's goal (88), boys who worked on the ball-propelling test were more tense than boys who simply observed the latter at work (85), and participants who passed notes to one another in which they commented on events during the experiment developed more tension than persons who did not pass their notes.

RESPONSES OF BOARD MEMBERS
TO ORGANIZATIONAL SUCCESS OR FAILURE

Some groups succeed consistently on work they repeatedly perform and other groups fail over and over. In a failing group how do they explain their organization's performance to themselves? Is success not important or do they employ some other criterion to judge the quality of their collective effort?

Questions such as these inspired the previously mentioned study of board members in local United Fund organizations (89). Response forms were received from 255 persons, half of whom belonged to 23 Funds that had failed to attain their campaign goal fours years in a row, and half to 23 Funds that had reached it four times. The towns were matched in size and economic wealth. On each board, in addition, half of the respondents were central members, persons who now hold or had held officer posts, and the rest were peripheral members with less responsible positions. Various findings from this survey have been useful in earlier chapters. These and other results will now be briefly summarized in order to illustrate the pattern of reactions within a group that has more freedom of movement than the experimental units we have been considering. The data relevant to this purpose, however, are too many and too varied for quantitative presentation. A running description of the findings will have to suffice. Where numerical results have been earlier supplied, this fact will be indicated by noting the number of the chapter in which they were mentioned.

Contrasting Reactions in Succeeding and Failing Funds

The significant differences in the responses of board members in successful and unsuccessful Funds can be summarized under several generalizations, ignoring for the moment whether the responses are by a central or a peripheral person. Initially, however, we note several background facts.

Assuming that the goal of a given campaign is an accurate indication of financial requirements in the welfare agencies supported by the Fund, failing Funds, by definition, are not meeting those needs. They are not meeting, moreover, the condition that gives the board members their greatest source of satisfaction (Chapter 5). Even though they set their goals at an easier level (considering the wealth available to local citizens), failing Funds, compared to succeeding ones, take in less per capita and solicit a smaller proportion of the campaign goal. Furthermore, when setting a goal for a new campaign, the boards in failing Funds set this goal at a greater distance above their past level of performance than do the boards of succeeding Funds (Chapter 2).

Generalization 8.   Failing organizations, compared to succeeding ones, pay less attention to the probability of success when selecting a campaign goal.

Members place less emphasis on the probability of success when explaining the reasons for a failing campaign than they do when explaining the reasons for a successful campaign. Despite the smaller amount of money solicited per capita, members in failing Funds express a greater dislike for lowering the goal after a failure and are more unwilling to support any proposal to that effect (Chapter 3). Those in failing Funds, compared to members of succeeding Funds, are conscious of the needs of the community and place more pressures on themselves to meet those needs by working longer hours for the agency. They also state that there is less value in lowering the goal after a failed campaign and more strongly believe that it would be difficult to do so. Board members of failing Funds, in short, seem to be more concerned (with good reason) about the needs of the local welfare agencies than are those in succeeding Funds and apparently allow the goal to be more determined by such matters than by an appraisal of what the Fund can reasonably be expected to raise.

Generalization 9.   Respondents in failing organizations, compared to those in succeeding ones, reveal a greater awareness of unfavorable consequences from the performance of their agency.

Members of failing Funds have less pride in their organization (Chapter 7), rate their own personal contribution lower (Chapter 7), blame the campaign workers rather than the board for a poor campaign (even though they themselves had a part in the solicitation of funds), say that too few people are willing to serve as volunteers for the organization, blame lack of volunteers as the cause of a poor campaign, and believe that they personally work harder than their colleagues in the Fund. Too few men are doing more work, and enjoying it less.

Generalization 10.   The respondents from failing organizations attach less importance to goal achievement as a criterion of success.

Board members in failing Funds, more than members in succeeding Funds, think that successful attainment of the goal is less important, work as often to beat last year's level of performance as to attain the official goal, would rather beat last year's performance than try to attain the goal, and would be pleased to do away with goals altogether. They are less confident, moreover, that their Fund can attain the goal for the campaign to be held in a few weeks.

Generalization 11.   The foregoing characteristics are not only the result of the contrasting experiences of success or failure, they probably contribute as well to the effectiveness of the agency itself.

Given the tendency of failing Funds to set unreasonably difficult goals, the beliefs in the failing groups perhaps predestine the groups to another failure. The above generalizations, in summary, form a sequence—a circular one. They suggest that failure may prepare the ground for further failure and that success may lead to further success, all else equal. These results are from an organization in which there are strong restraints against lowering its goal. They would be less applicable to an organization (if such exists outside the laboratory) where goals can be lowered whenever this seems necessary.

Central and Peripheral Members in Successful Funds.   When their Fund has been consistently successful, central board members, more than peripheral ones, derive greater satisfaction from the effective operation of their organization than they derive from meeting the needs of agencies dependent on the Fund. They believe that a campaign goal might conceivably be set too high because of a mistake in budgetary planning but not because the local agencies make unreasonable demands for money. Centrals, more than peripherals, recognize that lowering the campaign goal would arouse social pressures in opposition to such a move and oppose lowering of the goal themselves because doing so means that the Fund would be avoiding a challenge. Central members are more disposed than their peripheral colleagues to obtain satisfaction from successful outcomes of their personal efforts. More than peripherals, they believe that the goal must be placed at a reasonable level in order to ensure a successful campaign, that the leadership of the Fund must be effective, and that the support of influential citizens in the community must be obtained if the Fund is to be successful in its work.

Within a successful Fund, in summary, central board members, more than peripheral persons, derive greater satisfaction from their own individual efforts, and believe that success is assured for the organization if the goal is reasonable, the campaign is well run, and if the support of important citizens is obtained.

Central and Peripheral Members in Failing Funds. When their Fund has had a series of failing campaigns, central and peripheral members are strikingly different in their views about the proper placement of the goal. Centrals more often say that goals were set too high (so that their Fund failed) because the agencies' demands for money were too high, and because it was difficult therefore to lower the goals (Chapter 3). In failing organizations, centrals more than peripherals do not believe that lowering the goals would do much to ensure success anyway; citizens must be interested in supporting the welfare agencies if the Fund is to have a successful campaign and the failure of the Fund is largely because the citizens do not give large enough contributions. Central board members, compared to peripheral members, put in more time working for the Fund, devote more time working in the campaign itself, and believe that their personal efforts will be more important in determining the success of the upcoming campaign.

To summarize, central members in failing Funds believe that the goal is placed at a high level because of pressures from local welfare agencies to put it there; lowering the goal, furthermore, would not ensure success because a success requires more interest among the citizens and more sharing of the work to be done than has locally been available. In a failing Fund, compared to a succeeding one, a central person feels strongly obliged, and pressed, to set high goals and to work hard toward those ends even if he must do most of the work himself.

The results of this survey have demonstrated that a group's goal setting and its work toward that goal is accompanied by attitudes and actions that reveal the dispositions of members to approach or to avoid the task of the agency. These behaviors or beliefs, however, are not always useful in improving the performance of the organization; an adequate conception of motivated group behavior needs to recognize this possibility.

SUMMARY

In this chapter it has been assumed that the beliefs of members can be taken as indicators of the group-oriented motives possessed by participants. These beliefs were used as signs of the subjects' desires in examining the degree of support for a general proposition: events within a group that arouse an anticipation of favorable consequences generate beliefs that reveal a desire to approach the group's task while events that arouse an anticipation of unfavorable consequences generate beliefs that reveal a desire to avoid the group's task.

A brief explanation was offered of how certain consequences come to be valued or disvalued during the life of a group and how, as a result, a disposition is developed to approach or avoid these consequences. Results were described to show that the following conditions affect members' group-oriented beliefs: quality of group's performance, difficulty of the task, competence among members, individual differences in disposition to seek success, group discussions of such beliefs, and depth of involvement in the group. Sources of tension due to conflicting demands on participants were also discussed.

An extensive account was given of the contrasting beliefs among board members in failing and succeeding fund-raising organizations. These data revealed that beliefs (and apparently behavior as well) were in accord with the group-oriented desires one would expect to be dominant in such organizations. The expressed beliefs and behaviors, moreover, appeared to be parts of a circular-causal sequence such that a failure or success tended to predispose the organization toward a repetition of the same quality of performance.

| # Evaluation of Group and of Personal Performance

When a group has finished an attempt to reach a goal, the participants are interested in how well the group has performed—thus, they compare its output and its aspiration. If they give the group a poor evaluation when its score is below its level of aspiration and a good evaluation when its performance is above that level, they are using the aspiration as their criterion of success. Under what conditions are members more likely to appraise their group by referring to its aspiration level? When and why do they distort their evaluation of the group?

An important reason for examining the dynamics of group evaluation is that the output of a group may affect a member's evaluation of himself and may in turn determine his self-regard and the part he is willing to play in that group. How and why a member takes the score of his group as an indication of his own competence is given attention in this chapter. His evaluation of his own performance in his own role will be considered in Chapter 9.

MEMBERS' EVALUATION OF GROUP PERFORMANCE

Evaluation of a group has a restricted meaning here. It refers to appraisal of a particular performance at a particular time. Output on its current activity is evaluated rather than goodness of the group in all its activities. Most of the data we shall review were obtained from ratings made by subjects, near the conclusion of an experiment, to a question like the following: All in all, how well do you think your team has performed on this test? Because the results are from a variety of studies, it is again convenient to assemble them under a number of generalizations. The reader can assume, where there are contrasting conditions in an experiment, that the group levels of performance are not significantly different in these separate treatments of the study.

Generalization 12.   Members use the group's level of aspiration as their criterion for appraising the performance of their group.

In 11 investigations mentioned elsewhere in these chapters, subjects were asked to rate the quality of their group's performance. In every instance they made significantly more favorable ratings if their group had usually performed above its aspirations and less favorable ratings if it had performed below these aspirations. These judgments concern the average performance of the group during the entire series of trials in an experiment. Clearly, individuals evaluate the success or failure of their team by using its aspiration level as the criterion of a successful outcome, all else equal.

Generalization 13.   The degree of evaluation members assign to their group is a function of the direction and degree of discrepancy between the group's level of performance and its prior level of aspiration.

In three experiments described in Chapter 3 groups were exposed to social pressures to change its performance. In each experiment there was a control condition in which teams, all performing the ball-propelling test, did not receive such pressures. The data we first examine are from these control groups.

Consider the correlation between members' evaluation of their group and as is most typical, the amount the group's score, fell short of their group's aspiration level (the latter difference is hereafter called the *performance discrepancy*). In the first experiment this correlation was +.37 ($p < .01$); in the second it was +.16 (n.s.); in the third it was +.43 ($p < .05$). The evaluation was lower as the performance was poorer than expected.

It is of incidental interest that the observers in their control condition, that is, when the experimenter created no social pressures for the observers, rated the performing groups lower as the scores of the latter were farther below the observers' expectationss ($r = +.49$, $p < .05$).

Generalization 14.   A group aspiration established under the influence of social pressures from outside the group is more often taken as a criterion for appraising the group's performance when the pressures are toward harder levels than when they are toward easier levels.

Within the experiment in which a group's score was either comparatively worse or better than other units (*80*), participants set higher aspirations (and failed more often) under Unfavorable social comparisons than under Favorable ones. In the Unfavorable conditions the correlation between the evaluation of the group and the performance discrepancy was $+.37$ $(p < .01)$ and in the Favorable condition it was $+.16$ (n.s).

When the subjects received messages from observers indicating that the latter had either high expectations or low expectations for the group, the results were comparable in that members set higher or lower aspirations to match these pressures and failed more often in the former circumstance than in the latter. The correlations between evaluation of the group and the performance discrepancy was $+.74$ $(p < .001)$ when the observers sent high expectations and $+.11$ (n.s.) when they sent low expectations. Pressures from external sources apparently help to define a failure more than they help to define a success.

There is an alternative explanation for these results. Perphaps the personnel were not reacting to their failure to achieve their own aspirations but instead were responding to the unwanted discrepancy between their group's score and that suggested by an external source. This possibility cannot be excluded because failures to achieve aspiration levels were more common in the one condition and successes more common in the other, making it difficult to identify the degree that evaluation might have been affected by comparison with influences from outside. If the evaluations were largely caused by such comparisons rather than by performance discrepancies, it seems likely, however, that there would be more tendency (than we found) for members to approve their group whenever it performed better than the external criterion.

Generalization 15. When conditions make it important for a member to have a reliable appraisal of his group's performance, he is more likely to use the group's level of aspiration as a criterion for evaluation.

A plain example is found in the results of the questionnaires sent to the board members of United Fund organizations (*89*). The respondents were asked to evaluate the performance of several parts of the United Fund: the board, the campaign workers, and the United Fund in general as a service agency. Half of the members, it will be recalled, were in central posts with major responsibilities for the fate of the Fund and the other half were in peripheral roles. Because of their important part in its decisions and actions we assume that central persons, more than peripheral ones, need to make accurate judgments about how well their Fund might next perform so that an appropriate goal can be set for the coming campaign. To do this, they must be realistic about past performances of the organization. The central board members in consistently successful Funds evaluated their organization higher in all three respects than did those in failing Funds. The peripheral board members, in contrast, rated their Fund high in these same respects, regardless of whether it had a successful record or a failing one. The ratings by central members, in short, were more in accord with the facts than were the ratings by peripheral members.

Results based on quite different variables were similar to the ones just stated.

Group evaluations made by persons with a stronger need to achieve individual success (Ms) were compared with those made by persons with a stronger need to avoid failure (Maf) (86). It was assumed that people who are more strongly concerned about success will be more careful in estimating the probable performance of the group and therefore will pay more attention to any discrepancy between prior goal and subsequent score, and people who are more interested in avoiding failure will be less concerned about precision in such matters. In this experiment groups were allowed to set their aspirations as they wished and received accurate reports of their score; nevertheless some groups succeeded more often than they failed and other groups failed more often than they succeeded. Among the groups composed of persons with stronger Ms, successful groups were evaluated higher (mean = 5.04) and failing groups were evaluated lower (mean = 4.27, p of difference < .01). Among the groups composed of those with stronger Maf, evaluations of the group were not significantly different after a success and a failure (means 5.17 and 4.73). It appears that the members with a stronger interest in achieving success were more accurate in their evaluations of their group.

If the group's level of aspiration is used more often as a criterion when there is a greater need for reliable information, it follows that members who have ample opportunity to communicate with one another should develop views about their work that make it less necessary for them to use the group's aspiration level as their prime criterion of success. On the contrary, members who have no opportunity for such talk should make greater use of the aspiration level when evaluating the performance of their group. Support for this hypothesis occurred in the experiment that offered open communication among members (written messages passed around the group) in half of the groups, and no intermember communication in the other half of the groups. Among the groups where open communication occurred, the correlation between evaluation of the group and the performance discrepancy was nearly zero. In the groups where no communication was allowed, and presumably a need for making an appraisal was greater, this correlation was +.23 (p < .05).

Generalization 16. When observers have a stake in the score earned by the performing unit, the observers' evaluations of the performing group are more inaccurate than when they are less involved in that score.

As the observers watched the workers in action on the ball-propelling test, they were asked to agree among themselves on what score they expected the performing group would attain in the following trial. Half of the observers were led to believe that their expectations were communicated to the working group and the other half were told that the expectations were not delivered to the workers. At the end of the experiment the observers were asked to evaluate the working team.

When the observers understood that their expectations had been given to the performers, the correlations between their evaluation of the group's performance and the discrepancy between the group's score and the observers' expectations was $+.58$ ($p < .025$). This same relationship was nearly zero when the observers thought that their expectations had not been delivered. Perhaps in the former case observers felt a greater pressure to be accurate in their appraisal of the group.

The correlation between the observers' evaluation of the working group and the discrepancy noted above was larger when the observers perceived themselves as *not* being dependent on the performing group ($r = +.62$, $p < .01$) than when they perceived themselves as being dependent on that group, where the correlation is nearly zero. The observers also gave the group a higher rating in the former situation than in the latter. Thus, the observers judged the workers more realistically, and did not shift their evaluations upward, when they had less vested interest in perceiving that the workers had done well.

Generalization 17. Members are more inclined to misrecall the score obtained by their group if the group has failed than if it has succeeded.

At the conclusion of an experiment, Dustin (*19, 20*) asked participants to recall the score earned by the group on each of three trials. The members in groups that more often failed made more errors (in a direction that was more favorable to the group) than did members in groups that succeeded ($p < .01$).

A similar finding was observed in the study of United Fund board members. Here the respondents were asked to recall how much money their town had raised in the immediately prior campaign. In those towns where the Fund had repeatedly failed to achieve its goal, the board members recalled a larger amount than was actually raised ($p < .05$). The tendency to misrecall in this convenient manner appeared significantly more often among peripheral members than among central members of the board ($p < .05$). In successful communities the respondents, both central and peripheral, were reasonably accurate in recalling how well their town had performed in the previous year.

The tendency of those in failing groups to improve on things a bit when recollecting their group's past score has noteworthy significance. It implies that those in failing groups (assuming they recall their group's aspiration level accurately) are disposed to see less discrepancy between their group's score and its level of aspiration than is really there.

Generalization 18. When conditions promise greater potential satisfaction with the outcomes in a group, members give a more favorable evaluation to their group's performance, regardless of the actual quality of that performance.

The amount of satisfaction from completion of one task may be greater than that from another, whatever the score. The example noted most often is the contrast between the greater attractiveness of success on a more difficult task and the lesser attractiveness of success on an easier task. If more is to be gained from successful completion of a mission, members will perceive that their unit has performed better in that instance.

A simple illustration was evident in the results of the experiment that initially assigned groups either a difficult task or an easy one (82). Because the attractiveness of success on the more difficult task is greater than the attractiveness of success on an easier task and the repulsiveness of failure is less on a difficult task than on an easy one, we expect the evaluation of a group to be higher, regardless of its success or failure, as the difficulty of the task attempted by the group increases. The correlation between evaluation attributed to the group by participants and difficulty of the task was +.50 ($p < .01$). This correlation was strong both when the group succeeded more often ($r = +.35$, $p < .01$) and when it failed more often ($r = +.23, p < .05$). Working on a more difficult task induced a more favorable evaluation of the group.

In an additional study (83), members selected a level of aspiration for each new trial on an interdependent task but were given no reports on their group's score. In the latter situation, as noted in Chapter 2, the teammates consistently chose a more difficult level of aspiration than they had attempted in the previous trial. Members evaluated their group more favorably as they worked on these harder tasks: the correlation between evaluation of the group and average task difficulty was +.34 ($p < .01$). This correlation was larger in the well-formed groups (called "stronger" ones in that study) ($p = +.52$, $p < .01$) than in the weaker groups ($r \sim 0$).

In Chapter 5 we observed that an individual who knows that he is the group's most competent member is more interested in the outcome of the group than in his own fate, but one who knows he is the least competent man is more concerned about his personal outcome than that of the group. If one is an able member and devoted to helping his group, it seems reasonable that he would wish to perceive his group as competent. In accord with such an hypothesis, the persons with high personal competence gave their group an evaluation of 5.08 while those of low competence gave their group an evaluation of 4.39. These means are different at the $< .05$ level of confidence.

Generalization 19. When members perceive a higher probability that their group will succeed in the future, they assign a higher evaluation to their group's performance.

In a book-length report on the evaluations individuals give themselves on solo activities, Diggory (17) has demonstrated that subjects attribute higher evaluations to their solitary efforts as they perceive a higher probability of eventual success. Diggory used tasks in which the goal was fixed and could not be changed by subjects because he assumed that individuals tend to raise their goals when given a chance to do so and thus get discouraged as they discover in the course of events that their performance is worse than they had expected. His research was concerned with the conditions that cause an individual to perceive his probability of success to be high or low.

There have been studies of group evaluation that meet the general requirements advocated by Diggory and their results support his general findings.

In two experiments Forward and Zander attempted to generate a strong desire for group success in half of the groups and a weak desire in the remainder. This was done by having the subjects complete a short questionnaire when they entered the laboratory. The tests themselves were not scored but their wording was such that it was credible for the experimenter to assert, after he had pretended to score them, that the members in this group were highly alike in attitudes: strongly inclined toward attaining success on the one hand or little interested in such a matter, on the other. After this information was reported, the members were put to work on an activity described in Chapter 8. They were not allowed to choose their level of difficulty, which was assigned by the experimenter, and they were not asked for a group level of aspiration.

At the conclusion of the test period the members were invited to evaluate the performance of their group without knowing the score it had obtained. In the first experiment those who were induced to have a strong desire for group success rated their group considerably higher than those who were induced to have a weak desire ($p < .001$). In the second study the results were similar, and these were replicated in a third investigation (92). It seems likely that the initial information was taken by the subjects as evidence about how well their group would perform, and nothing happened during the experiment to contradict this view. It is possible that the early comments by the experimenter had a different meaning to the subjects than the above interpretation of them. Perhaps his instructions meant in the one case that "this is a fine group of strivers who are worthy of your respect" and in the other case that "this is an apathetic lot, worthy of your derogation." There is no way of telling if that occurred.

There are other studies relevant to this generalization. Fouriezos *et al.* (30), as noted earlier, observed that members of a committee were less satisfied with its work if a good proportion of the acts during meetings were intended to service a participant's personal needs rather than the needs of the group. In such a situation, presumably, the perceived probability of success by the group would be low since many members manifestly ignore the group's task in favor of their own individual desires. In a similar vein, Rosenthal and Cofer (61) report that members rated their group as more inept when it had a casual and indifferent member within it (an employee of the research project, planted in the group by the experimenters) than when they had no such burden. In the questionnaire study of the criteria students used as their bases of satisfaction in a classroom project, described in Chapter 5, it was observed that men gave more favorable ratings to their group as their perceived probability of group success increased.

An interesting variation on the theme in this generalization has been provided by Deutsch (16). He noted that members rated their group as more capable in its work if it had a success, but only if the motivation of the members was known to be low; and rated their group as less capable after it had failed, but only if the motivation of members was known to be high. Thus, in this instance, a success is taken as a sign of competence if the members succeed even when they are not interested in doing so and a failure is taken as a sign of incompetence if members fail when they clearly wish to succeed.

MEMBER'S EVALUATION OF HIS OWN PERFORMANCE

In many organizations as in prior experiments a member periodically receives reasonably good information about the performance of his group but no adequate evidence about how well he is doing. If he wishes to make an appraisal of his own effort, he can make a rough judgment of this by referring to the quality of his group's score; thus, he thinks his performance is good if his group has done well and bad if his group has done poorly. One can imagine a situation, however, when he feels that he cannot give himself credit for his group's success or blame himself for its failure. Under what conditions is a member more likely to reject the group's score as an appropriate indicator of his own performance? When will he accept the group's score as relevant evidence?

The data we consider now are again from a variety of studies, provided by subjects when responding to a questionnaire near the end of an experimental session. The relevant question was: "Considering everything, how well do you think you personally performed during this test?" As previously, it is convenient to summarize the results in the form of generalizations.

Generalization 20. Members of successful groups evaluate their personal performance better than do members of failing groups.

In the experiment that provided Favorable comparisons for some groups and Unfavorable comparisons for others (80), the groups were more often successful in the former case than in the latter. Members thereafter rated their individual contributions higher in the successful groups (mean = 5.7, on a 7-point scale) than in the unsuccessful groups (mean = 5.1) ($p < .01$). Also during the experiment with domino designs (82), members of successful groups gave higher ratings to their personal performance (5.63) than did those in failing groups (3.78) ($p < .001$). And, among the board members of United Funds, those in consistently successful organizations rated their personal contributions higher (3.54) than those in repeatedly failing organizations (3.11) ($p < .01$).

These bits of evidence suggest that participants often use the quality of their group's performance as an indicator of their personal competence.

Generalization 21. A member with comparatively more commitment to the group is more likely to evaluate his performance in accord with the group's quality of outcome.

A clear example is found in the experiment that placed participants in either central or peripheral positions (55). The central members gave their personal performances high ratings if the group succeeded and low ratings if the group failed; the peripheral members, however, gave themselves high ratings, regardless of the group's success or failure ($p < .01$).

In an experiment employing sets of 6-8 college women, Zander *et al.* (78) assigned the participants to a task that required coordination of their efforts in several different roles while they made judgments about the best combinations of colors for parts of a lady's costume on different occasions. They understood that the judgments by their set would be compared to standards proposed by the American Institute of Fashion Design (a fictitious organization) and that members would be told whether their group had done well or poorly in reference to those standards. Through certain instructions and activities half of the sets were led to perceive themselves as a group with high unity; the other half, as a collection of separate individuals, a set with low unity. It was assumed that persons in more unified groups would have a greater involvement in the work of their team than would persons in less unified sets and thus would more often refer to the group's score when judging their personal performance. The results supported this expectation. In groups with higher unity, members of successful sets gave themselves higher evaluations (mean = 7.58) and members of failing units gave themselves lower ratings (mean = 7.10) (*p* of difference $< .025$). In groups with low unity, however, participants gave themselves evaluations that were not significantly different in successful and failing groups (means = 7.82 and 7.55, respectively).

We noted in Chapter 5 that the men in classroom committees took greater responsibility for the work of their group than did the women. The men thereupon gave more favorable evaluations to their own performance if they perceived the group as doing well and unfavorable self-ratings if they saw the group as not doing well. The women did not base their self-ratings on apparent progress of the group.

A member will attach more personal meaning to the success (or failure) of his group then if he has had a greater responsibility in producing the group's score.

Generalization 22. Members of failing groups, compared to those in successful units, less often evaluate their personal performance in accord with the quality of the group's outcome.

Saying this another way—in a successful group members rate themselves as favorably as they rate their group but in a failing unit they rate themselves better than the set. This tendency was first noted in the experiment that provided either Favorable or Unfavorable comparisons (*80*). In one condition individuals worked alone on the same task as that performed by the teams. Solo persons rated their own performance high if they succeeded more often and low if they failed more often. The members of teams evaluated their personal efforts in the same direction, but the difference in successful and failing groups was not large; members in failing groups did not evaluate themselves as poorly as did individuals who failed, all else being equal. It appeared that membership in a group was a convenience insofar as self-appraisal is concerned. One can evaluate himself well if his group does well but need not evaluate himself poorly if the group fails.

A direct test of this last conjecture was made by Dustin (*20*). He provided standardized scores and standardized levels of aspiration to groups so that in one condition all groups failed to attain their level of aspiration by the same amount and in another condition exceeded this level by the same amount. He then made comparisons of the evaluations members gave to their teams and to themselves. In the better-performing groups members rated their teams better than they rated themselves, in the poorer groups members rated themselves higher than they rated their teams ($p < .01$). In still another study (*83*) members judged their group's performance to be lower than their personal performance when the group had failed more often, but they rated the group and themselves about the same when the group succeeded more often. When the group failed, the mean ratings of team and personal performance were 3.21 and 4.67 respectively ($p < .001$), but when the group succeeded, the comparable ratings were both about 5.00. Johnston and his colleagues have reported similar results (*39, 41*).

This is perhaps the best place to mention failure to find support for a relevant hypothesis. On the basis of the foregoing and other notions it was expected that individuals might privately give their teams less favorable appraisals than they would during a group discussion. In order to test this hunch the members of each group, after each individual had privately evaluated the group, were asked to make a unanimous evaluation of their unit as the very last activity in an experiment by Zander and Ledvinka (*82*). The results of the group decisions were no different from the average rating members made in private. Thus, group discussion did not generate a greater tendency to approve or to disapprove of the group than members had previously developed. The hypothesis is worthy of more careful study.

Generalization 23. Regardless of the discrepancy between the performance of a group and its level of aspiration, when members have a stronger desire for group success they evaluate their personal contributions more favorably.

In an unpublished experiment, Forward and Zander induced contrasting degrees of desire for group achievement. The participants were not given information about the performance of their group or themselves (on a task that required exertion of full muscular effort). Members in the groups with the supposed higher desire for group success gave higher evaluation to their personal performance than those in groups with less desire ($p < .001$). Zander and Ulberg observed a similar effect (92).

The responses of central and peripheral board members in United Funds are relevant. Evidence reported elsewhere reveals that central persons have a greater desire that their Fund achieve its goal than do peripheral members. Accordingly, central members gave themselves a rating the mean of which was 3.54 and peripheral members gave themselves a rating with a mean of 3.20 ($p < .025$).

As has been shown, members who have a stronger motive to approach success (Ms), compared to those with a stronger motive to avoid failure (Maf), are more concerned about the success of their group. It is anticipated then that individuals with a stronger motive to achieve success will assign more favorable ratings to their performance as members. In the experiment that provided evidence to members about their own competence on the group's task (86), those who received favorable reports judged their own contributions better of course, than those who received unfavorable reports. The personal motive to approach success, however, modified these ratings. Members of high competence were more satisfied with themselves when they had a stronger motive to approach success (Ms > Maf); in contrast, members of low competence were more *dissatisfied* with themselves when they had a stronger motive to approach success (Ms > Maf) ($p < .05$). Thus, greater interest in personal success generated greater satisfaction with self among good performers and greater dissatisfaction with self among poor performers.

There was a tendency noted in one experiment for persons with Ms exceeding Maf to assign themselves more favorable ratings than persons with Maf exceeding Ms when they were in a peripheral position but not when they were in a central position (88), regardless of the performance of the group. It seems likely that an individual with a stronger motive to approach success will not only want more accurate facts so that he can make suitable judgments about himself and can set his future sights at an appropriate level, as noted earlier; he will also wish to believe that success has indeed occurred whenever the facts are ambiguous on this matter. It would be helpful to know, on the one hand, when and how a member's motive to approach success presses him to be careful in appraising himself and, on the other hand, pushes him to distort the outcomes toward a favorable direction.

SUMMARY

In this chapter we have examined results bearing on two different types of evaluation: appraisal of a group's performance and ratings of personal performance. A number of generalizations were presented. Their major points can be stated briefly.

The personnel in a group use the group's level of aspiration in judging the performance of their unit; a score that exceeds the level is considered to be a good one and a score that falls short is a poor one. The degree of discrepancy between a group's level of aspiration and its subsequent score determines the amount of value members assign to that performance.

The valuations members assign to their group's output are more highly correlated with its performance discrepancy when conditions require participants to be more accurate about the quality of their group's performance. Yet, distortions occur. After a failing performance members tend to misrecall the score to a greater degree (in a direction that is more favorable to the group) than they do after a success. When members perceive that they will obtain more satisfaction from the performance of their group, they evaluate the group more favorably, regardless of its score. In groups where the goal is fixed or the members have no information about the score of the group, members tend to give it more favorable appraisals when its properties make it apparent that success is more probable.

If it is assumed that more frequent use of the level of aspiration as a criterion of success can be taken as a sign that members attach greater importance to attainment of that level, these results are in accord with those in prior chapters. They indicate that members operating under personal or social requirements that their group be successful are more likely to pay careful attention to the true relationship between prior goal and subsequent performance, but these same persons also have an inclination, which they ordinarily curb, to perceive their group as doing better than the facts warrant when the consequences from a good performance are seen to be unusually favorable.

Concerning the effect that a group's quality of performance has on a member's self-evaluation, it was noted that one who knows the score and aspiration of his group is inclined to appraise his own effort unfavorably if the group has been unsuccessful and favorably if the group has been successful. The group's attainment of its level of aspiration has more effect on a member's self-evaluation if he is more responsible for the group's score; thus, a marginal member is less likely than a central member to take the group's quality of output as an indicator of his own performance. There is good evidence, moreover, that a member (particularly a peripheral one) rejects the group's failure as a sign of his own competence but readily accepts a group's success as such a sign. He denies, in short, that a group failure says much about his own performance, but he believes that a group success is reliable evidence on this issue: a central member however rates himself in accord with the group's attainment no matter how well or poorly his unit has performed.

When a group gets no score and sets no level of aspiration, persons who have a greater desire for group success are more likely to perceive that they themselves performed well.

In general, it seems, group members assign more favorable appraisals to their own output than to their team. When rating their team's performance, members are inclined to give more negative than positive evaluations. When rating their personal contribution, they are less ready to accept a failing group performance (than a successful one) as an indicator of personal competence. As a result, members of a failing group do not look to the group's output as a source of personal satisfaction, and of course find little satisfaction in the failing performance of the group itself. The most comfortable position in a group then is a peripheral post. In that type of role a man can give himself credit for the group's success and can avoid any self-blame for the group's failure. The most uncomfortable place is a central one in a failing unit.

It is interesting to press this line of conjecture a bit further. A person who has a strong need for achievement presumably will want to get ahead in any organization he joins—this means that he takes or is given greater responsibility for the output of his group. But a person's self-regard is more influenced by the performance of the group if he is in a central role than in a peripheral one. Thus, it may be that one with a high need for achievement gravitates toward a social position that makes him vulnerable to self-derogation since, in the long run, his group (in many types of tasks) may fail more often than it succeeds. Perhaps it is too much to assume that an individual with a high need for achievement recognizes this possibility and for this reason avoids group activities when he has the opportunity to do so, as was noted in Chapter 5. It would not be surprising, however, to find that a person with a higher need for personal achievement is more likely to leave an organization than one who has a higher fear of failure. Probably, a person with a need to avoid failure can adequately defend his own self esteem when he is a member of a group.

| **Motives, Aspirations, and Group Performance**

Everyone knows that members of a group work harder when they are more motivated and that harder work yields better results. When a team pulls on a rope or pushes a heavy object it finishes the job faster if more vigor is applied. Most tasks however are not as simple as these; in more complicated cases "what everyone knows" is hardly sufficient. If a group's activity calls for different contributions from separate members, greater use of energy may not be an important ingredient of effective performance, or may not be desirable at all, the amount of coordination among participants is more telling and excessive enthusiasm may reduce the care needed for smooth collaboration. In a complex activity a group might not produce well even though its members earnestly desire it and have the required skills.

The beneficial effects of motives and goals can be attenuated for varied reasons. In a group that sets a level of aspiration the participants do not strictly need a remarkable score to obtain satisfaction from its endeavors. If necessary, they can lower the unit's aspiration level so that an unimprovable output becomes satisfying when it previously was not. Often they can avoid the task, or convince themselves that the output is not a true indicator of the group's ability. They may choose a different motive, if desirable, so that they are less involved in unattainable ends and more appreciative of achievable ones.

As in most of the experiments previously mentioned, the production by all members is usually taken as the measure of a group's performance. In some groups however, it is necessary that only one person, no matter who, come up with correct action to have a successful group; in other groups the score is decided by the output of the man who finishes first; in yet others it is decided by the one who comes in last. When the work of all participants decides the group's score, a member's group-oriented motivation is likely to affect the production of the group. When the work of one member can determine the success of the group, a member's person-oriented motivation may be more important in deciding the score.

In order to study the effects of motivation on group performance, a scholar must reduce the confounding created by conditions such as those just mentioned. But when he does so he still has problems. What measure, for example, should he use to calibrate the unit's output? Shall he observe the number of items produced, the quality of work, the energy exerted, the accuracy of movement, the cost of these actions, or what? This is not an idle choice since one type of measure can be more susceptible to motivation than another. The various indicators of group performance in this chapter were chosen because they were reliable or were convenient to use. They are admittedly different in content, but the results of future research are needed in order to know how much they contrast or supplement one another in reflecting the motives of members.

We begin with the simple assumption that variations in any of the parts that determine the tendency to approach (Tgs) or the tendency to avoid (Tgaf) will under certain circumstances, affect the score a group earns, all else equal. We recall that Tgs is a resultant of the multiplicative relationship among the desire to attain the consequences of group success (Dgs), the perceived probability of group success (Pgs), and the incentive value of group success (Igs). Tgaf is a function of the desire to avoid group failure (Dgaf), the perceived probability of group failure (Pgf), and the incentive value of group failure (Igf). If we assume that Tgs and Tgaf determine the member's movement toward the task of his group, and that the several conditions named create the strength of these tendencies, it is reasonable that differing degrees of such conditions cause differing amounts of effort toward the group's task. If the situation is right, better output ought to occur. Testing this assumption will be one purpose of this chapter. A second purpose will be to determine if the output of a group varies on tests of differing difficulty.

FEEDBACK AND PERFORMANCE

In a way of life accustomed to coordination among athletes, collaboration among space travelers, and orchestration of workers on an assembly line, there is ready acceptance of the proposition that a group can improve its performance if it makes proper plans to do so. In Chapter 1, it was asserted, however, that actions in behalf of such plans need to be checked and that members must then introduce whatever changes are necessary, in its goals or procedures, if effective effort is to occur. An essential part of adaptive group action is that plans be informed by evidence concerning past performance, that action be based in short upon adequate feedback. The availability of feedback has been a characteristic in most of the groups studied thus far.

Before continuing, it is necessary to establish that performance of a group can be affected simply by the presence of feedback, ignoring the motivation or aspiration of members. Will the performance of a group meet a given criterion more effectively when feedback is given to members than when it is not supplied? The answer to an additional question is useful: which kind of feedback is most effective, that concerning the group score alone, that concerning the performance of individual members, or both?

Glaser and Klaus (33) studied contrasts in team performance when feedback was provided and when it was not. The participants in a number of three-man teams worked 1½ hr. a day, 5 days a week, for 3–10 weeks. On each of the numerous trials in their investigation, a subject had to press a button for what he estimated to be either a 2-sec or a 4-sec interval of time. Interdependence was created in the task by requiring one of the subjects on each team to indicate whether he judged the estimates of his colleagues to be accurate. The team was successful on a given trial only if all three persons, two button pressers and one judge, were correct—any other pattern of performance was a failure. As is typical in studies of reinforcement contingencies, the groups first were given feedback on quality of performance (correct or not correct) until they were producing consistently at a preset criterion of accuracy, then the feedback was omitted for several days. When it was stopped, performance deteriorated. Reintroduction of feedback caused performance once more to improve and absence of feedback at a later time again caused deterioration. Improvement in performance was clearly a function of the availability of feedback. It is also noteworthy that individual practice and feedback on individual efforts, introduced routinely throughout the study, did not cause improvement in a unit's performance; feedback on the performance of a team was necessary for better output by the team. This was true even when it had initially become highly efficient. These authors comment, "Thus, it is not how well the game is played that counts but whether the game is won."

In some group activities a good performance is not required by everyone, the rule instead is that appropriate behavior by any single member or subset is enough for a group success. Glaser and Klaus studied the effects of feedback in this type of situation. When feedback describes only the score obtained by the group, they reasoned, a member who functions incorrectly does not learn that he has done so. Because his group has succeeded, he presumes that his effort was also successful. It follows that the more often such inaccurate feedback occurs, the more the performance of the inept member deteriorates. In a group operating under the rule stated above, the performance of the group should gradually worsen with feedback rather than improve since inept members gradually get the idea that they are doing well when in fact they are not. An experiment to test these notions was in most respects similar to the previous one. Under this rule feedback eventually caused the team to do worse than it had done on earlier trials.

In many instances a member gets information about more than the output of his group; he obtains feedback as well about his own personal contribution and that of each of the others. To study the effects of more complete feedback, Zajonc (74) compared two types. In one, each member was informed about the success or failure of the entire unit, his own individual performance, and the performance of each member—three separate kinds of information. In the other type, a member was told only about the success or failure of the group as a whole, the procedure employed by Glaser and Klaus.

Groups of seven members were observed. The task again was simple. On signal, each member pressed a button as quickly as he could; the length of his reaction time, measured by an electric clock, was the score for his performance. Each participant had a panel at his place with a set of lights that revealed the success or failure of any part of the team. A description of this equipment, called a *Group Reaction Time Apparatus*, has been provided by Zajonc (76). A lengthy series of trials was run in which the quality of the group's performance was determined by how long it took for the slowest member to complete the task. The results showed that more complete feedback was better than less. That is, the speed of the group improved more when the members received feedback about the success of the group, each member, and themselves. Information about the group's score alone was weaker in determining its speed.

It is concluded that groups perform better when they receive feedback than when they do not, and fuller feedback is better than less. These last experiments used simple motor movements. Will feedback have comparable effects in a situation that demands more coordination and verbal interaction among participants?

Zander and Wolfe (81) compared the effects of several forms of feedback on a group task that allowed members to collaborate with one another, or not, as they thought necessary. The participants, five men in a group, were members of 23 district coordinating committees in a large utility, each committee being a near duplicate of the others in the composition and character of the members. The task was described to the subjects as a test of "work group intelligence" and required them to make predictions about which two of four possible events might occur in each of a series of trials. For each success they earned a number of points. To do this reliably, each man could get the answer from the experimenter (at a cost of all the points he would ordinarily win for being correct) or could buy or beg it from a colleague. All communication was by written messages; participants were allowed to give or sell information they possessed; they could also contribute some of their own points to anyone else in the group if they felt altruistic enough to do so. This task was first performed for six trials without any feedback. During the next six trials each group was given feedback publicly in one of the following ways: (a) *Group,* the sum of the scores of all members; (b) *Individual,* the separate score of every member; (c) *Group and Individual,* every member's score and the sum of these; or (d) *Control,* no feedback given.

A significant improvement in group performance ($p < .02$) (compared to the amount of change in the Control condition) occurred only when Group and Individual scores were simultaneously provided (type c above). Neither the feedback of Group scores (a), or of Individual scores (b), created a reliable change in output. Thus, even in a complex task, requiring some thought and care about others' needs, the more feedback members obtained, the better.

These results provide no direct evidence about the motivation of members although a better performance probably means that participants had a stronger desire to do well. It seems likely, too, that feedback was needed in order for any motivation to be aroused and maintained; if members were to commit themselves to a group task, they needed to know whether their efforts would be worthwhile. Might the stronger effect of reporting both individual and group scores be due to the arousal of both person and group-oriented motives? We will return to this issue later.

DESIRE FOR GROUP ACHIEVEMENT
AND PERFORMANCE OF GROUP

The basic proposition now is that the tendency to approach the task of the group (Tgs) is a resultant of the desire for the group to attain success, times the perceived probability of success, times the consequences to be derived from that success. Because there is reason to believe that Tgs will vary as the difficulty of the task is higher or lower, it is necessary to keep the difficulty, and thus the incentive value, constant. When probability and incentive are unchanging, the only variable that will determine the strength of Tgs is the strength of the desire for group success. Thus, the hypothesis to be tested is that greater desire for group success causes better group performance, all else equal.

Support for this hypothesis has been provided in an unpublished study by Horwitz *et al.* (36). They were concerned with the effects that certain group properties might have on the goal a member selects for his group and on his certainty that this choice is a reasonable one. They were also interested in the accuracy, speed, and persistence of members on the group's task, the data most relevant to our purpose. They did not, however, mention the concept Dgs.

Horwitz *et al.* used 40 five-man groups. All participants were strangers except in Treatment 1 (below). The task required the subjects to work together in assembling a five-piece jigsaw figure. They were seated around a table, separated from one another by wooden shields, but could see an outline picture of a locomotive in the center of the table's surface. They were each provided one part of the locomotive-pattern and were instructed to push their piece into its place by using a long stick. They were told that speed and accuracy of placement determined the final score for each trial. After the figure was assembled, the experimenter disassembled it and the task was repeated for at least 40 trials or 80 min.

Before each trial a participant privately provided three judgments about: (a) the *goal* for the next trial, stated in terms of a percentage "grade"; (b) his *confidence* in this estimate, and; (c) his degree of *satiation* indicated by his response to the question: How do you feel about doing this particular task again? Ratings were made on a 6-point scale varying from "some interest" to "intensely distasteful."

There were four experimental treatments and one control condition. The variables within each treatment follow.

1. Group is high in cohesiveness (i.e., a team from a fraternity), each member is told that he and others are in close agreement on goals for group, and group is given accurate feedback about the time taken for each trial.

2. Group is low in cohesiveness, each member is told that he and others are in close agreement on goals for group, and no feedback is given.

3. Group is low in cohesiveness, each member is told that he and others are in disagreement about goals for group, and no feedback is given.

4. Group is low in cohesiveness, each member is given no information about agreement on goals, and no feedback is given.

5. (Control) Member sets no goal for group and is given no information about goals or the group's performance.

It is plausible to suppose that Treatment 1 generated more desire for group success than the others, especially Treatment 4. The results are displayed in Table 8-1.

TABLE 8-1 EFFECTS OF EXPERIMENTAL CONDITIONS ON GROUP PERFORMANCE[a]

	Condition					F
	1	2	3	4	Control	
Mean score (minutes per trial)	.92	1.16	1.11	1.17	1.36	6.03**
Mean satiation score	2.48	2.85	3.07	3.28	3.54	3.96**
Mean inaccuracy score	5.10	3.45	3.75	3.66	3.57	3.29*
Mean level of goal (%)	79.06	72.87	66.94	62.68	—	16.15**
Mean confidence in accuracy of goal estimate	3.06	2.82	2.27	2.44	—	11.35**
Frequency of atypical shifts in goals	13	16	26	25	—	(χ^2 = 9.45*)

[a]After Horwitz *et al.* (36).
*p < .05.   **p < .01.

Members worked more rapidly and showed more persistence on the task (felt less satiation) as more of the properties were present that favored the development of Dgs. As the conditions favoring group-oriented motivation were increased, however, the accuracy became worse, suggesting that members put more energy than care into their actions.

Although only Condition 1 provided true feedback on the time a group consumed for a trial, the authors adopted the convention that any deviation in a group that was larger than 20 sec from the average of all groups was discernable by the subjects and thus provided a rough degree of feedback. With this working assumption the researchers could observe whether members followed the rule: "performance improves, raise goal; performance worsens, lower goal." It can be seen in Table 8-1 that adherence to the rule was more common as the conditions presumably creating greater Dgs were present. Finally, it is of interest, given that all members worked on the same task over and over, that the chosen goals were higher as Dgs presumably increased, and that members in that condition felt more certain they were correct in chooosing harder goals. In general, stronger Dgs created better performance.

In an unpublished study, Forward and Zander examined the effects of desire for group success on the physical effort members expended for their group. The subjects were 144 high school boys in 48 groups of three members. In order to control on effects due to personal motives, members within separate treatments were matched on their strength of Ms and Maf, in ways previously described.

As the subjects arrived in the experimental room, they were asked, without explanation, to answer a brief questionnaire. While they were doing so, the experimenter took each participant, one at a time, to a place removed from the others and described the operation of a hand dynamometer (an instrument for measuring strength of grip). On the pretense that he was adjusting the machine to the boy's size of hand, the experimenter asked the boy to squeeze the grip, as hard as he could two times. These scores, not reported to the subject, provided the base-line measures of strength, prior to the introduction of the experimental instructions.

When the questionnaires were completed, the experimenter ostensibly "scored" them and then explained that he was conducting a survey of "team muscle control and coordination." The questionnaire, which did not measure anything, made it credible for the experimenter to assert that they had just taken a test that indicated "how much each of you is inclined toward working for group goals." After assuring them that there is nothing good or bad about different scores on this test, he told them the average team in this school got a score of 28, and that 50 was the maximum. As a point in passing he remarked to half of the groups that they had a score of 42 (High Dgs condition) and to the other half a score of 14 (Low Dgs condition).

The strength of grip on a dynamometer is shown by a pointer moving over a dial; the pointer remains at its highest level until it is manually returned to zero. For the present need the instrument was enclosed in a wooden box with a hinged cover. Thus, the subject could not see his score but the experimenter could do so when he lifted the cover to return the pointer to its starting place. Wires were taped on the sides of each machine and a cable connected the three instruments. An additional length of cable extended to a separate table where relay boxes, yellow lights, and buzzing sounds at several frequencies were located. These latter pieces of apparatus were alleged to be an "accumulator" which electrically transposed the separate contributions of members into one score for the group as a whole. Each squeeze, all subjects in unison, constituted a trial. There were six trials with 20 sec rest between each. After every other trial the members were told that their group was doing a little bit better than average. Talking among subjects was not permitted.

The mean results are shown in Fig. 8-1. Members given the High Dgs induction performed considerably better, compared to their base-line level of performance, than did members who were given the Low Dgs induction $(F = 7.45, p < .01)$. The levels of difficulty included in Fig. 8-I were assigned to the groups by the experimenter and may be ignored for the moment.

Although the grip measure is a reliable and uncomplicated indicator of the effort exerted, the experimenters were struck during the rehearsals of this experiment that it was a rather boring and isolating activity. In order, therefore, to give participants a stronger feeling of working in a group, the grip measures in

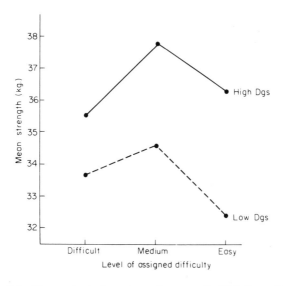

Fig. 8-1   Mean output of members of groups with High Dgs and Low Dgs.

every condition were preceded by a separate "test" in which free oral interaction and close collaboration among members was possible. A team was given 30 dominoes spread out randomly on the table and asked to build an ordering among them in which the numbers on the dominoes would proceed from double blank to double nine and down again to double blank. Each member took his turn in putting the next piece in place. They were allowed to assist one another in finding a needed block (which they did with gusto) and, after they had finished one trial, to discuss ways of improving their performance. The group's score was determined by the speed of completion. The subjects believed that this activity was part of the testing program. They were not told their score.

We do not intend to take seriously the data from this informal exercise. It is interesting, however, that on the first trial the High Dgs groups did worse than the Low Dgs groups. The difference was not a significant one ($p < .15$), but it serves as a reminder that High Dgs is not always a cause of a better performance, if the activity is a complicated one. Part of the reason for this is suggested by the finding that members in the High-Dgs condition talked considerably more than those in the Low-Dgs condition while working on the domino task ($F = 5.72$, $p < .05$).

In a later study (Zander & Ulberg, 92) boys were given a paper and pencil questionnaire to measure their latent desire for group success in any group. Homogeneous four-person groups were then composed of persons with either uniformly high scores or uniformly low scores and the basis of their group's formation was reported to each group by the experimenter. Because the measure of desire for group success was previously untried, one cannot be sure how much the members actually differed in that respect before they heard the experimenter's report of their scores. Regardless of the source of the difference, it was clear that High-Dgs groups performed considerably better than Low-Dgs groups. The task in this experiment was a simple one; it required members to count holes in electronic data processing cards as rapidly and accurately as they could. High-Dgs groups were both faster ($p < .001$) and more accurate ($p < .05$) than Low-Dgs groups.

It can be concluded that greater group-oriented motivation to achieve success causes better performance on a simple task. But the method used for creating the different degrees of Dgs was not a wholly satisfactory one. Perhaps the experimenter's instructions did no more than warn subjects in the Low-Dgs treatment that there was little sense in trying hard since no one else in the group intended to make much effort. Thus, the treatment called High Dgs may not have been high, but merely not low.

Such a potential criticism does not seem warranted in the observers' experiment mentioned several times in previous pages (85). In that study, groups led to believe that the observers were dependent on them for a good score performed better on the ball-propelling test than groups that were told the observers were not dependent ($p < .10$). Bowers and Seashore report that salesmen performed better, and more in accord with goals of their unit, if they placed more value on the achievement of company goals (9).

In the studies mentioned thus far the variables were unitary properties of the group. Differing conditions within a group may also generate greater or lesser amounts of desire for achievement of group success. As has been shown, participants in an organization may develop greater concern for the fate of the group because of their particular position, their responsibility, or their personal makeup. In Chapter 5 it was demonstrated that members who believed they had a more important part in a group performed better in behalf of the organization than members who thought they had a less important role, even though all subjects were unknowingly engaged in the same activity (Pepitone, 57).

The same line of approach was developed further by Burnstein and Zajonc (10), who allowed subjects to decide among themselves how important each person's role in the group would be. These authors used four-person groups and the members worked on the reaction-time test over a long series of trials. Each member was able to see how well he did and how well others performed. At regular intervals he was asked to vote secretly on which members should occupy which status positions. In a higher position an occupant's performance counted more in determining the group's score. The intervals in measuring reaction time were very brief so that it was possible for the experimenter to control the feedback concerning the performance of separate members without anyone being aware that he was doing so. Thus, he made it appear that one member was gradually getting better on the task while another was gradually getting worse. As a person's reported performance "improved" he was typically chosen for the most important position by his colleagues and as his performance worsened he was typically chosen for the least important one.

It was found that an increase in a member's elected importance was followed by an improvement in his *actual* speed of performance and a decrease in his importance was followed by a slowing in his performance. Perhaps the axiom is true that a man will improve the quality of his effort to fill a more important social position; but it is equally true that he will depress his output to suit a less important post.

The performance of the military men on the four-day trek through snow, mentioned in the previous chapter, could not be measured reliably since each unit had a somewhat different route to follow. The observers' ratings nevertheless revealed that individuals with high initial involvement in the group's task displayed more effort ($p < .01$) and more adaptability to changing conditions ($p < .02$) than did those who were less concerned with the quality of their performance. Immediately following the long trek, all teams were required to engage in an 18-hr evasion exercise during which they moved through more urbanized territory. The most appropriate measure of performance on this shorter trek is the proportion of hikers who were captured by the "enemy." About one-fifth of all participants were caught. Of this number 62% were individuals with less desire for successful achievement and 38% were ones with a strong desire ($\chi^2 = 5.22$, $p < .03$). Although an individual motivation was heavily involved here, it was clear in both the longer and shorter hikes that effective performance required that each man help the others in his squad.

The experiment by Zander and Forward described at the end of Chapter 4, in which individuals chose to work either for a group or for themselves, contained participants who were strong in the personal motive to approach success (Ms) or strong in the motive to avoid failure (Maf). When working for the group, members with greater Ms performed significantly faster ($p < .05$) and had better overall scores ($p < .05$) than members with greater Maf. Similar results occurred when they were working for themselves.

Taken in sum, there is encouraging evidence that the degree members desire group success affects the amount of effort they exert for their organization. There are several indications, however, that stronger Dgs may create too much bull-in-a-china-shop behavior when the task requires care rather than vigor.

Although the evidence is encouraging, it is far from faultless. Findings have been pulled together from a variety of sources; studies done for other purposes were reinterpreted for the present interest. There is a need for research that is better pointed toward the issues discussed in this section. Moreover, the desire to avoid group failure may have an impact on the performance of a group, but no studies have yet observed the influence of this motivation.

In these investigations the arduousness of the group's task was kept constant at something like a moderately challenging level. In light of the fact that difficulty is itself a determinant of a task's attractiveness, perhaps we should not expect that mere motivation is enough to generate a better performance unless the task is also a harder and more attractive one.

DIFFICULTY OF GROUP TASK AND PERFORMANCE OF GROUP

In previous chapters, when considering the origins of a group's aspirations, the difficulty of the group's task was given attention in two seemingly different approaches. In the first, it was assumed that members favor harder tasks over easier ones because the consequences of success on a task that is seen to be more difficult are perceived to be more favorable, and the consequences of failure on such a task are simultaneously perceived to be less repulsive. The tendency of a member to work hard, whether it be to attain success or to avoid failure, ought then to be stronger on a subjectively harder level than on an easier one, and the performance of a social unit should be better on a subjectively more difficult task than on an easier one, all else held constant.

In the second approach, stress was laid on the effect of achievement motivation in deciding the level of the goal most preferred by members. In Chapters 4 and 5 it was stated that members with stronger Dgs are more careful than those with weaker Dgs in the sense that they place future aspirations for the group closer to their past level of performance. They are more attracted to and have a greater desire to attain the favorable consequences of success but they also weigh the probability that success will in fact occur. As a result, they favor levels they perceive to be in the intermediate range more than levels away from that range. Then it should be expected that groups with greater Dgs will perform better on tasks of intermediate difficulty *for them* than on tasks they perceive to be harder or easier.

Atkinson and Feather (*4*, p. 329) cogently emphasize the importance of a motive in determining the attractiveness of medium goals for an individual. They say:

> The tendency to achieve success should be strongest when a task is of intermediate difficulty, but the difference in strength of the tendency to achieve success that is attributable to differences in difficulty of the task (Ps) will be substantial only when Ms is relatively strong.

And:

> When difficulty of a task is held constant, the tendency to achieve success is stronger when Ms is strong than when it is weak, but this difference due to Ms will be substantial only when the task is of intermediate difficulty.

In fact, it was noted in Chapters 4 and 5 that the amount of difference between High Dgs and Low Dgs groups in their preference for the intermediate range was very small when compared to the number of difficulty levels they had to choose among. The smallness of this difference causes one to wonder if the separate desires for group success are strong enough or can be made so to make the most intermediate level stand apart from others as a more attractive goal when action, rather than mere choice of aspiration level is involved.

At first glance the two approaches appear to suggest different preferences for the group's level of aspiration, a more difficult level on the one hand, and a medium level on the other. In order to avoid confusion it should be clear that the more difficult task is favored when the motivation of members is held constant, its attractiveness is greater because it is a path to more favorable consequences. The moderate level is preferred (closer to the prior score) when the motivation of members is stronger—a more difficult level is still more attractive, but it must not be so difficult that success is not reasonably well assured. Members with greater Dgs pay attention to the probability of success and thus prefer more moderate goals in the light of past performance by the group. That is, tasks are preferred with a Pgs of .50. We turn now to studies that are relevant to both these approaches. The effects of task difficulty are observed as well as the way in which varied degrees of motivation modify these effects.

The first study in which the difficulty of the group's task could be related to performance was the one that obliged each subject to circle one or more fields of numbers on an IBM card and to pass the card to his neighbor. This experiment was described in Chapter 4 (83). Groups freely chose their own level of aspiration, the number of fields they would try to complete within a standard time interval, but the group's success or failure in achieving its preferred level was controlled by the experimenter—some groups succeeded more often and others failed more often in a balanced design, regardless of their actual speed. The measure of performance was the length of time taken to complete a trial divided by the number of fields attempted on that trial. Half of the groups were treated in a way that was intended to make them Strong (High Dgs) and the other half were to be Weak (Low Dgs). It was found that the strength of the group had no effect upon the speed of performance.

The groups were to choose among 13 different levels of difficulty. When the speed of performance was examined in relation to the difficulty of the task attempted, there was a rather regular pairing, the greater the number of fields attempted, the faster was the performance per level (see also Locke and Bryan, 50). This relationship is illustrated in Table 8-2. There was no indication that the strength of the group modified the relationship between performance and difficulty of the task.

In order to be sure that subjects were aware that their task was either easy, hard, or difficult, Zander and Forward assigned levels of difficulty to groups as a part of the "grip-test" experiment earlier described. The experimenter told the subjects during the introduction to the experiment that they would choose the goal their group would attempt on each of a series of trials. "However," he added, "we have found it helpful to run some practice trials first so that you can get used to this test and get used to coordinating your efforts as a team." This was said so that there would be a reason for his assigning a particular level to the team and to make it appear that his assignment was a part of the learning period with minimal pressure from the experimenter. There were in fact no test trials and all results were from subjects who believed they were practicing for the real thing to come.

The experimenter displayed a chart with a vertical scale showing scores from 0 to 100 and explained that a score of 25 is very easy, a score of 55 is

TABLE 8-2   PERFORMANCE OF GROUPS AT DIFFERENT LEVELS OF DIFFICULTY

Difficulty of task	N of trials	Performance speed (%)		
		Slow	Faster	Fastest
Easy level	57	49	36	15
Medium level	61	22	47	31
Hard level	79	2	47	51

medium-hard, and a score of 85 is very difficult. The chart revealed for each level the proportion of teams that usually attain that value. Then, he said: "For these trials I want you to stick to the (very easy, or medium, or very difficult) level, that is, to work for a score of (25, 55, or 85) where (80, 50, or 20%) of the teams have been successful." Each team was given one of the three levels of difficulty to work on during the entire session. The scores were said to be a combination of the member's strength, muscle control, and coordination (ability to squeeze at exactly the same moment). The last was mentioned in order to emphasize the interdependence among members in the work to be done.

The results were shown earlier in Fig. 8-1. It is evident that the performance was better at the medium level than at the extreme levels within both the High Dgs and Low Dgs condition, but not significantly so in either case when tested by orthogonal comparisons (High Dgs, $p < .15$; Low Dgs, $p < .12$). Performance at a more difficult level, moreover, was not better than at the other levels. The most likely reason for these hollow results is that members did not fully perceive that the level of difficulty assigned to their group was in fact, high, medium, or low as was specifically intended *for them.* Instead, according to answers on a postsession questionnaire, members believed that they had a moderately difficult task regardless of what level their group had been assigned. Several other pieces of evidence suggested that the members were awaiting further indications about the performance of their group before fully committing themselves to the task. The experimental activity itself was tiring, and maybe was seen by a subject as one in which he had a ceiling he could not exceed no matter how hard he tried; thus, during these practice trials he had better conserve his energy.

Because of these uncertainties about the experimental procedure, it was decided to repeat the study with "improvements." In the replication subjects worked on the group-reaction time apparatus. This is a less fatiguing activity than is squeezing a hand dynamometer and made it possible to complete many more trials during an experimental session. Subjects were allowed to choose a level of aspiration for their group every ten trials, by private ballots. The results of the vote, however, were reported in such a manner that every group worked on all three levels (hard, medium, or easy) in a balanced order. The scores reported to the members were also standardized so that each group had the same evidence when selecting a group level of aspiration. Every ten trials the groups were told that their performance was about average. They understood that they were taking the actual test, not just practicing to do so. Half of the groups were given the High Dgs induction and half the Low Dgs induction, as in the prior study. The results again were negative. There was no difference in the speed of performance at the different levels of difficulty regardless of the presumed Dgs of members. Groups performed somewhat better on more difficult tasks than on easier ones, but not significantly so.

In the last three studies it is clear that stronger group-oriented motivation did not generate better performance at the intermediate levels of difficulty compared to other levels. Whether this is because the induced desire for group success was too weak, the different levels of difficulty were not perceived as such by the subjects, or some other reason, cannot be stated.

Let us drop the desire for group success momentarily, therefore, and concentrate on the more promising finding, the direct relationship between task-difficulty and performance. A hunch is that more difficult levels did not yield a better performance in the last two experiments because subjects had no trustworthy information about the quality of their own group's performance and thus could not confidently gauge their own probabilities of success. In such a case an objectively more difficult goal may not be a more arousing one because members cannot know it is more difficult for them. A field experiment in a large manufacturing section of a company, done by Stedry and Kay (*64*), is relevant to this issue.

Work groups making similar products were assigned goals of varying difficulty in two important aspects of their output, quality and quantity. On the basis of the past performance record of each group during the previous six months, it was given either of two goals, a *normal* goal or a *difficult* one. A normal goal was set at a level which the crew had achieved at least half of the time in the base period. A difficult goal was set at a level which it had achieved only 25% of the time.

Two weeks after the goals had been assigned, the foreman of each unit was asked how difficult the goal was for his crew. The responses of the foremen fell into either of three categories, as follows: (*a*) a *normal* goal, requires no additional effort, 8 chances out of 10 of attaining it; (*b*) an *impossible* goal, 2 chances out of 10 of making it; and (*c*) a *challenging* goal, between 3 and 7 chances in 10 of reaching it. The difficult goals assigned the groups were seen to be either impossible or challenging.

The output of the groups then was observed and made public each week as had been the custom prior to this study. Concerning the quality of work, when the goals were perceived as challenging, there was a 28% improvement; when the goals were seen as normal, there was a 16% improvement; when the goals were believed to be impossible, there was a 35% *decrease* in quality. Quantity results were more difficult to change, but were in the same direction,—a 3% increase if the goals were either normal or challenging and a 7% *decrease* if the goals were viewed as impossible. Groups with challenging and impossible goals were reliably different in both quality and quantity.

Thus, performance by the group depended upon how difficult members *perceived* their task to be, not its objective difficulty. A challenging goal generated improvement, but an impossibly difficult goal caused a slowdown. It is interesting that older men were more likely to see their group's new goal as impossible while younger men more often saw it as challenging.

TABLE 8-3 d VALUE AND SUBSEQUENT PERFORMANCE PER CAPITA IN UNITED FUND CAMPAIGNS[a]

d Value (goal for year $y + 1$)	No. campaigns N	Change in performance (year y to $y + 1$)		
		Decrease or none (%)	Moderate improvement (%)	Much improvement (%)
Negative	129	58	36	7
Moderately positive	244	21	53	26
Large positive	220	27	27	46
		$\chi^2 = 478.15$, $p < .001$.		

[a]After Zander and Newcomb (87).

In the investigation of 149 United Fund campaigns over four years (87), the relationship was determined between the change in goal relative to the prior year's income (the d value) and the increase or decrease in performance relative to the previous year's income. In this analysis the previous year's performance served as a common base for observing both changes in goal and changes in performance while preserving the appropriate chronological sequence between them. The results, shown in Table 8-3, indicate that as the d value increased the performance improved. Harder goals generated better output.

Recall, however, the larger d values were set by failing Funds and smaller d values by succeeding Funds. Board members in failing funds, moreover, were much less confident they could attain their goal than were those in succeeding funds. Thus, it would be well to examine the relationship between d value and improvement in performance separately in failing and succeeding communities. In Funds with more successes than failures this correlation was +.76 ($p < .001$); in Funds with equal numbers of successes and failures the correlation was +.73 ($p < .001$); but in Funds with more failures than successes the correlation was −.18 (n.s.). It appears that the larger d values in failing agencies were too great to serve as a stimulus for improvement in performance. The more modest goals in the successful Funds helped to generate a better output.

In an experiment, described in Chapter 3 (29) and modeled after the conditions faced by a United Fund, group members were induced to establish unreasonably large d values, through Unfavorable comparisons of their group with others, or very small d values, through Favorable comparisons. In this instance the correlation between the size of d value and improvement in performance was −.73 ($p < .05$) in the Unfavorable comparison condition and .12 (n.s.) in the Favorable comparison condition. Here, a very large d value preceded a worsening rather than an improving in performance and small d values had little effect on performance.

A related finding from United Funds is also of interest. In the survey of board members, 30 Funds were originally identified as having failed in their campaigns for four years in a row. In the goal set for a new, fifth-year campaign, the d values in ten towns were small, in another ten were medium, and in the remaining ten were large. The correlation between percentage of improvement in the fifth-year campaign and the size of the d value was .88 ($p < .001$) when the d value was small, .98 when it was medium, and .33 (n.s.) when it was large. This analysis could not be made for 30 succeeding communities as their d values were uniformly small and their improvement in performance was similar.

In sum, the findings suggest that there may be a curvilinear (inverted U) relationship between the size of the d value and improvement in performance. The evidence is not complete enough, however, to warrant that as a firm conclusion. Instead, a more specific and narrow, conclusion is more appropriate: a goal that is higher than past levels of performance generates an improvement in output but only if the discrepancy between future goal and prior score (the d value) is not greater than some optimal amount. The new task must, in short, be a challenging one, not an impossible one, closer to the .40 level of probability, say, than to the .20 level. In the rather special sense implied, then, a task closer to the intermediate range arouses greater effort than one that is much more difficult.

If the criterion for achievement should not be too far removed from the past level of performance in order to arouse greater effort, we can expect that gradual increases in the difficulty of the goal, each step a small one, will cause members to press themselves harder at each upward move. Their improved performance may not necessarily be good enough for the group to attain each of the ever more difficult criteria, but, it should nevertheless be a gain of a noticeable amount. By the end of a series of trials the group should be performing considerably better than it was at the outset.

Zajonc and Taylor (75), working with the reaction-time test, trained individual members on a series of trials until they reached a level of performance they apparently could not exceed,—they had reached the ceiling of their ability. This was taken to be their base line of individual competence. The subjects were then asked to work on the reaction-time task with other persons and were constrained to react rapidly enough to beat a particular time limit set for the group as a unit. Feedback, provided by placing an electric clock in a location visible to all, showed in milliseconds how long it took for the group to react. No information was given about the reaction times of separate members but they were informed about how many of the members had finished the task rapidly enough to meet the criterion. Each group had seven members.

Increased difficulty of the task was made operational in two quite different ways. In one case it was increased by enlarging the number of persons who had to perform successfully in order for the group to succeed. The easiest level asked only that one person do so and each successively harder level required more members to succeed until, at the hardest level, all had to react before the failure light flashed. The length of time necessary for a success was set at a moderate level and remained the same throughout all trials. In the other operation the task was made more demanding by requiring, every ten trials, an ever faster performance in order to attain success. The easiest level was one that an average group could attain on almost every trial and the hardest level was one that could be achieved on only 10 or 15% of the trials. While difficulty was being varied in this last way, there was a standard rule that at least four members of the seven react quickly enough to beat the failure light. There were 70 trials with seven levels of difficulty in each type of operation.

The results revealed that as the difficulty of the task regularly increased the performance of the group regularly improved ($p < .001$). This was true for both methods of determining difficulty and there was no significant difference between them. Meanwhile, as the degrees of difficulty regularly increased, the proportion of successes by the group regularly decreased; again, there was no difference between the two types.

DIFFICULTY OF THE TASK AND PERFORMANCE OF INDIVIDUAL MEMBERS

If the best performance is forthcoming from a group when the task is seen as a challenge but not excessively difficult, it is evident that the demands laid upon members will, because of differences in competence among them, be greater for some participants than for others. The effects of task difficulty on members who have different degrees of competence might therefore illuminate the origins of better group performance.

In a relevant experiment, the degree of difficulty in the group's task was varied by Zajonc (74) in the manner just described, increasing the number of members who had to perform their part successfully in order for the group to succeed. The two types of feedback, previously mentioned, were employed. One provided complete information about the performance of each member, the subject himself, and the group as a whole; the other provided information only about the score of the group as a unit. It was noted earlier that the fuller feedback was more potent in improving group performance than feedback of only the group's score. More complete feedback was also more effective in improving the scores of individual members than was feedback based solely on the score of the unit.

Given the way in which the task was made harder or easier for subjects in this study, it is clear that the easy level, when only one person need respond well in order to have a successful group performance, makes a faster member more responsible for the group's success. When all members must complete the task successfully in order for the group to have a good output, however, the slower member is more responsible for the group's success. Accordingly, Zajonc compared the performance levels of the members who had been faster and those who had been slower in the base-line measures of competence made before work in the group began. He found that initially slower persons improved considerably more than initially faster persons after they began working as a group member.

Slower persons, however, were more affected by increasing difficulty of the group's task than by the feedback. That is, the slower members improved their performance most when they were most likely to affect the group's performance. The effects of greater difficulty (noted above) were primarily due then to the improvement among initially slower members. The faster persons, in contrast, were more affected by feedback than by the difficulty of the task. They did better when they received fuller feedback on the performance of others, self, and groups than when they received only the unitary score of the team. Thus, the effects of fuller feedback (noted earlier) were primarily due to the improvement among initially faster members.

It appears then that the improvement in a group's performance due to increases in the difficulty of its task is largely traced to the bettering output of the originally less competent persons. This improvement, Zajonc makes clear, was not due to learning or practice. The procedure used to create greater difficulty in this study was one in which the importance of the slower person for the success of the group increased as the more difficult end of the scale was approached. Thus, the more difficult level was in effect harder for him than it was for the other members. Clearly, he rose to the occasion as the pressure mounted.

In a followup study Zajonc and Taylor (75) compared the effects of the two different operations they used for creating difficulty in a group task, the one that constrained more and more members to perform well for the group to be successful, and the one that required at least four members to perform successfully on each trial while the time criterion was made more and more demanding. They observed that the performance of the members improved as difficulty of either of these types increased—the same result noted a moment ago for the group as a whole.

The improvement in individual performance was greater, however, when more members had to respond correctly than it was when the speed required of subjects was gradually made more stringent. Furthermore, this last contrast was larger for the slower subjects than for the faster ones. Thus, the initially slower subjects were aroused more in the situation where the need for a good performance was more directly at work upon them. Eventually they were as fast as the initially faster members.

Results reported by Johnston and his colleagues (40, 41) supplement these last findings well. The authors report that a person improved less when working on a team task if he was better than his partner and improved more on such a task if he was worse than his partner. More inept members improved most if they had a partner that was better, but not extremely so, next most when the partner was very good, and least with a poor partner. It appears that the least competent person in a social setting is more aroused to perform well than is the most competent person, but the demand on him must not be too great.

How can one account for the difference in the group performance of slower and faster members? Recall that these labels refer to the reaction times of the subjects during the base-line trials prior to work on the group's task. The results indicate that a member's base-line speed of reaction may be a cue to the motivational disposition of the participant.

Consider the members who had slower speeds on the base-line individual measures. During the subsequent group tests these persons improved in performance, when all members had to perform well in order for the group to succeed, until they were as good as the originally faster persons. Thus, slower individuals in fact were not less able than faster ones; during the base-line trials they were slower, perhaps because they were not aroused to do as well as they could—they did not covet a satisfying successful individual performance. They may have had a weak personal motive to approach success.

These slower members began to improve, more than did faster members, when they became members of a group; their speed of improvement increased more as the task became more difficult. The greater difficulty was accompanied by an increasing demand, stemming from the needs of the group, that each and every member perform well. Thus, one can say that the increase in group performance was contributed most by those members who became most aware of the needs of the group. Separate forms of feedback, it may be added, gave slower members incorrect information about themselves—when the group succeeded they were probably led to believe that they themselves had performed adequately. Thus, it is not surprising that the slower members with weak personal desires to perform well did not greatly improve as a result of receiving feedback. Seemingly, it took a need of the group to arouse them.

Considering now the subjects who originally were faster in the base-line trials, it is clear for reasons given that they were not physically more competent than the slower members. Their faster performance in the base-line trials may be an indication that they personally wanted to do well on the individual task and had a stronger desire to achieve a satisfying success on that task, alone. This disposition doubtless continued during their participation in the group and therefore they were more stimulated to improve their performance when they had fuller feedback—a source of evidence about how well they personally were doing toward the successful achievement they yearned to have. They were aroused relatively less by the group's need for an adequate performance since this was something they were providing to a satisfactory degree.

In summary, the improvement in a group's performance due to a moderate increase in the difficulty of its task may in large part be the result of increasing awareness that an adequate group performance demands the best from every member (especially from the less ambitious ones). When this awareness is not present, improvement in the group's performance may be the result of efforts by certain members to satisfy their person-oriented disposition to achieve, but they need rather complete feedback on their own competitive position in order to do their best in the group.

All in all, the data suggest that a group's performance will improve if a number of things happen: if members are aroused to have a high degree of desire for group success, if each new goal is placed moderately higher than the past level of successful performance, if members are made aware that the group needs each person's best effort, and if feedback is provided on the score of the group as well as the scores of individual members. Such a net of conditions should be enough to catch within it each of the above aspects that appear to improve performance. Doubtless, research not touched upon in these pages, and studies yet to come, will widen this net and narrow its mesh.

SUMMARY

This chapter began with several reminders that stronger group-oriented motivation among members may not always lead to a better performance by a group because the complexity of an organizational task and the need for appropriate collaborative arrangements as well as the variety of motives members bring to that setting may be such that effective performance cannot occur even when it is strongly desired.

If we wish to examine the causes of better performance by a group, we need to establish that members can make necessary changes in their collective behavior when available evidence indicates this is necessary. Thus, the findings from a set of studies were presented to demonstrate that a group shows more improvement when it is provided feedback on its performance than when it is not. Generally speaking, information concerning the output of separate parts of the group as well as the group as a whole is superior to feedback about either the performance of each member or the group's score alone.

Other results revealed that when the difficulty of a group's task is held constant, a stronger desire for group success seems to generate a better performance than a weaker desire. If the task is highly complex and demands care or precise collaboration among participants, stronger motivation may disrupt rather than improve the group's performance. Nothing is known about the effects that desire to avoid group failure has on the score of a group.

When the difficulty of the group's task is varied, matters become more complicated. No confirmation was found for the hypothesis that groups in which members have a stronger desire to achieve group success perform better on their preferred tasks: those in the intermediate range of difficulty. Nor did comparisons among harder, easier, or intermediate tasks seem to get better work out of members who had stronger or weaker motives.

Fairly consistent findings suggested instead that a group develops a better output on a task that is more difficult than its previous level of performance, but the difficulty must not be too great. If it is, performance may worsen instead of improve. Such results suggest we may eventually find that the relationship between size of d value and subsequent improvement in performance is curvilinear, in the shape of an inverted U.

A final set of results revealed that improvement due to increases in difficulty was largely caused by the bettering of output among individuals who had been slowest in their initial base-line measures of competence, before they had begun work on the group task. Improvement due to more complete feedback was caused by a greater speed among individuals who had worked harder when the base-line individual measurements were made. A slower member improved most when the need of the group became most pressing for him. A faster member improved most when he had evidence of how well he was doing compared to the others. It seems plausible that the latter persons, compared to the former had a stronger need for individual achievement.

The last section in this chapter has considered the requirements a group may place upon a member. Once a group sets a goal, the members develop expectations about the ends each should attain. How and why is a group more effective in having its goals determine the goals of individuals in the organization? The answer to this question is a prime interest of Chapter 9.

| # Group's Aspiration for a Member

When members jointly select a group level of aspiration, they naturally expect one another to help attain that end. In certain instances this expectation is the same for everyone, in other cases it differs; a higher achievement is needed from some, a lesser one from others. The quota for a particular person is conceived as a *group's aspiration for that member.*

As he works in the group, an individual develops a private prediction about his own performance. The demand he makes of himself may be the same or different from that which his colleagues propose for him. Under what conditions does he accept (or reject) his group's aspiration as the goal for his own behavior? What determines whether he sets his personal aspiration close to the one posed for him by his colleagues? It is known that a solo person's aspiration can be affected by social pressures. Thus, we suppose that his aspiration in his role as a member (at least his public statement of it) will be affected by the wishes of group mates. When under social pressure is his publicly stated aspiration the same as the one he privately plans to attain?

Often, one member has the authority to establish a goal for others and to ensure that the latter conduct themselves as expected. A person with such authority is frequently beholden in his actions, moreover, to agents outside the group. When and why do participants accept the views of an authority as their own personal goal?

The experiments in this chapter do not directly examine the effects of personal motivation because they were completed prior to those we have already considered, before the potential effects of individual motives on role aspirations were appreciated. There is interesting work to be done here because conditions that influence a member's aspiration affect the nature of his motives; this will be seen in later pages.

STRENGTH OF INFLUENCE ON A MEMBER'S ASPIRATIONS

An initial investigation was based on the simple belief that a member will be more likely to place his level of aspiration at the location proposed for him by his peers if events in the group somehow have more importance. In a pilot study to explore such matters, Rasmussen and Zander (58) asked high school teachers about their own aspirations and the aspirations of their colleagues, being curious to see what degree of congruence there was between "other" and "own" aspirations and whether this similarity tended to be larger when the views of associates had more value.

The teachers were asked to identify (state the names of members in) two separate groups inside their faculty, one group in which he was a member and one in which he was not a member. They were next invited to describe on rating scales their ideal level of performance as a teacher and to describe the level of performance those in the membership and nonmembership groups presumably favored. Several findings are notable:

1. The teachers placed their personal ideal closer to the preference they attributed to the membership group ($r = .46$, $p < .001$) than to the one they attributed to the nonmembership group ($r = .10$, n.s.).

2. They placed their personal ideal closer to the one they attributed to groupmates as the attractiveness of that group increased ($r = .36, p < .001$).

3. They placed their personal ideal closer to the one they attributed to colleagues as they perceived this matter to be more important to the others ($r = .58$, $p < .001$).

Because the respondents answered both for themselves and their friends, and because the faculty groups were unlikely to have set true group aspirations for these issues, one cannot put much confidence in these results. They encouraged us, however, to make a somewhat more restricted statement of conditions that could foster congruence between one's own aspiration and an aspiration proposed for one. The general proposition went like this: a member will place his own aspiration closer to the one advocated for him by his group as he becomes more aware that his actions are instrumental to the group's achievement. Two conditions, among many, might affect a member's belief about the instrumental value of his efforts: (a) the relevance of his work for accomplishment of the group's task, and (b) the strength of his teammates' expressed wish that he perform at a given level.

Relevance of Role. A central hypothesis in an experiment by Stotland and co-workers (65) was that a member more readily aspires to obtain the level groupmates expect of him as the relevance of his activity in the work of the group increases.

In this investigation, subjects were asked to work privately on the solution of a complicated puzzle while a number of others in the room did likewise. In half of the groups they were led to believe that the product of their effort was needed in order that the group might be able to perform the next part of the experiment (*relevant* condition); the other half were told that the task was a preliminary activity in preparation for unspecified later procedures and had no direct relevance to the group's task (*nonrelevant* condition). Prior to work on their individual puzzles, all members completed ballots which described how well each expected the others to perform. The results of this ballot were said to be that the majority desired either a high level of performance (*difficult* expectation) or a "do the best you can level" (*easy* expectation).

After their work on the puzzle was finished, the participants were told whether their performance was or was not up to the standard set in their group. When asked to evaluate their performance on the puzzle, their evaluations were lower if they failed to achieve their group's expectation in the relevant condition than if they failed to do so in the nonrelevant condition ($p < .05$), indicating that the group's expectation was more often accepted in the former case than in the latter. Members who succeeded in attaining the group's expectation judged their performance favorably regardless of the relevance of the task.

Strength of Pressures on Member. In an experiment conducted by Zander, Natsoulas, and Thomas (77), it was predicted that the amount of congruence between a member's level of aspiration and one proposed for him by his groupmates is greater as his colleagues express a stronger desire for him to achieve a given level of performance.

Six to eight subjects were seated in separate cubicles and asked to find, within a set time limit, as many marked beans as possible, stirred in among a large number of unmarked beans, and to place these in a narrow-necked bottle. The members were informed that the group as a unit should increase its productivity by at least 4% on each of the seven trials if it was to attain a reasonably adequate score.

Before each trial members privately indicated what percentage of increase they wished the group to reach on that trial (their aspiration for the group) and how strongly they desired this increase. The average of the members on these two items was then reported to the subjects, excluding the member's own vote; this average is the group's aspiration for the member. In order to standardize the average in separate conditions, the experimenter substituted preplanned values. For half of the groups the members were said to expect a very large increase on each trial and for the other half a moderate increase, but above the minimally successful degree of improvement. Within each of the two conditions just described, half of the groups were told that the remaining members strongly desired this increase and in the other half that the members weakly desired it.

Prior to every trial, after obtaining the above information, each member stated how much he proposed to improve his own output (his personal aspiration level).

The similarity between the member's own level of aspiration and the group's aspiration for the member was greater, regardless of the level proposed by the group, as the strength of the group's expressed wish to attain that level increased ($F = 18.31$, $p < .01$). Members who placed their personal aspirations closer to those suggested for them by the group were also more concerned that the group improve its output ($p < .001$) and that they increase their personal output as well ($p < .001$).

A further finding is reminiscent of earlier noted aspiration preferences. The members were aware that a 4% increase was needed on each trial for an acceptable output. In half of the groups they learned that groupmates desired a 6.85% improvement on the average (*moderate* increase) and the other half that their teammates proposed an 11.14% increase (*difficult*). The aspiration levels members set for their personal output were closer to the moderate levels than to the difficult levels ($p < .01$). Doubtless they saw the request for a larger increase to be more than it was possible to attain.

Although the results of these experiments are not surprising, they assure us that members are more likely to accept an individual aspiration level proposed by teammates when they perceive their actions have greater salience for the group's attainment. The more that members desire successful achievement by their group, it follows, the more they ought to behave as just proposed.

OVERT AND INTERNAL LEVELS OF ASPIRATION

When an individual puts his own level of aspiration close to the one suggested by his group this does not always mean that he takes the goal to heart. He may, under some circumstances, state a particular personal aim in order to conform to the wishes of others, or to avoid interpersonal disagreements, while having little intention of guiding his actions by this criterion. This latter might have been happening in the study just described because members performed better under weaker pressures from others than under stronger ones ($p < .05$).

A distinction may be made between an overt level of aspiration and an internal one. An *overt* level is the value publicly expressed by a member when he is requested to report the score he expects to attain on his next trial. An *internal* level is a hypothesized value a member privately uses as a standard when judging his performance as a success or a failure. A person's overt and internal levels can be the same or can differ. They would more often differ when there is some gain for the person from making this distinction. It is assumed that the internal level is a more important criterion than the overt one and is more often used by a member in directing his energy and in evaluating his performance.

It is not easy to establish whether there is a true difference between what a person publicly says he expects of himself and what he privately feels he should do. A rough approximation of this difference can be detected, however, by comparing the reactions among persons exposed to conditions that have either stronger or weaker effects upon internal aspirations. An approach for doing this is suggested by the work of French and Raven (32). They propose that a person's internal cognitions are more effectively determined by pressures from groupmates when these pressures are based on referent power than when they are based on coercive power, assuming that the pressures in these two types are approximately equal in strength. *Coercive* power is the ability of colleagues to influence a member because of the latter's desire to escape punishment that will be forthcoming if he does not act as he is being pressed to do. *Referent* power is the ability of colleagues to influence a member because of the latter's desire to be similar to the colleagues.

In order to observe the effects of these separate bases of influence, Zander and Curtis (79) presented three qualitatively contrasting conditions to subjects: a coercive one in which a member was pressed by teammates to achieve at least a given level of performance, with the threat of punishment if he did not do so; a referent condition wherein a member learned the scores that attractive others had obtained on the task he was to perform; and, a control condition in which no external standards of performance were provided.

The hypothesis was this: A member will place his internal level of aspiration closer to the level he perceives his teammates expect of him when he has a referent relationship with them than when he has a coercive relationship.

In the experiment a subject worked alone on the ball-propelling test with the understanding that he had been chosen for membership on a team that would compete with units from other schools on similar tests of skill and that his score would be reported to his teammates. In the coercive condition he was informed that the purpose of the test on this day was to determine if he is good enough to make the team—the potential punishment was possible removal if his performance was inadequate. In the referent condition he was told that today's test was simply for him to see how well he could do. As is typical, a subject was asked to state a level of aspiration prior to each trial after he had been told (in the coercive and referent conditions but not in the control) the scores made by his teammates. The teammates' reported prior scores were consistently higher than the ones the subjects were attaining. The results are given in Table 9-1.

Note first that participants in both the coercive and referent conditions placed their overtly stated aspirations well above their levels of performance and significantly higher than those in the control condition. The pressures in the two experimental situations apparently influenced participants to choose higher overt aspirations.

TABLE 9-1 MEMBER'S REACTIONS TO GROUP INFLUENCE ATTEMPTS BASED ON COERCIVE AND REFERENT POWER[a]

	Control mean (A)	Coercive mean (B)	Referent mean (C)	t of differences		
				A–B	A–C	B–C
Overt levels of aspiration	29.8	33.6	34.4	4.00***	4.89***	n.s.
Performance scores	28.0	27.8	30.5	n.s.	2.77**	1.83
Satisfaction with performance	3.4	3.2	2.5	n.s.	2.64	2.05**
Importance of doing well	5.4	4.4	5.1	2.84**	n.s.	1.88*
Effort exerted to do well	5.8	5.1	6.0	2.50**	n.s.	3.21***
Importance of meeting others' expectations	4.8	4.4	5.6	1.29	2.58**	3.80***
Interest in others' evaluations	4.9	3.8	5.2	2.75**	n.s.	3.50***
Desire to remain on team	5.8	4.3	5.2	3.26***	1.30	1.96*
Desire to be like others	5.0	4.4	5.7	2.50**	2.91**	5.42***
Validity of score	4.5	3.6	4.0	2.43*	1.35	1.08
Importance of ability	6.2	5.4	5.4	2.58**	2.58**	n.s.

[a]After Zander and Curtis (79).   *P < .05.   **p < .01.   ***p < .001.

If a member in a referent relationship places his internal level of aspiration closer to the (high) level proposed by his team, and if he is more likely to evaluate his performance in the light of his internal aspiration than his overt one, a man in the referent relationship should evaluate his performance lower than one in a coercive relationship because his internal aspiration is higher in the former situation. It can be seen in Table 9-1 that this is indeed what happened. In the coercive and control conditions a subject apparently used a lower criterion level in judging his performance than he did in the referent condition.

The string of results in the remainder of Table 9-1, from questionnaires completed at the end of the experiment, show that in the referent treatment they were more involved in the task, and more concerned to do well, than in the coercive one. Participants in the latter situation indicated in many ways that they were more ready to withdraw from the experience, had a weaker desire to do well, and were largely concerned with avoiding the unfavorable consequences that follow a poor performance. It is particularly striking in the light of the above that subjects had better performance scores in the referent situation than in the coercive one.

In sum, when a member states an aspiration level that matches one proposed by his team, he is more likely to internalize this goal in a referent group than in a coercive one and is more likely to develop a desire to do well on the test. A referent condition appears to generate a desire to approach the consequences of success while a coercive one arouses a disposition to avoid the consequences of failure.

RELATIONS WITH A PERSON OF AUTHORITY

In the last experiment the pressures on a subject were from an ambiguous source, were brief in duration, and were based on the arousal of some one motive beyond the need for achievement. Outside the laboratory, agents of influence probably appeal to a variety of motives over a longer period of time; a superior who is responsible for the behavior of others may have a wide repertoire of motivational appeals to call upon.

What is the comparative effectiveness of an authority person's efforts to influence members' aspirations when these attempts appeal to different motives? In order to explore such matters a questionnaire was given to 400 high school boys in which they were asked about the grade they aspired to attain in mathematics and about their assessment of the expectations their teacher had for them in that respect. Thus, the students themselves were used as informants about the motives teachers most often tap in the classroom (Rosenfeld & Zander, 60).

Teachers, it was assumed, expect a student to work up to his capacity (not more, or less) and have a reasonably good estimate of each student's ability. It was assumed that students know this is the standard teachers set for them, and eight out of ten indicated that this was so. Therefore, the students were asked to make an estimate of their *capacity grade* (the one they should be able to get) and then to state their *aspired grade* (the one they expect to get) for the current semester. The central question was the relationship between various forms of behavior (students said were) shown by teachers and the degree of congruence between an aspired grade and a capacity grade. Each form of teacher behavior was conceived as a particular basis for her social power. The stronger the correlation between a given form of power and the congruence just mentioned, the more that form of power was being effectively used by the teacher to influence the students' aspirations.

These correlations confirmed the results of the Zander–Curtis study. Noncoercive actions by teachers, more than coercive ones, were related to the congruence between capacity and aspiration. In fact, a student who perceived his teacher to be using coercion, and especially indiscriminate coercion, tended to place his aspiration farther away from his capacity than closer to it. Other findings concerning interest in mathematics during the term, liking for the teacher, desire to do well, and actual performance in the subject indicated that noncoercive forms of power were associated with a stronger tendency to approach the task at hand, while coercion was associated with a disposition to avoid. Approach was apparently most strongly aroused when the teacher's power was perceived to be legitimate and when she gave rewards by approving of the student as a person. Kay *et al.* (*42*) and Bachman *et al.* (*5*) also observed that a superordinate who employs coercive power tends to arouse withdrawal in his subordinates while his use of noncoercive forms stimulates them to seek success.

The effects of different bases of social power on the aspirations of members are worthy of further attention; they provide a promising approach for explaining the impact of an authoritative person on his subordinates. Much has been written about the ability of a superior to "motivate" his followers and about the beneficial effects of one style of leadership behavior over another. Often, an implicit emphasis in this writing is that a person with greater power is a "threat" to those under his purview, and that members take steps to avoid that threat. The meanings of such terms as "motivating another," "leadership style," and "threat" are not always entirely clear. A useful way to conceive of these terms is that actions by a superior may arouse in members an awareness of the unfavorable consequences of failure, while contrasting actions may emphasize for them the favorable consequences of success. If it can be shown in later research that separate behaviors of powerful persons arouse these quite different motives in members, we would then have a means for linking the acts of superiors to the group-oriented or person-oriented motives of subordinates and could do this in ways that would increase our knowledge about motivational processes in groups.

A variety of researchable questions follow from such a frame of ideas. Among these Zander and Curtis studied just one: the tendency of individuals to foster mutual withdrawal from a situation when undesirable consequences occur for them because standards established by an authority are too difficult (84). Along with the results just considered, the experimenters were stimulated by an observation of Stotland (66) that individuals are more willing to reject impositions by an authority if they have social support in doing so, and by Cohen's belief (13) that boys in lower socioeconomic level neighborhoods appear to form gangs when they cannot easily meet the requirements of society; the gangs create group standards that are different from those set for them in school or work. The main supposition was that standards proposed by a superior are more often dimissed, and easier ones favored instead, when the standards are too high and individuals agree with one another that this is the case, but only if they reach this agreement when the authority is not within earshot. The members help one another, in short, to escape a situation in which excessive demands have generated in them a tendency to withdraw.

High school boys in groups of five or six members were given a paper-and-pencil test of their ability in using "insight." This ability was chosen on the presumption that boys would be uncertain about their capacity in this respect. Prior to administration of the test, the experimenter (the authority in this instance) informed half of the groups that a score of 15 was the minimum for a satisfactory score and told the other half that it was not yet known what a satisfactory result is for boys of their age. These are called the *standard* and *no-standard* conditions respectively. The students in most of the groups received private information indicating that their scores were rather low on the test, the members in the remaining groups received high scores.

Immediately after the authority had given each subject his score, written on a small slip, he "discovered" that preparations for the next test in the series had gone awry and that he must be excused for several minutes. For half of the low-score groups (within each of the standard and no-standard conditions) he then left the room and stayed out of sight for 10 min. For the other half he sat himself at one side, close enough to hear anything the boys might say, and worked on papers. In both conditions the boys were told they were free to discuss anything they wished. These are the *authority-absent* and *authority-present* conditions, respectively.

Immediately after completion of the test, but before they had received their slips, the subjects were asked what score they expected to get. The mean naive aspiration for all subjects was 14.01 and there was no significant variation from this average in any treatment of the experiment. Thus, boys in the no-standard

TABLE 9-2   REACTION TO STANDARDS AND SURVEILLANCE BY AUTHORITY
AFTER GROUP DISCUSSION[a]

	Authority sets standard		Authority sets no-standard		p of difference			
					A vs. P	S vs. Ns	Inter- action	SA vs. SP
	Present	Absent	Present	Absent				
Level authority favors for S	15.02	13.48	9.29	9.83	—	**	*	**
Level S favors for self	13.43	11.28	10.53	10.79	—	*	—	**
Validity of test	3.93	3.21	4.29	4.36	—	**	—	*
Liking of test	4.00	3.06	4.20	4.28	*	**	**	**

[a]After Zander and Curtis (84).   *$p < .05$.   **$p < .01$.

condition had almost precisely the same naive expectation as those in the standard one.

After the pupils had received their scores and had engaged in conversation, either in the presence or absence of the authority, they were asked several questions. The mean responses are shown in Table 9-2.

It is seen that persons in the no-standard condition perceived the authority to have a much lower standard than did those in the standard condition. The presence or absence of the authority during the group's discussions, in itself, however, did not significantly determine the standard that subjects attributed to him. Rather, students asserted he had a lower (easier) standard than he had previously stated when they had held a meeting in his absence. The same pattern of results occurred in their judgments about what a person should earn on this test. Thus, the discussions when the authority was absent aroused a belief among the boys that the authority's standard was lower and caused them to lower their own criterion level as well, but only within the standard condition, a clear and convenient misrecall of the superior's desires.

The test was rated as less valid when the authority provided a standard than when he did not and, within the standard condition, when subjects met in his absence then in his presence. As stated earlier, avoiders typically are derisive about work they are constrained to perform.

It was not possible to eavesdrop on the group discussions during the authority-absent condition. Instead participants were asked to recall what they had discussed in their meetings, and written descriptions were obtained. The content of these reveal that the test was the major topic of conversation and that negative features of it were mentioned more often in the authority-absent condition than in the authority-present one. Apparently, in the former situation, subjects provided more cues to one another that supported their derogatory reactions to the test and to the standard established by the authority. Among those who reported that their group discussions were unfavorable about the test, remarks were significantly more often attributed to their group as a whole in the authority-absent condition than in the authority-present one.

Subjects who received high scores recalled the standard setter's criteria accurately, set high standards for themselves, and were strongly positive toward the whole experience whether or not they held a meeting. All in all, it appears that social support for avoiding the unfavorable consequences was more likely to develop when persons were outside the surveillance of an authoritative person.

SUMMARY

A group may set an aspiration level for a member and a member may have his own aspiration for the activity he is to perform in the group. What determines whether he sets his own aspiration close to the one proposed for him by the other? In contrast to earlier chapters, a member now knows his own amount of output, not only that of the group, and is pressed to become aware of the relations between his personal aspiration, the goal presented for him, and his own level of performance.

Results of a pilot study suggested that a member places his own goal closer to one he perceives originating in a group if he is a member, the issues are important to colleagues, and he is attracted to that group. Experimental results revealed that congruence between one's own goal and a group's requirement is greater if the member's task is more relevant to the work of the group, the members of the group press him more strongly to perform at a particular level, and the goal is a more moderate challenge, not an excessively difficult one.

A member may have both an internal level of aspiration and an overt level; these two may be the same or different, but the internal one is the more demanding criterion, we assume. A member appears to place his internal level of aspiration closer to the level he perceives his teammates expect of him when he has a referent relationship with them than when he is coerced by them. Generally, a person under referent power is more likely to approach his task and one under coercive power is more likely to avoid it. In a questionnaire study of students it was again observed that noncoercive forms of social power stimulated tendencies to approach their task while coercive forms of social pressure aroused a disposition to avoid it.

When individuals provide social support for one another, they more often encourage avoidance of a difficult task imposed on them by an authority when they are away from his surveillance than when they are under his purview.

One can conclude then that a member will place his own level of aspiration closer to the level originating for him in the group when he perceives that his actions have instrumental value for the group or he is strongly pressed by his mates to perform at the level they propose. These social pressues are more effective, however, if they are noncoercive in nature. Under coercion members are likely to become concerned with the consequences of failure, seek to avoid these and help one another to do so, if the superior is not keeping them under too close surveillance. When a member's internal aspirations are strongly influenced by outside agents, one should notice, he loses the ability to move his aspiration freely so that he might obtain a maximal sense of success or a minimal sense of failure, as may be necessary.

CHAPTER 10 | **Summation and Interpretation**

We have surveyed an assortment of findings from a number of studies. Now we need an overview that reveals the coherence among results, explains what leads to what, and prepares the way for further investigation. To meet these needs, this chapter first presents a set of basic assumptions and the outcomes of research related to each, then a more integrated summary is offered that discusses the effects of major conditions.

The approach in these inquiries was partly deductive, through experimental tests of derived predictions, and partly inductive through survey measures of group behavior. The deductive approach, however, was one in which many of the hypotheses to be weighed were derived from assumptions that did not immediately concern collective processes. Many of the experiments therefore were more inductive than deductive in spirit as they sought to determine whether theories of individual aspiration and motivation were useful for suggesting explanations of purposeful group behavior.

Because of this research strategy, the following assumptions are of several kinds: (a) those that were clearly in mind when these studies were initiated, (b) those that were developed as a way of accounting for unanticipated findings, and (c) those that were developed while this chapter was being written. By an assumption is meant a description of a consistent interaction among two or more abstractly stated concepts. For the present there appears to be little value in noting whether a particular one was originally a "given" or was later invented; thus, each will be offered as a lawlike statement.

Most of the results are presented in the form of hypotheses even though they sometimes summarize or rephrase generalizations created after the data were known. It is better to advance the findings as though they were derivations since many results can be briefly summarized in that way and because each along with others gives operational meaning to the assumptions. Unsupported hypotheses and findings that do not follow from the assumptions are noted. They reveal where the central propositions are open to question and where additional ones are necessary to encompass a wider range of phenomena.

At the outset certain working decisions were made in order to limit the domain for these studies. A group goal was conceived as part of a unit's ongoing procedure in doing work, subject to change as a result of feedback about its performance as a whole. Distant or fixed goals, to be reached only once, were generally excluded in favor of repeated tasks. Because decisions in a social entity are made by individuals, even when these are the result of a joint vote, both a member's goal for his group and a group's goal for the group (i.e., a group goal) were observed. A member's presence in a purposeful organization may arouse his motives, either those he brings into it or those he develops after he has joined, those that are person oriented or those that are group oriented. Accordingly, assumptions and methods were selected that best provided a natural linkage between group behavior and member's motives. These considerations suggested that the theory of aspiration setting, and later, of achievement motivation, could provide useful concepts and procedures for research.

In order to work within the decisions just mentioned, attention was limited to situations with the following properties:

(1) A group of members exists for doing work.

(2) All members interdependently engage in the group's activity.

(3) Any member, compared to others, may perceive that he has more or less responsibility for the score of the group.

(4) The group performs its task repeatedly for a number of trials.

(5) A member knows the score of his unit but does not know his personal score.

(6) One out of a number of group scores may be earned on any trial.

(7) These scores each occupy some point on an objective scale of difficulty from easier to harder.

(8) The difficulty of attaining a given score can be quantitatively described in terms, for example, of the probability of group success.

(9) The subjective probability of group success attributed to each score by a member may be different from the objective difficulty inherent in reaching that level.

Although this list is a long one, a variety of goal-setting bodies are probably covered by them all.

Assumptions and hypotheses are now presented under six topic headings: (a) sources and functions of a group level of aspiration, (b) effects of group success and failure, (c) reactions to social pressures arising outside the group, (d) group-oriented motives, (e) person-oriented motives, and (f) group's aspiration for a member. Under each of these topics four kinds of results are discussed: placement of a group's level of aspiration, motivated beliefs of members, evaluation of performance, and performance of the group.

THE SOURCES AND FUNCTIONS OF A GROUP ASPIRATION LEVEL

Why does a group establish a level of aspiration? What function does it serve for the members? The conditions that precede the development of a group aspiration are not really known since groups in the laboratory are asked to select a level and they courteously do as requested; outside the laboratory the issue has not been studied. Real-life groups often establish such levels, formally or otherwise; thus, it may be enlightening to make some guesses about their origins. If these conjectures are wrong, it will do no harm to the ideas that follow. We believe that a level of aspiration arises, speaking first in summary terms, when the quality of the group's performance begins to have a meaning for members and they develop a sense of satisfaction or dissatisfaction in their group's output. The level of aspiration, how well the members expect their group will do in a future trial, then serves as a standard for appraising the group's score.

In the early trials of a new activity the members do not know what to expect of their group and, if they think about it all, have difficulty in deciding if the performance of their unit has been superior, inferior, or average. After a few scores have been earned, and contrasts among them have become evident, the members are able to speak of their past record, their best score, or their poorest showing, and are able to judge (roughly) what the chances are of getting a given score. This assumes that there is no normative information on hand showing how well other groups have done in similar work. It assumes also that the group has reasonably reliable feedback about its own performance; if not, these events cannot occur.

Assumption 1.   When members working as a unit jointly perform an activity for more than a few trials, in which the group's scores are arrayed along a scale of difficulty, they become aware that some scores have a higher probability of attainment by their group than do others.

A member's *subjective probability of success by his group* (Pgs) is his judgment as to the probability, from 0 to 1.00 that his group will successfully attain a given score. This perceived probability will be smaller for a difficult score and larger for an easier one. A member's *subjective probability of failure by his group* (Pgf) is his judgment as to the probability that his group will fail to attain a given score. This probability will be larger for a difficult score and smaller for an easier one. The subjective probability of failure is the inverse of the probability of success, that is, perceived probability of failure decreases as perceived probability of success increases and the sum of the two probabilities equals unity.

When these comparative estimates of probability are on hand, members react to a later score obtained by their group in a way that is no longer simply cognitive; they now respond as well either with satisfaction or dissatisfaction. The *incentive value of group success* (Igs) is the amount of satisfaction with his group that a member develops following its attainment of a given score. The *incentive value of failure* (Igf) is the amount of dissatisfaction with his group that a member develops following its failure to attain a given score. Any earned score, in short, now serves as a source of more or less satisfaction or more or less dissatisfaction.

Assumption 2.   A member's satisfaction in his group's attainment of a given score (Igs) is inversely related to the perceived probability of group success in attaining that score (Pgs), that is, satisfaction is greater after attaining a harder score than after attaining an easier one. A member's dissatisfaction in his group's failure to attain a given score (Igf) is inversely related to the perceived probability of failure (Pgf) to attain that score, that is, dissatisfaction is less after a failure to reach a harder score than after a failure to reach an easier one.

The awareness that different scores have different degrees of probability for the group, that attainment of more difficult scores provides more satisfaction as well as less dissatisfaction, and that attainment of easier scores provides less satisfaction as well as more dissatisfaction, implies that maximal satisfaction can occur only if the most difficult score of all is achieved. It also implies that maximal dissatisfaction can occur only if the easiest score of all is failed. Assuming that their subjective estimates of probability are reasonably accurate, it is likely that the group will seldom attain the extremely hard scores and will usually do better than the very easy ones. The scores obtained by the group thus will provide less satisfaction than the maximal, and less dissatisfaction than is possible. If the competence of the group does not drastically change, which in turn would change the location of Pgs and Pgf, members (as already stated) begin to anticipate a particular score from their group in the future. In order not to anticipate too much so that its output is likely to be a dissatisfying failure, in order not to expect too little and obtain little satisfaction from success, and in order for members to know if they have arrived or are still on their way, it becomes useful before each new trial, to decide what expectation level is most appropriate. The chosen level is the one that best resolves the conflict between the attractiveness of success, the repulsiveness of failure, and the perceived probabilities of success and failure. The level is set at a locus that will provide as much satisfaction as is reasonably probable. This expectation has a further value, it allows members to avoid future disagreements about the criteria to use in appraising their group's performance and reduces the likelihood of later differences among members when making these appraisals.

A *member's aspiration for his group* is the level of performance he expects his group to attain successfully on a future trial. A group's *aspiration for the group* is a decision jointly reached by members concerning the level of performance they expect the group to attain successfully on a future trial.

Assumption 3.   A member's aspiration for his group is placed at the score level with the greatest perceived probability of group success (Pgs) times the incentive value of that success (Igs), minus the perceived probability of failure (Pgf) times the repulsiveness of that failure (Igf). The member's aspiration either maximizes the expected satisfaction from success (Pgs $\times$ Igs) or minimizes the expected dissatisfaction from failure (Pgf $\times$ Igf).

Under Assumption 1 it was asserted that Pgs is the inverse of Pgf. Thus any value of Pgs will always provide a zero for the formula (Pgs $\times$ Igs) – (Pgf $\times$ Igf). The formula moreover will provide a useful prediction only if (Pgs $\times$ Igs) is greater than (Pgf $\times$ Igf), or vice versa. The motivation of members usually decides which of the two terms is greater, as will be seen in Assumptions 8, 9, and 10.

When members explicitly establish a group level of aspiration and choose a new one at a later time as the group's performance makes this necessary, they are engaged in a process of comparing prior aspiration and subsequent performance. The aspiration level becomes a standard of excellence. A *successful* performance, thereafter, is one that equals or exceeds the level of aspiration and a *failing* performance is one that falls below the level of aspiration. A primary function of an established level of aspiration is to provide a standard for appraising the quality of a group's obtained score.

A *group performance goal* is an end toward which the joint effort of members is directed. A group level of aspiration is not necessarily a goal. It functions in a fashion similar to a goal under conditions that make attainment of success particularly important to the members—a matter discussed later. A goal moreover is not a level of aspiration, even though the attainment of the goal level may appear to be a source of satisfaction or dissatisfaction for the members. In the latter case we prefer to say that the goal happens to be at the same location as the aspiration level; attainment of the goal then means that the level of aspiration also has been attained. A score designated as a goal often, but not always, may be determined by the same conditions as those involved in selecting a level of aspiration, noted in Assumption 3. When it is determined by only those matters, it is placed at the same level as the aspiration. If it is determined by other matters, it will be at a different location. A goal and a level of aspiration may not be similar because the former is so vaguely stated, for example, that its exact location is not known. Even when precisely defined, a goal may be put forward at a level different from the aspiration in order to indicate a general direction of effort, to state a policy, to describe a need, to encourage effort of members, or to state a forecast without any intention that it be used as a criterion for judging future success or failure. A performance goal that is imposed upon a group because of that unit's relations with other groups may quite often be different from its own level of aspiration. More than a level of aspiration, a goal may be greatly influenced by conditions other than members' feelings of satisfaction in the group's achievement. These are matters relevant to the efficiency of the group's procedures, or the desire for other rewards, outside the realm of this book. The central assumption appears to be this.

Assumption 4.   A group's performance goal and a group level of aspiration may be based on quite similar determinants or quite different ones. As the determinants of the goal and aspiration increase in similarity, the two become more congruent in location and function.

The validity of this assumption has not been directly tested but something like it is needed to account for the observations that a criterion that has a function of determining the satisfaction or dissatisfaction in a group's performance (a level of aspiration) often is at the same level as a group's objective for its efforts—to account for a goal that apparently arouses satisfaction from success or dissatisfaction from failure, and to account for a goal that seems to arouse little satisfaction or dissatisfaction whatever the group's performance. The assumption reminds us in brief that a given goal level may or may not invoke the incentives Igs or Igf and a given level of aspiration may or may not serve to guide the work of members; members may not, for example, realistically expect to attain a level of aspiration that is placed at a very difficult level. In the paragraphs that follow little will be stated about goals as such; interest, however, will center upon the conditions that cause a level of aspiration to serve the function of a goal in guiding the effort of members. Later, it will be shown that goal and aspiration are most likely to be similar when members strongly desire success (see discussion of Assumption 9).

In many organizations the aspiration choice does not describe which *score* the group is expected to achieve among an array of possible scores, instead it indicates which *task* out of a set of tasks a group might be able to perform successfully. If these tasks can be arrayed along a scale of difficulty from easier to harder, everything said up to this point applies equally well to such a task. An aspiration level thus can be expressed in terms of the task that members expect their group to accomplish successfully in the future. A number of hypotheses follow from what has been said thus far.

Placement of the Level of Aspiration

1.   During a series of trials on a group activity a group's mean level of aspiration exceeds its mean level of performance (II).*

2.   When members receive no information about their group's score on a series of trials, their group's level of aspiration is higher than when they receive this information (II).

3.   Observers of a group who have information about the score obtained by that unit select the same levels of aspiration as participants in the group select (III).

A tangential finding is that certain members privately set an aspiration level for their group on any given trial that tends to conform with the announced decision of the group on the previous trial (II). This conformity occurs more often among members who have higher need for affiliation and lower individual need for achievement (V). Conformity to views of teammates is more frequent when sources outside the group press for levels of performance that do not fit the tendencies of members in the light of the group's prior performance or the strength of member's group-oriented motives (II, III). There tends also to be a greater similarity among members' privately selected aspirations for the group when the group has been working on objectively more difficult tasks (II), and when the group is more often successful than unsuccessful on these (II). Both conditions make the given task more attractive. Seemingly, explicit or implicit pressures toward uniformity operate to help determine the level of a group's aspiration because members wish to work in the same direction and to judge their group by the same standard.

Evaluation of Performance

Operationally, a member's evaluation of his group is his rating, after his group has performed a series of trials, in response to the question: "All in all, how well do you think your team has performed on this test?"

---

*An arabic numeral preceding a statement indicates that it is an hypothesis that has been reliably supported. A roman numeral (within parentheses) indicates the chapter in which this hypothesis is more fully discussed. Unnumbered paragraphs express regrets, asides, or interpretations.

1. Members assign a more favorable evaluation to their group's performance as its mean score exceeds its mean level of aspiration and a less favorable evaluation as its mean score is below its mean aspiration (VII).

2. When members have no information about the score their group has achieved, they appraise its performance more favorably than when they have full information about that score (VII).

3. After a series of trials, when the frequency of a group's successes and failures have been fairly equal, members evaluate that performance more favorably if it has worked on difficult tasks than if it has worked on easy ones (VII).

4. When members are asked to recall the score of their group, they are fairly accurate after a successful trial but err in a direction favorable to the group after a failing trial (VII).

EFFECTS OF GROUP SUCCESS AND FAILURE

Assumption 5. An experience of group success strengthens a member's expectancy of future success in attaining that score, that is, Pgs becomes larger, and an experience of group failure strengthens the expectancy of future failure in attempting to attain that score, that is, Pgf becomes larger.

Because available scores are arrayed in a scale of difficulty, a change in the subjective Pgs or Pgf of a given score will change the perceived Pgs and Pgf of other scores. Recalling the relationship between incentive and probability, it is assumed that a group success increases the desirability of success for members and a group failure increases the repulsiveness of failure for them. Thus, the perceived potential attractiveness of success is greater and the potential repulsiveness of failure is less, the more difficult the score is perceived to be (the lower the Pgs). Also, the perceived potential attractiveness of success is less and potential repulsiveness of failure is greater, the easier the score is perceived to be (the higher the Pgf). Success, in sum, heightens the attractiveness of success and failure the repulsiveness of failure. Although it is not yet necessary to do so, one might assume that success has prepared the way for developing a desire to approach success (Dgs) and failure for developing a desire to avoid the unfavorable consequences of failure (Dgaf) (see Assumption 7).

Placement of a Group's Level of Aspiration

1. During a series of trials, the direction of changes in a group's aspiration levels follows the rule: succeed, raise; fail, lower (II).

2. During a series of trials there is closer adherence to the "succeed, raise" part of the rule than to the "fail, lower" part (II).

3. The amount of shift in the level of a group's aspiration from Trial X to Trial Y is larger after the group has had a success than after it has had a failure (II).

4. The discrepancy between a subsequent level of aspiration and a prior group score (the d value) is greater after a failure than after a success (II).

5. As the number of failing trials increases in a group the size of the d value becomes larger, and as the number of successes increases the size of the d value becomes smaller (II, VI).

6. Observers who watch a group perform during a series of trials change their predicted scores for the group in accord with the rule: succeed, raise; fail, lower. Here, success and failure are determined by the relationship between the score of the observed group and the expectation of the observer (III).

It is interesting, but not easy to explain, that shifts in expectations by observers were more in accord with the "succeed, raise" part of the rule than were shifts in aspirations made by those in the observed group; there was no difference, however, between observers and workers in adherence to the "fail, lower" part of the rule.

Motivated Beliefs of Members

Motivated beliefs are views expressed by members implying that they are satisfied by and prepared to approach further participation in a group's activity or dissatisfied by and ready to avoid such participation. Beliefs indicating satisfaction and tendency to approach are revealed by favorable responses to such matters as: effort anticipated from colleagues, importance of doing better than other teams, helpfulness of colleagues, or amount of energy exerted by teammates. Beliefs indicating dissatisfaction and a tendency to avoid the activity are revealed by unfavorable responses to such matters as: perceived personal responsibility for the group's score, perceived part in the work of the group, helpfulness attributed to teammates and self, attractiveness of the group, value in the group's success, validity of the group's score as a measure of its ability, or willingness to abandon the process of setting goals.

1. General hypothesis*: After engaging in objectively more difficult tasks for a series of trials, members describe themselves and colleagues as interested in the group's activity and eager to do well, but after engaging in objectively easier

*A general hypothesis is stated in broader terms than the remaining hypotheses. It briefly summarizes a number of hypotheses employing different operational measures.

tasks, members reveal a desire to withdraw from the activity and little interest in doing well (II, VI).

2. Members in a unit that fails more than it succeeds, as compared to those in a group that succeeds more than it fails, express less confidence that their group can attain a future level of aspiration (II, VI).

3. Members in a unit with a consistent history of failure compared to those in a group with a consistent history of success are more willing to have their group cease setting a goal for each trial (VI).

4. General hypothesis: After a series of trials, when a group has succeeded more often than it has failed, members say they are interested in the activity of the group and want their group to do well; but when the group has failed more than it has succeeded, they say they wish to avoid the group's activity and seek to evade the negative outcomes of failure (VI).

5. General hypothesis: The motivated beliefs as well as actions in a successful organization are more likely to enhance the ability of the group to succeed in the future, whereas the beliefs and actions of members in an unsuccessful organization are more likely to reduce the ability of the group to succeed in the future (VI).

The support for this hypothesis is from the study of United Funds, an organization in which the annual goal may not always be at the same locus as its level of aspiration because, especially in failing funds, the level of the campaign goal apparently is influenced by matters other than Pgs and Pgf. The hypothesis merits further study as most organizations outside the laboratory probably have social pressures acting on their goal selection.

Evaluation of Performance

1. During a series of trials a group is likely to have more failures than successes (II).

2. After a series of trials, members of a group are more likely to give the group an unfavorable evaluation than a favorable one (VII).

Observers who watch a group at work use their expectations for that group in appraising the latter's quality of performance (VII). The observers' evaluations are higher when they are dependent on the working group than when they are not dependent; a vested interest in the group's score apparently arouses a tendency to distort the score upwards (VII).

We should note that a desire to obtain a higher evaluation does not reliably predict the direction of changes in aspiration levels. These levels are often selected so that the possibilities of obtaining a better evaluation are reduced rather than improved and this happens more often in groups that are already poorly appraised by their members.

REACTIONS TO SOCIAL PRESSURES ARISING OUTSIDE THE GROUP

The members of a group frequently receive information from external sources that can have, intended or otherwise, an impact on the group's level of aspiration.

Assumption 6. Social pressures acting on members of a group, originating in an external source, and directed toward either harder or easier levels of performance, cause members to choose harder or easier aspiration levels, respectively, than they select in the absence of such pressures.

Placement of a Group's Level of Aspiration

1. Members generate a larger d value in setting their group aspiration if they learn that their group's score is worse than the average score of groups like their own, and a smaller d value if they learn that their group's score is better than the others (III).

2. Members generate smaller d values (nearly zero) if observers predict the group's score will worsen than if observers predict the group's score will improve (III).

3. In groups that perform better than similar groups, the level of aspiration is more influenced by awareness of this favorable social comparison and the level of aspiration is set *below* its typical level of performance in very early trials before the ability of the group is clearly evident to members than in later trials when members are more certain about how well their group can perform (III).

4. The opportunity to compare the performance of own group with that of other groups (Favorable or Unfavorable comparison), the awareness of need in an organization of which the group is a part (High need or Low need), and the presence or absence of pressures to raise the group's goal, apparently operate independently of one another and generate additive effects upon increasing the group's d value (III).

5. If the direction of an external pressure is unexpected in the light of the group's prior experience of success or failure, members pay less attention to the outside influence and more attention to the views of teammates in selecting an aspiration for the group, holding constant the shift in aspiration level after a success or after a failure (III).

6. When members of a group receive a request to perform at a higher level than they had been attaining and this request is accompanied by an offer of a reward for doing so, the attractiveness of the reward and the attractiveness of attaining a satisfying success apparently summate to provide a stronger tendency to choose a more difficult aspiration level than either of these incentives generate alone (III).

In several experiments it was evident that members placed their group's aspiration closer to the level of performance advocated by an external source when the external standard was hard than when it was easy. These results suggest that a difficult external standard is more influential than an easier one. The results of a carefully controlled experiment described in Chapter 3, indicate, however, that the greater congruence between aspiration and harder external standard can be due to the greater preference for harder aspiration levels and not at all to the stronger influence of a harder external standard. Further study is needed to determine what conditions cause members to conform to external standards or only appear to do so. There is reason to believe that members of a group may be more vulnerable to pressures arising outside the group if these generate feelings of failure rather than feelings of success.

Suppose that members learn trial by trial that their group is performing at a level worse than most groups like their own or that observers believe they soon will fail to achieve the level of performance they have thus far reached. Such information implies that the probability of a poor performance by their group is greater than they may have thought and that failure is again likely on the same level or even on easier levels. Such a message at the same time of course underscores the dissatisfaction potentially facing the group. As a result, the members become more concerned about unfavorable consequences than they would have in the absence of this doleful information and they develop a desire to avoid this prospective dissatisfaction. But what should they do? The next choice is uncertain. Should they raise their aspiration (which enhances the likelihood of failure next time) thus promising greater satisfaction if they succeed and less satisfaction if they fail? Or, should they lower their expectation (which increases the chances of success), thus assuring themselves more dissatisfaction from a failure and less satisfaction from a success? The message arising outside the group sharpens uncertainty as it makes potential dissatisfaction more salient.

There is ample evidence that a person is more likely to be influenced by another, when making a choice, as his uncertainty increases (12, 32). Thus, information from an external source that implies a preferred shift in aspiration level, and is accompanied by derogatory implications will have a strong impact on members since it suggests a way of resolving the uncertainty generated by that information itself.

Imagine instead that members of a group learn repetition by repetition that their unit is performing at a level better than most groups like their own, or that observers anticipate they can successfully attain an even better score than they have thus far achieved. Such information suggests to members that the probability of a good performance is better than they may have thought and that future success is likely on the same or even harder levels. This information simultaneously emphasizes the continued satisfaction ahead for the group, a state the members will be eager to maintain. Their past practices in performance and goal setting have led to satisfying outcomes and it appears they will do so in the future. The thing to do then is more of the same. Any change, such as the one implied in the information from external sources, is not necessary or welcome. Consequently, complimentary information from outside the group, under these conditions, has little effect upon the group's level of aspiration.

It had been expected that performers would give more credence to predictions made by observers who have a vested interest in the group's score than to observers who have no vested interest in that score. There was no indication however that this was so (III). Apparently comments from external agents, when there is no reason to question their ability to make predictions about the group's performance, are accepted as credible, regardless of the observers' vested interest or lack of interest in the quality of the group's score.

No support was obtained for the hypothesis that information concerning how well other groups have performed (an Unfavorable comparison) will influence the predictions observers make for the group before their eyes (III). The observers' role seems to make them more concerned about the accuracy of their predictions than about the desirability of success or the undesirability of failure in the group they are observing.

Motivated Beliefs

When members received information that their group was doing better or worse than other groups, their attitudes in these two situations were in sharp contrast, as one would expect, indicating satisfaction and a desire to approach in the former case and dissatisfaction plus a desire to withdraw in the latter one. When members, however, received predictions from observers about their future performance there were no differential reactions to the task itself. Instead, the complimentary observers were praised (even though they made predictions that were impossible to fulfill) and the derogatory observers were rejected (even though their predictions were easy to exceed). Clearly approaching or avoiding behaviors were in large part reactions to the implications attributed to the observers' predictions. It is an interesting paradox that the predictions from approved sources were less accepted than the predictions from disapproved sources.

Evaluation of Performance

Even when a level of aspiration has been influenced by outside sources, it is often used as a criterion for evaluating the group's performance. This means either that the aspiration level the group was induced to accept is taken as a true criterion for appraising the group, or that the members judged their group in terms they believed external agents might use. Although there is no certain way of choosing between these two interpretations with the presently available data, it seems plausible that members would ordinarily put more faith in criteria they felt were their own than in criteria proposed by others. Thus, members may overtly select an aspiration level when under the influence of external agents but privately use this as a standard for appraising their group only if they personally believe in it.

GROUP-ORIENTED MOTIVES: DESIRE FOR ACHIEVEMENT OF GROUP SUCCESS AND DESIRE TO AVOID THE CONSEQUENCES OF FAILURE

After a member is aware of the desirability of group success and the undesirability of group failure, he becomes disposed to seek future success and to avoid future failure. No doubt colleagues mutually reinforce these inclinations within a group.

Conceive of two group-oriented motives. The *desire for group success* (Dgs) is a disposition on the part of a participant to experience pride and satisfaction with his group if it successfully accomplishes a challenging group task. The *desire to avoid group failure* (Dgaf) is a disposition on the part of a member to experience embarrassment or dissatisfaction with his group if it fails on a challenging task.

Assumption 7. A member's experiencing satisfaction in group success and dissatisfaction in group failure eventually generate, respectively, the desires Dgs and Dgaf in the member. He develops a motive for that group.

A group oriented desire is not an impulse for action, it is rather a disposition that will influence actions perceived to be pertinent in attaining preferred consequences. The impulse to take part or not to take part in a given activity is called a *tendency*. The *tendency to achieve group success* (Tgs) is an inclination to have the group approach a task with interest and the intent of performing it well. The *tendency to avoid group failure* (Tgaf) is an inclination to have the group resist performance of the activity because it is expected to lead to failure.

Tgs expresses an interest in goal achievement, Tgaf expresses an interest in avoiding an activity in order to evade anticipated failure.

Assumption 8. The tendencies Tgs and Tgaf are determined by the effect of Dgs and Dgaf on the perceived probabilities Pgs and Pgf as well as the incentives Igs and Igf, as follows:

$$Tgs = Dgs \times Pgs \times Igs$$
$$Tgaf = Dgaf \times Pgf \times Igf$$
Resultant tendency to action by group = Tgs—Tgaf.

The inverse relationship between probabilities and incentives continues to hold here as earlier.

Assumption 9. As members' strength of Dgs increases in a group, their preference for group scores perceived to be in the intermediate range of difficulty increases and as members' strength of Dgaf increases, their preference for group scores perceived to be away from that intermediate range increases, when selecting a group level of aspiration.

For reasons stated more fully in Chapter 4, the motivelike desires Dgs and Dgaf generate resultant tendencies to engage in group activities with different perceived levels of probability. Among persons in whom Dgs is stronger than Dgaf, the resultant tendency to engage in a group's task is strongest where the perceived Pgs is .50 since this is where the expected value of success is maximal for thesee persons. Among members in whom Dgaf is stronger than Dgs, the resultant tendency to avoid, given that they are required to engage in the activity, is greatest where Pgf is .50; therefore, they would least prefer to engage in a task with that subjective probability. Literally speaking, members with strong Dgaf prefer to avoid the activity altogether because it is expected to lead to failure. If they are constrained to participate, they will prefer levels of difficulty they perceive to be away from the intermediate range. One important consequence of these separate inclinations is that members with stronger Dgs move their group's aspiration very little from the past level of performance while those who have stronger Dgaf tend to move it a great deal. The former are more cautious than the latter, when setting aspirations.

If members choose a group aspiration while they have a strong tendency to seek success (Tgs), one may presume that the members will be likely to work (put out effort) toward that level because the strong Tgs implies that the aspiration setters have made a choice that is largely influenced by their impulse to act. Attainment of the chosen level is important, so important that *the aspiration level has the same function as a goal.* Thus, the presence of strong Tgs is a reasonable guarantee that members will have set an aspiration level that functions as a goal does. (At the same moment there may be another goal in the group, or many goals, relevant to outcomes other than achievement-oriented ones. The conditions that cause the latter goals to have the same location are not known. It seems likely, however, that their similarity to the level of aspiration may be greater as the strength of Tgs increases.)

If strong Tgaf has been aroused among members, one cannot be certain that the level of aspiration a group chooses will function as does a goal since a group level of aspiration for such persons has been largely influenced by an impulse to minimize the undesirable consequences of failure and to avoid the task if possible. The presence of stronger Tgaf does not mean that members have no goal; it simply implies that a group goal is likely to be at a different location than a level of aspiration, the criterion for judging success or failure.

We have seen that the quality of a group's performance can generate group-oriented motives. However, conditions in a group other than its past successes or failures can teach members to develop the dispositions Dgs or Dgaf, and can arouse these inclinations in members when these desires have been developed. In order to create Dgs among members it is necessary, for example, to make successful achievement of the group's aspiration level more important to members. Likewise, in order to invoke stronger Dgaf, it is necessary to make the outcomes of group failure highly unfavorable. The logic in the following hypotheses then is to demonstrate that a particular condition, which is taken to generate some degree of Dgs or Dgaf, on grounds too extensive to review here (see Chapter 6), stimulates behavior among members that one would expect from the presence of those desires.

Placement of the Group's Level of Aspiration

1. During a series of trials on a group activity members of a strong group are more likely to select group aspirations in the intermediate range of difficulty than are members of a weak group (IV).

A *strong* group is one of high unity (members are aware it is a group) and high cohesiveness (members are attracted to the group); a *weak* group is one of low unity and low cohesiveness. Dgs, it is assumed, is more strongly aroused in a strong group than in a weak one.

2. A member in a central position in a group, compared to one in a peripheral position, is more likely to select aspirations in the intermediate range of difficulty for his group (IV).

In a *central* position the occupant is largely responsible for facilitating completion of the group's task; in a *peripheral* post he has little such responsibility. It is noteworthy that a central position in the flow of work arouses more perception of responsibility for the group's fate than does centrality in selecting the group's goal. Behavior most typical of one with High Dgs was invoked in a member when he was central in *both* the group's task and the selection of its goal (V, VI).

3.   During a series of trials, members more often select a group's aspiration in the intermediate range of difficulty if they are in a reward condition than if they are in a cost condition.

In a *reward* condition participants are told that the consequences of their group's performance is a gain in points if their score exceeds their level of aspiration, the more difficult the level on which they succeed the greater is the reward. In a *cost* condition members are told that the group will lose points if the performance of the group is below its level of aspiration, the easier the task on which they fail the greater is the loss in, points. The reward condition is assumed to be an arouser of Dgs while the cost condition is a stimulant of Dgaf.

Motivated Beliefs

When the attitudes of members within contrasting experimental conditions were examined, where it was intended to create different degrees of Dgs, it was observed that more approaching beliefs were offered in presumably High Dgs conditions (strong group, central member, reward, members informed that group mates were eager to do well) than in presumably Low Dgs conditions (weak group, peripheral member, cost, members informed that group mates are not eager to do well). These findings support the belief that contrasting degrees of Dgs aroused the appropriate reaction of members toward the task (VI).

1.   After a series of trials, a member who consistently prefers a higher group aspiration than the group selects, reveals a greater desire to withdraw from the group's activity than a member who consistently favors a level that is closer to the group's choice (VI).

Thus, the unreasonably difficult aspirations, which often characterize the behavior of a member with stronger Dgaf, were accompanied by beliefs indicating a tendency to withdraw from the task and to avoid the consequences of failure.

A potentially promising lead was provided by the finding that a group meeting, in which members discussed their group's effort, generated more approach reactions and more avoiding reactions than the same members privately displayed prior to that discussion. The discussion enhanced whatever tendency was already present among the members (VI). There is a good basis for the nation that groups over the long run "naturally" are more likely to develop Tgs than Tgaf (IV).

Performance of Group

1. General hypothesis: Groups with stronger Dgs perform better than those with weaker Dgs (VIII).

This hypothesis received better support when the activity of the group was simple, requiring little coordination of effort among individuals who had different duties, than when the activity of the group was complex. Persons with greater Dgs perhaps have too much zeal and take insufficient care for effective coordination on complex tasks. Nothing is known about the effects of Dgaf on the performance of a group.

No reliable support was obtained for the hypothesis that a group with stronger Dgs will perform better on a task in the intermediate range of difficulty than on an easier or harder one (VIII). Perhaps strong Dgs was not really aroused where it was supposed to be present, or perhaps members did not perceive the intermediate task to be any different from the harder and easier ones. A more differentiated hypothesis or set of hypotheses should be tested that more precisely predict which level of difficulty will invoke greater expenditure of energy under what conditions. Note, for example, the following.

2. General hypothesis: The larger the d value a group generates in selecting a level of aspiration for a given trial, the more the performance of the group improves on that trial, up to some maximal size of d value; beyond that maximum, performance deteriorates rather than improves (VIII).

Simply stated, a level of aspiration that is too different from the group's past level of performance loses its capacity to stimulate a better performance, but up to that level, each increment of difficulty creates an increment of improvement. This finding implies that in a special sense a goal closer to the intermediate range (as perceived by members) is more motivating than one unreasonably removed from that range. Conditions that cause members to set moderate aspirations for their group are also those we recall that generate a desire to do well on the task.

If further research establishes that Dgs and Dgaf have notable consequences for the goals, beliefs, and performance of members, it will be useful to determine if differences in the bases of power used by those who attempt to influence the behavior of colleagues can arouse more or less of these desires. There are indications in various places that this may occur and that differences in the reactions of participants to success or failure of their group may be, to a degree, a function of the group-oriented motivation aroused by powerful persons in the unit (IX). Coercive power appears to generate Dgaf while noncoercive power arouses Dgs.

PERSON-ORIENTED MOTIVES AND GROUP ASPIRATIONS

When a person joins a group, he brings with him a propensity to react to challenging activities in a certain way. He will have some degree of the *motive to achieve success* (Ms), defined as an individual's capacity to experience satisfaction from the successful achievement of challenging tasks, and some degree of the *motive to avoid failure* (Maf), defined as a capacity to experience dissatisfaction when faced with potential failure. The performance of a group on a challenging task stimulates a member's Ms or Maf.

A member's personal *tendency to achieve success through his group* (Ts(g)) and his *tendency to avoid failure through his group* (Taf(g)) depends upon the perceived probability and incentive value as in the following.

Assumption 10.

$$Ts(g) = Ms \times Pgs \times Igs$$
$$Taf(g) = Maf \times Pgf \times Igf$$

Resultant $T = Ts(g) - Taf(g)$, where relations between P and I are as stated earlier.

It is plausible that concern with one's own needs and with the needs of a group may be separable matters. Thus, the following can be stated.

Assumption 11. Motives Ms and Maf are separable and independent from desires Dgs and Dgaf. This independence implies that person-oriented and group-oriented motives may supplement one another in an additive manner, increasing the strength of the total tendency to approach or avoid, or that the two types of motives may act in contrasting directions, each weakening the effect of the other.

Placement of the Group's Level of Aspiration

1. During a series of trials, members in groups composed wholly of persons with Ms exceeding Maf more often select group aspirations in the intermediate range of difficulty than do members in groups composed wholly of persons with Maf exceeding Ms (V).

2. General hypothesis. Members in whom Ms exceeds Maf more often prefer intermediate group aspirations when Dgs is strong than when it is weak, and members in whom Maf exceeds Ms less often prefer intermediate group aspirations when Dgaf is weak than when it is strong (V).

There was no statistical interaction in the values for the person-oriented and the group-oriented variables in the data relevant to this last hypothesis, suggesting that the variables are independent in origin and effect. More important, support for this hypothesis indicates that group-oriented and person-oriented motives can summate or can contradict the effects of one another.

We expected that a member who learns he is the most competent performer on a group's task, compared to one who learns that he is the least competent, would develop greater Ms and thus would be likely to prefer group aspirations in the intermediate range. This prediction did not work out (V).

Motivated Beliefs

1. After a series of trials, members in whom person-oriented motives Ms and Maf are dissonant with group-oriented desires Dgs or Dgaf become more tense than members in whom these dispostitions are consonant (V, VI).

2. During a series of trials, a member reveals more avoiding behavior if he is coerced by his group mates, and more approaching behavior if he is given the opportunity to refer his own behavior to theirs (IX).

Coercion in this instance was based on the threat of punishment if a member did not perform as well as his colleagues asked of him and the referent relationship was based on knowledge of the average score obtained by attractive colleagues.

It is reasonable to suppose that some members of a group may be more inclined to see satisfaction in the performance of their group while other members look for satisfaction in their own personal performance. In a study of committees, all working on the same type of project for ten weeks, some members were more alert to the satisfaction they might obtain if their group were to be successful (the men, in this case) while others were more aroused by the satisfaction they would obtain from interpersonal relations in the group (the women in this case) (V).

Among high school boys, when asked in a questionnaire whether they would rather work on a challenging task as a member of a group or work alone for a personal score, two-thirds preferred to work for their own score and the remainder preferred to work for a group score (V). A laboratory experiment on the same issue provided comparable data (V). Persons with Ms exceeding Maf strongly preferred working alone rather than for the group, while individuals with Maf exceeding Ms had a weak preference for working with others (V). These results support the proposition that either a person-oriented or a group-oriented desire can be stronger in a given person at a given time.

Managers in a business firm had a stronger desire that the group they supervise attain a satisfying level of performance than that the company do so. They were as much concerned about the fate of the group as they were about their own personal performance (V).

Evaluation of Performance

1. Members in groups composed of persons with Ms exceeding Maf appraise their group's performance more accurately than members with Maf exceeding Ms (VII).

2. A member occupying a central position in a group, compared to one in a peripheral position, is more likely to evaluate his own personal performance in accord with the group's quality of outcome (VII).

This hypothesis indicates, it should be noted, that peripheral members are less likely to take the group's quality of work as evidence of their own individual competence—they tend to rate themselves favorably even if the group does poorly.

3. Members in groups with a history of success appraise their personal performance more favorably than those in groups with a history of failure (VII).

4. Members of groups with a history of success evaluate their personal performance in accord with the quality of the group's outcome; members of failing groups rate their personal performance higher than the quality of the group's performance (VII).

5. Regardless of whether their group has more often succeeded or failed, members evaluate their group more favorably as their strength of Ms increases (VII).

Performance of Group

The effects of individual motives Ms or Maf upon group performance were not directly studied since reports of research on such issues are available elsewhere. Observations reported by Zajonc and summarized in Chapter 8 were interpreted in ways that are pertinent, however, to understanding the joint impact of group-oriented and person-oriented needs on performance. He has noted that improvement in the productivity of a group occurs either as the task becomes more difficult or as fuller feedback is made available about both the score of the group and each member.

Enhancement of group output due to increasing difficulty of the task apparently occurs because members who have little interest in attaining an outstanding individual performance are more susceptible to the needs of the group. Improvement of group performance because of feedback seems to develop because members who have a stronger personal motive to succeed obtain the relevant information, by means of feedback, to arouse their efforts and to guide them to the proper level of output. Thus, the individual motives and group-oriented motives of members are aroused by quite different conditions which separately affect their efforts in behalf of the group. It follows from the above that persons with Ms exceeding Maf might show more improvement in their performance on a group task if they are given fuller feedback about how their personal performance compares with that of other members while those with Maf exceeding Ms might improve more if they are given fuller information about the needs of their group.

GROUP'S ASPIRATION FOR A MEMBER

A group may set an aspiration level for a member and a member may have his own aspirations for the activity he individually is to perform within the group. What determines whether he sets his own aspiration close to the one his colleagues prefer him to have?

Assumption 12. The congruence between a member's level of aspiration and the one his group provides him is greater as he is more aware that his actions are more instrumental to the group's achievement.

The objective of research in the light of this assumption is to determine if conditions intended to enhance the perception in a member that his actions are important to the group's achievement generate greater congruence between the group's requirement of him and his personal aspiration level. Several relevant hypotheses have received support.

1. The amount of congruence between a member's aspiration level and the one he perceives other members value is greater as the attractiveness of the group increases (IX).

2. The amount of congruence between a member's aspiration level and the one he attributes to his colleagues is greater if he perceives this aspiration to be more important to the others (IX).

3. A member develops a greater desire to do as well as his group mates expect of him if his personal activity is more relevant to the work of the group (IX).

4. The amount of congruence between a member's level of aspiration and one proposed for him by his group mates is greater when his colleagues express a stronger desire to have him achieve a given level of performance (IX).

5. The amount of congruence between a member's level of aspiration and the aspiration proposed for him by others is greater if the proposed increase is moderately difficult than if it is extremely difficult (IX).

Overt and Internal Levels of Aspiration

A member may have an overt level of aspiration and an internal one. An *overt* level is the value publicly expressed by a member when he is requested to state the score he expects to attain on his next trial. An *internal* level is a hypothesized value a member privately uses as a standard when judging his performance as a success or a failure. These levels can be the same or can differ. One anticipates that a person's internal level of aspiration will be more similar to his overt level and that both types of aspiration will be more congruent to a level arising in an external source when the proposed level is the property of a referent group than when the proposed level is supported by coercive power (IX).

6. A member places his internal level of aspiration closer to the level he perceives his teammates expect of him when he has a referent relationship with them than when he has a coercive relationship (IX).

Subjects were clearly more involved in their own task, more concerned to do well, and in fact performed better, in the referent situation than in the coercive one. It appears that the referent situation aroused either Ms, Dgs, or both, while the coercive condition stimulated Maf, Dgaf, or both.

7. Members more readily encourage one another to avoid the unfavorable consequences of their personal performance, on a task assigned by a higher-status person, when he is absent than when he is present (IX).

CAUSES OF GROUP-ORIENTED BEHAVIOR

The form of presentation up to this point was suitable for discussing why aspiration processes happen as they do. The findings can be organized in a different way that illustrates what leads to what without intervening comments on cause and effect. Such an ordering may have more value to readers who seek ideas for use in practical settings. Accordingly, we now consider a number of variables in turn, with a view to identifying briefly the events that follow from the presence of each.

Feedback on Performance of Group

This term refers to information that a group periodically obtains about its output. There is no way of knowing what proportion of producing entities in the world of work receive some kind of feedback, but available evidence suggests that most do not. When feedback is available, certain events are more likely to occur. The quality of the group's productivity improves, whether its activity is simple, requiring little collaboration among participants, or complex, demanding considerable interaction among them. The improvement in quality increases as the completeness of the feedback increases, that is, feedback on the score of the group as a whole and of each individual member is more effective than either of these two types of information separately; it appears probable that the performance of individuals who have a stronger need to achieve success is more enhanced by this fuller feedback. When feedback is available, moreover, members make a more accurate evaluation of their group's performance because the information allows them to establish a more appropriate criterion for appraising events in the group.

Influence on Group from External Sources

If an observer of a group has information about the group's performance, he is likely to prefer the same aspiration for the group as the members do. Nonetheless, if the observer proposes a goal for the unit that is different from the one that members select, this difference is probably due to some gain he might obtain from influencing the group's objective and production.

The level of performance an external agent suggests (intentionally or otherwise) does not have as much influence on a group's aspiration as does the suitability of the suggestion in the light of members' experience; social pressures from outsiders are apparently more influential if they emphasize the repulsiveness of failure than if they stress the attractiveness of success. At the same moment, members will support one another in avoiding or derogating a task from an external source that is too difficult for them, provided they can do this without fear of reprisal from that source. If the agent threatens to use coercion, moreover, there is an even greater likelihood that members will withdraw from the task. It appears then that arousing an awareness of the undesirability of failure creates conforming behavior, but simultaneously induces a tendency to avoid the task and to use private criteria in judging the group's success.

Difficulty of Task

A harder group task is more attractive than an easier one. When members select a more challenging task, but not an unreasonably difficult one, certain events occur. The participants are more interested in what they are doing, they produce more, they have more favorable feelings about the group, and they evaluate the group's performance better. A difficult task generates more failures than successes, but there is a greater sense of satisfaction following a success, and less sense of dissatisfaction after a failure.

An easier task is less attractive than a harder one. When members work at that level, they are less enthusiastic about the work to be done, produce less, are more derogatory toward their group and evaluate its performance less favorably. A task at this level results in more successes than failures, but the successes are not satisfying ones.

In general, groups gravitate toward a more difficult aspiration level since a success is then more pleasing and a failure less repulsive than similar events on an easier level.

Success versus Failure

If a group achieves its level of aspiration, the immediate consequences, and the subsequent train of events, are sharply different from those that follow a failure.

After repeated success, members perceive that the future promises a greater likelihood of success at that level of difficulty, raise their anticipated level of aspiration, develop feelings of success and pride in the group, assign a favorable evaluation to their group's performance, attribute greater value to future success, develop a disposition to seek further successes, perceive their group to be an attractive one, and become committed to the process of setting future goals. Individuals who have more responsible positions are more likely to have the reactions just described than are those with less important roles.

After repeated failure, members are less inclined to be concerned about the probabilities of future failure, or success; instead, they seek means that will help them to avoid the unfavorable consequences of failure. They tend to: lower their group's goal or stick with the one they have failed to reach, give an unapproving evaluation to their group's performance, see the activity as less important, believe the success on the task is less desirable, are less attracted to their own group, and would like to judge the group in relation to its past performance rather than its goal attainment—they would gladly abandon altogether the practice of setting aspiration levels. Members in such a group have a distinct preference for unreasonably difficult tasks, in the light of their past performance, making them highly vulnerable to subsequent failures.

Desire For Achievement of Group Success

A number of conditions arouse a desire that one's group attain the pleasing side effects of a success. Chief among these, perhaps, is that the group sets an aspiration level for a series of trials, that the group is successful, and that the member perceives he has a responsibility for or a commitment to the group.

If and when members develop a stronger desire for achievement of group success, a number of events regularly occur. The members are cautious in setting an aspiration level, choosing one that will stretch the group but is still attainable nearly half the time. As the desire is stronger, the members perform better, have more favorable attitudes toward the group and its task, perceive that the product of the group depends upon their own effort, set their personal goals in accord with those proposed for them by colleagues, evaluate their personal performance in accord with the score obtained by the group, and support one another in the belief that achievement of success is important.

Members also develop a desire to avoid unfavorable consequences that follow a failing performance by their group. This motivation is stimulated when agents in the environment underscore the repulsive features of failure, when the group fails, or when a member feels that he is responsible for that failure. When the desire to avoid has been induced in members, their behavior reveals a concern not so much to prevent another failure as to ensure that the effects of such an event will not reach them. Thus, they tend to favor unreasonably difficult goals and to act in the ways earlier described for persons whose group has failed.

The dominating characteristic in the purposive behavior of members depends on which of these, the desire for success or the desire to avoid failure, is the stronger.

Individual Motives for Achievement

Because membership in a working group provides a challenge, a participant is aroused to attain personal success or to avoid personal failure. When the nature of the available feedback is such that he can attain a sense of achievement only through accomplishment by the group, because he gets no information about his own contribution, his personal motive causes him to be most directly concerned with the selection of a challenging, but not too difficult group goal. When he has feedback available concerning his own output, as well as that of the group, he is more concerned with his competitive position in relation to his colleagues and is primarily interested in the achievement of individual excellence. He will be less interested in group membership, moreover, and will prefer, if the choice is available, to work for himself rather than for the group.

Some members bring to a group a stronger inclination to avoid the by-products of a failure. When this motivation is aroused, an individual has a stronger preference to work in a group than on his own. In the group he tries to be a helpful member since he is uniquely sensitive to its needs and works hard in its behalf when it becomes evident that this is necessary. Furthermore, if he is placed in a central position, he tends to act like a person with a motivation to succeed, an inclination that is not aroused when he is in a less responsible role.

Competence of Member

Among a set of persons, all of whom are performing the same task for their joint benefit, a member who has objective evidence that he is more competent than the others develops greater interest in the fate of the group and works harder for its success than does a less competent member. The latter individual devotes his effort to improving his own record in competition with the others.

Centrality of Position

A member whose activities have a greater effect upon the success of a group either because of the work he performs or his influence on the group's aspiration level is in a more central position. One in a central post, compared to one in a peripheral position, is aware of his greater responsibility for the outcome of the group, has a stronger desire for the group to be successful, prefers moderately challenging goals for the unit, develops greater tension when working for the group, works harder, produces more, and evaluates his own output in accord with the quality of the group's performance. The reactions by the person with a more central position are stronger if his role is important in the flow of the group's work than if he has the power to determine the group's aspiration level.

Sources of Better Group Performance

A group's performance will be better if a number of things happen: if members are aroused to have a strong desire for group success, if each new goal is placed moderately higher than the past level of successful performance, if members are made aware that the group needs each person's best effort, and if feedback is provided on the score of the group as well as the scores of individual members.

References

1. Anderson, B., & Cockcroft, J. D. *Control and cooptation in Mexican politics.* Technical report, Laboratory for Social Research, Stanford: Stanford University, 1965.
2. Atkinson, J. W. *Motives in fantasy, action and society.* Princeton: Van Nostrand, 1958.
3. Atkinson, J. W., & Litwin, G. H. Achievement motive and test anxiety conceived as motive to approach success and motive to avoid failure. *Journal of Abnormal & Social Psychology,* 1960, **60,** 52-63.
4. Atkinson, J. W., & Feather, N. T. *A theory of achievement motivation.* New York: Wiley, 1966.
5. Bachman, J. G., Smith, C. G., & Slesinger, J. A. Control, performance and satisfaction: An analysis of structural and individual effects. *Journal of Personality & Social Psychology,* 1966, **4,** 127-136.
6. Bem, D., Wallach, M., & Kogan, N. Group decision making under risk of aversive consequences. *Journal of Personality & Social Psychology,* 1965, **1,** 453-560.
7. Bennis, W. Organizational developments and the fate of bureaucracy. *Industrial Management Review,* 1966, **4,** 41-55.
8. Blake, R. R., & Mouton, J. Overevaluation of own group's product in intergroup competition. *Journal of Abnormal & Social Psychology,* 1962, **64,** 237-238.
9. Bowers, D., & Seashore, S. Predicting organizational effectiveness with a four-factor theory of leadership. *Administrative Science Quarterly,* 1966, **11,** 238-263.
10. Burnstein, E., & Zajonc, R. Individual task performance in a changing social structure. *Sociometry,* 1965, **28,** 16-29.
11. Cartwright, D. The nature of group cohesiveness. In D. Cartwright & A. Zander (Eds.), *Group dynamics research and theory.* New York: Harper & Row, 1968, pp. 91-109.
12. Cartwright, D., & Zander, A. Pressures to uniformity in groups. In D. Cartwright & A. Zander (Eds.), *Group dynamics research and theory.* New York: Harper & Row, 1968, pp. 139-151.
13. Cohen, A. K. *Delinquent boys.* Glencoe, Ill.: Free Press, 1955.
14. Cowen, J. Test anxiety in high school students and its relationship to performance on group tests. Unpublished doctoral dissertation, School of Education, Harvard University, 1957.
15. Deutsch, M. The effects of cooperation and competition upon group process. *Human Relations,* 1949, **2,** 129-152, 199-231.
16. Deutsch, M. Some factors affecting membership motivation and achievement motivation in a group. *Human Relations,* 1959, **12,** 81-95.
17. Diggory, J. *Self evaluation, concepts and studies.* New York: Wiley, 1966.
18. Dreyer, A. Aspiration behavior as influenced by expectation and group comparison. *Human Relations,* 1954, **7,** 175-190.

19. Dustin, D. Member coping with group success and failure. Unpublished doctoral dissertation, The University of Michigan, 1963.

20. Dustin, D. Member reactions to team performance. *Journal of Social Psychology*, 1966, **69**, 237-243.

21. Emerson, R. Mount Everest: A case study of communication feedback and sustained goal striving. *Sociometry*, 1966, **29**, 213-227.

22. Feather, N. Valence of outcome and expectation of success in relation to task difficulty and perceived locus of control. *Journal of Personality & Social Psychology* 1967, **7**, 372-386.

23. Ferguson, C., & Kelley, H. Significant factors in overevaluation of own-group's product. *Journal of Abnormal & Social Psychology*, 1964, **69**, 223-227.

24. Festinger, L. A theory of social comparison processes. *Human Relations*, 1954, **7**, 117-140.

25. Festinger, L. *Theory of cognitive dissonance.* Evanston, Illinois: Row, Peterson, 1957.

26. Fiedler, F. *A theory of leadership effectiveness.* New York: McGraw-Hill, 1967.

27. Forward, J. Group achievement motivation and individual motives to achieve success, to avoid failure and to seek social approval. Unpublished doctoral dissertation, The University of Michigan, 1967.

28. Forward, J. Group achievement motivation and individual motives to achieve success and to avoid failure. *Journal of Personality*, 1969, **37**, 297-309.

29. Forward, J., & Zander, A. Choice of unattainable group goals and effects on performance. *Organizational Behavior and Human Performance*, (in press).

30. Fouriezos, N., Hutt, M., & Guetzkow, H. Measurement of self-oriented needs in discussion groups. *Journal of Abnormal & Social Psychology*, 1950, **45**, 682-690.

31. French, E. Effects of the interaction of motivation and feedback on task performance. In J. Atkinson (Ed.), *Motives in fantasy, action and society.* Princeton: Van Nostrand, 1958.

32. French, J. R. P., Jr., & Raven, B. The bases of social power. In D. Cartwright (Ed.), *Studies in social power.* Ann Arbor: Research Center for Group Dynamics, The University of Michigan, 1959.

33. Glaser, R., & Klaus, D. A reinforcement analysis of group performance. *Psychological Monographs;* General and Applied, 1966, **80**, Whole No. 621.

34. Gross, B. What are your organization's objectives? *Human Relations*, 1965, **18**, 195-216.

35. Harbison, F. H., & Coleman, J. B. *Goals and strategy in collective bargaining.* New York: Harper, 1951.

36. Horwitz, M., Exline, R., Goldman, M., & Lee, F. *Motivational effects of alternative decision making processes in groups.* Technical report to U. S. Office of Naval Research, Group Psychology Branch. Urbana, Ill.: Bureau of Educational Research, University of Illinois, 1953.

37. Horwitz, M. The recall of interrupted group tasks: An experimental study of individual motivation in relation to group goals. *Human Relations*, 1954, **7**, 3-38.

38. Hughes, C. L. *Goal setting.* New York: American Management Association, 1965.

39. Johnston, W. Self evaluation in a simulated team. *Psychonomic Science*, 1966, **6**, 261-262.

40. Johnston, W. A., & Nawrocki, L. Effect of simulated social feedback on individual tracking performance. *Journal of Applied Psychology*, 1967, **51**, 145-151.

41. Johnston, W. Individual performance and self evaluation in a simulated team. *Organizational Behavior and Human Performance*, 1967, **2**, 309-328.

42. Kay, E., Meyer, H., & French, J. R. P., Jr. Effects of threat in a performance appraisal interview. *Journal of Applied Psychology*, 1965, **49**, 311-317.

43. Korten, D. C. Situational determinants of leadership structure. *Journal of Conflict Resolution*, 1962, **6**, 222-235.

44. Learned, E. P., & Sproat, A. T. *Organization theory and policy*. Homewood, Ill.: Irwin, 1966.

45. Lewin, K., Dembo, T., Festinger, L., & Sears, P. Level of aspiration. In J. McV. Hunt (Ed.), *Personality and the behavior disorders*. Vol. I. New York: Ronald Press, 1944.

46. Lewin, K. Frontiers in group dynamics. *Human Relations*, 1947, **1**, 5-41.

47. Lewis, H. An experimental study of the role of the ego in work. *Journal of Experimental Psychology*, 1944, **34**, 113-126.

48. Likert, R. *The human organization*. New York: McGraw-Hill, 1967.

49. Litwin, G. Achievement motivation, expectancy of success and risk-taking behavior. In J. W. Atkinson & N. Feather (Eds.), *A theory of achievement motivation*. New York: Wiley, 1966.

50. Locke, E., & Bryan, J. *Goals and intentions as determinants of performance level, task-choice and attitudes*. Silver Springs, Md.: American Institute for Research, 1967.

51. Mandler, G., & Cowen, J. Test anxiety questionnaires. *Journal of Consulting Psychology*, 1958, **22**, 228-229.

52. McBurney, W. J. *Goal setting and planning at the district sales level*. New York: American Management Association, 1963.

53. McClelland, D. *The achieving society*. Princeton: Van Nostrand, 1961.

54. McClelland, D. Toward a theory of motive acquisition. *American Psychologist*, 1965, **20**, 321-333.

55. Medow, H., & Zander, A. Aspirations for group chosen by central and peripheral members. *Journal of Personality and Social Psychology*, 1965, **1**, 224-228.

56. Pelz, D., & Andrews, F. Detecting causal priorities in panel-study data. *American Sociological Review*, 1964, **29**, 836-848.

57. Pepitone, E. Responsibility to group and its effects on the performance of members. Unpublished doctoral dissertation, The University of Michigan, 1952.

58. Rasmussen, G., & Zander, A. Group membership and self evaluation. *Human Relations*, 1954, **7**, 239-251.

59. Riecken, H. Some problems of consensus development. *Rural Sociology*, 1952, **17**, 245-252.

60. Rosenfeld, H., & Zander, A. The influence of teachers on the aspirations of students. *Journal of Educational Psychology*, 1961, **52**, 1-11.

61. Rosenthal, D., & Cofer, C. The effect on group performance of an indifferent and neglectful attitude shown by one group member. *Journal of Experimental Psychology*, 1948, **38**, 568-586.

62. Rotter, J. Level of aspiration as a method of studying personality. *Journal of Experimental Psychology*, 1942, **31**, 410-422.

63. Schachter, S. *The psychology of affiliation*. Stanford: Stanford University Press, 1959.

64. Stedry, A., & Kay, E. *The effects of goal difficulty on performance*. Crotonville, N. Y.: Behavioral Research Service, General Electric Co., 1964.

65. Stotland, E., Thorley, S., Thomas, E. J., Cohen, A. R., & Zander, A. The effects of group expectations and self esteem upon self-evaluation. *Journal of Abnormal & Social Psychology*, 1957, **54**, 55-63.

66. Stotland, E. Peer groups and reactions to power figures. In D. Cartwright (Ed.), *Studies in social power*. Ann Arbor, Mich.: Research Center for Group Dynamics, The University of Michigan, 1959.

67. Terhune, K. Motives, situation, and interpersonal conflict within Prisoner's Dilemma. *Journal of Personality & Social Psychology*, Monograph Supplement, 1968, **8**, 24 pp.

68. Thomas, E. J. Effects of facilitative role interdependence on group functioning. *Human Relations*, 1957, **10**, 347-366.

69. Thomas, E. J., & Zander, A. The relationship of goal structure to motivation under extreme conditions. *Journal of Individual Psychology*, 1959, **15**, 121-127.

70. Thompson, J. D. *Organizations in action*. New York: McGraw-Hill, 1967.

71. Wallach, M. A., Kogan, N., & Bem, D. J. Group influence on individual risk-taking. *Journal of Abnormal & Social Psychology*, 1962, **65**, 65-68.

72. Wallach, M., Kogan, N., & Bem, D. Diffusion of responsibility and level of risk taking in groups. *Journal of Abnormal & Social Psychology*, 1964, **68**, 263-274.

73. Willerman, B., Lewit, D., & Tellegen, A. Seeking and avoiding self evaluation by working individually or in groups. In D. Wilner (Ed.), *Decisions, values and groups*, Vol. I. New York: Pergamon Press, 1960.

74. Zajonc, R. B. The effects of feedback and probability of group success on individual and group performance. *Human Relations*, 1962, **15**, 149-161.

75. Zajonc, R. B., & Taylor, J. The effects of two methods of varying group task difficulty on individual and group performance. *Human Relations*, 1963, **16**, 359-368.

76. Zajonc, R. B. The requirements and design of a standard group task. *Journal of Experimental Social Psychology*, 1965, **1**, 71-88.

77. Zander, A., Natsoulas, T., & Thomas, E. J. Personal goals and the group's goal for the member. *Human Relations*, 1960, **13**, 333-344.

78. Zander, A., Stotland, E., & Wolfe, D. Unity of group, identification with group, and self-esteem of members. *Journal of Personality*, 1960, **28**, 463-478.

79. Zander, A., & Curtis, T. Effects of social power on aspiration setting and striving. *Journal of Abnormal & Social Psychology*, 1962, **64**, 63-74.

80. Zander, A., & Medow, H. Individual and group levels of aspiration. *Human Relations*, 1963, **16**, 89-105.

81. Zander, A., & Wolfe, D. Administrative rewards and coordination among committee members. *Administrative Science Quarterly*, 1964, **9**, 50-69.

82. Zander, A., & Ledvinka, J. Difficulty of a group's task and collective coping behavior. In A. Zander & H. Medow (Eds.), *Group aspirations and group coping behavior.* Report to U. S. Office of Education, Cooperative Research Project 1143. Ann Arbor, Mich.: Research Center for Group Dynamics, The University of Michigan, 1964.

83. Zander, A., & Medow, H. Strength of group and desire for attainable group aspirations. *Journal of Personality*, 1965, **33**, 122-139.

84. Zander, A., & Curtis, T. Social support and rejection of organizational standards. *Journal of Educational Psychology*, 1965, **56**, 87-95.

85. Zander, A., Medow, H., & Efron, R. Observers' expectations as determinants of group aspirations. *Human Relations*, 1965, **18**, 273-287.

86. Zander, A., & Wulff, D. Members' test anxiety and competence: Determinants of a group's aspirations. *Journal of Personality*, 1966, **34**, 55-70.

87. Zander, A., & Newcomb, T., Jr., Group levels of aspiration in United Fund Campaigns. *Journal of Personality & Social Psychology*, 1967, **6**, 157-162.

88. Zander, A., & Forward, J. Position in group, achievement motivation and group aspirations. *Journal of Personality & Social Psychology*, 1968, **8**, 282-288.

89. Zander, A., Forward, J., & Albert, R. Adaptation of board members to repeated success or failure by their organizations. *Organizational Behavior & Human Performance*, 1969, **4**, 56-76.

90. Zander, A. Students' criteria of satisfaction in a classroom committee project. *Human Relations*, 1969, **22**, 195-207.

91. Zander, A. *Manager, group, and company, A report to the Pripp's Company.*

Stockholm, Sweden: Swedish Institute for Administrative Research, 1969, mimeographed, 41 pp.

92. Zander, A., & Ulberg, C. The group level of aspiration and external social pressures. *Organizational Behavior & Human Performance*, in press.

93. Zander, A. The purposes of national associations. Report in preparation.

Subject Index

A

Achievement
  group, desire for (DgAch), 7, 56-57, 201
  motivated beliefs, evident in, 113-128
  need (n Ach), 7, 54-56
Affiliation, need (n Aff), 101, 106-111
Aspiration level
  group
    assumptions about, 17, 178-189
    change, amount, 16-18, 24, 41-44, 63, 182-188
    change, direction, 12-17, 24-25, 33-34, 182
    difficulty, see Difficulty, group aspiration level
    evaluation, criterion for, 129-140, 183, 185-186
    goal of group, 70-71, 180-182
    individual level, compared, 12, 58
    mean value, 12, 22, 25, 68-70
    measurement, 11
    member's aspiration for group, 12, 120-123
    origins, 178-183
    performance change, relation to, 12-15, 18-21, 182
    research procedure, 10-12, 177
  group's for member
    authority, influence of, 170-174
    relevance member's role, 165-166
    social pressure, 165-167, 197-198
  member's for group
    changes in, 60-63, 94-96, 182-184, 186-188
    definition, 6, 180
    deviant from groupmate's, 120-123
    individual motives, influence of, 90-106, 109-110

measurement, 11, 60-63
similarity among members, 25-27, 41-44, 70-73, 95-96, 110-111, 120-122, 182, 192
member's personal, 164-174
overt and internal, 167-170, 198

B

Ball-propelling task, group, 10-11, 23, 90-93

C

Centrality
  group decision, 60-63
  social position
    affiliation need, 107-111
    aspiration for group, 60-63, 97-101, 107-109, 191
    effects of, 58-63, 97-101, 126-128, 133, 139, 151, 202
    experimental procedure for, 59-60, 97
Coercive social power, 44-48, 167-174, 195
Communication among members, effects, 72, 106, 118-119, 132, 150, 192
Consequences, task effort
  favorableness anticipated, 113-127, 133-134
  group versus individual preferred, 73-79, 83-90
Competence of member, 92-96, 159-162, 202
Cost condition, 66-68, 101-106, 192

D

d Value
  external pressures on, 31-48, 186-188
  group property, effect of, 103-105
  nature of, 18-21

209